Strategic Index Investing

Strategic Index Investing

Unlocking the Power of
Exchange-Traded Index Funds

Richard D. Romey

ISBN 1-58597-295-9

Library of Congress Control Number: 2004097015

A division of Squire Publishers, Inc.
4500 College Blvd.
Leawood, KS 66211
1/888/888/7696
www.leatherspublishing.com

This book is dedicated to

my wonderful and loving wife, Debbie,

my two sons,

who provide great happiness and joy in my life,

and to my parents,

for all they have done for me.

ACKNOWLEDGMENTS

In writing this book, I have relied greatly on the help and wisdom of several people. Above all, Debbie Romey, who was mainly responsible for editing, correcting, and advising me throughout this project. Without her help, support, and hard work this book would never have been completed. For all of her help I am truly grateful.

Vince Pastorino, a friend and trusted associate, contributed greatly to the organization and structure of the book. His suggestions, insights, and editing added tremendously to the overall quality of the final product. His reading and reviewing of the material is much appreciated and will not be forgotten.

Linda Romey brought a professional perspective to the project and helped me take it to the next level. I appreciate her willingness to review and edit the manuscript in its earliest stages. She provided me with much needed help and confidence at a critical time.

I would also like to thank all of my many friends, family, and associates who have helped with this endeavor. In particular, Arvin Pfefer, who provided the early inspiration needed to undertake such a project and for the years of trusted advice and friendship he has given me.

CONTENTS

INTRODUCTION

A Remarkable New Investment Product

A little over ten years ago, a watershed event occurred in the area of personal finance when the American Stock Exchange (AMEX) began trading shares of a unique, new investment product called Standard & Poor's Depositary Receipts (SPDRs) or "Spiders." Simple, flexible, low-cost, and tax-efficient, Spiders were the first of an entirely new type of investment product commonly referred to as *Exchange-Traded Funds* (ETFs) or *Exchange-Traded "Index" Funds* (ETIFs).

Exchange-traded index funds exist at the intersection of traditional index mutual funds and common stocks, incorporating the most attractive features of each structure. They are like stocks – flexible, easy to use, and actively traded throughout the day. At the same time, they are like index mutual funds – tax-efficient, cost-effective, diversified, and designed to track the performance of a given market index or benchmark. Shares of exchange-traded index funds can also be created or redeemed at the fund's net asset value (NAV) per share on any business day, similar to traditional mutual funds.

Like other revolutionary innovations, such as the automobile, television, or Internet, many initially dismissed the value of exchange-traded index funds. They were called "index funds for traders" and "unnecessary" by some financial professionals. Mutual fund companies went on the attack, as well, going to great lengths to discourage investors from using this new product. "Stick with what you know," was their advice, referring to traditional mutual funds. Ironically, many of the same mutual fund companies that once openly criticized exchange-traded index funds now offer them.

Not everyone was so quick to dismiss the value of this powerful new portfolio management vehicle. Large institutional investors, such as pension and hedge fund managers embraced them almost immediately. Even some mutual fund portfolio managers found exchange-traded index funds the perfect tool to quickly and efficiently gain exposure to a specific asset class or segment of the market. As is often the case, when institutional investors embrace a new product retail investors soon follow. It wasn't long before individual investors were using exchange-traded index funds to meet a variety of portfolio management needs.

Today, barely ten years since first introduced, there are over 120 exchange-traded index funds available covering virtually every possible asset class, investment style, market capitalization, economic sector, industry group, country, and geographic region. As of December 2004, total assets under management (AUM) for all exchange-traded index funds exceeded $175 billion and on any given day they account for over half of all trading volume on the American Stock Exchange. Based on the growth in popularity we have witnessed, it's safe to say that exchange-traded index funds are rapidly becoming the investment tool of choice for millions of investors.

A Portfolio Management Revolution Is Underway

Exchange-traded index funds are the most important financial innovation of the last thirty years and the catalyst behind a powerful new approach to portfolio management, called Strategic Index Investing. Unlike the vast majority of portfolio management strategies used today, Strategic Index Investing is not based on picking the right stock or finding the next "hot" mutual fund. Instead, the focus is on the use of index-based investments to access the key drivers of portfolio performance – investment style, company size, sector, industry, geographic region – in conjunction with proven active portfolio management strategies. In essence, Strategic Index Investing is where the efficiency of indexing meets the art of active portfolio management.

Strategic Index Investing is a comprehensive approach to portfolio management based on the use of exchange-traded index funds, the diversification benefits of asset allocation, the efficiency of indexing, and the flexibility of active portfolio management. It is designed for investors seeking to avoid the costs, tax inefficiencies, and erratic performance most often associated with traditional mutual funds and individual common stocks in conjunction with buy-and-hold investing. Most importantly, Strategic Index Investing offers every investor a way to construct a highly customized portfolio based on his or her specific goals, risk tolerance, and investing time horizon.

The Purpose of this Book

This book is designed to serve as a practical guide to the art of active index investing. As such, it has two primary objectives. First, to introduce, explain, and demonstrate the benefits associated with a powerful new portfolio management tool called exchange-traded index funds. Second, explain the principles of Strategic Index Investing. A portfolio management methodology based on the premise that actively managing a portfolio of passive assets represents the best way to maximize performance while minimizing risk.

In the process, the most popular investment products and strategies used today, such as actively managed mutual funds and buy-and-hold investing, are called into question. While new ideas are often difficult to accept and letting go of old habits is even harder, it's my sincere hope that you will approach the material put forth in this book with an open mind. And, if appropriate, use the ideas presented to improve your investment results.

What this Book Is Not

This book is not a get-rich-quick guide. It will not divulge a top secret trading strategy or foolproof moneymaking system. Such outlandish claims will be left to others so we can focus on constructing fundamentally sound portfolios based on proven financial principles.

After twenty years in the investment management industry, I've learned one undeniable fact: there is no such thing as a consistent, surefire, quick and easy way to make money in the stock market. Portfolio management is hard work. It takes planning, consistency, determination, and time. Fortunately, for those willing to pay the price the equity markets offer tremendous wealth creation potential.

How this Book Is Organized

When discussing portfolio management, it's important to understand that a limited number of key factors will ultimately determine success or failure. Investors who focus on these key factors will more often than not be successful while those who play it from the hip usually fail. In this book, I present what I believe are the key factors of portfolio management within the framework of Strategic Index Investing. To accomplish this goal, this book has been divided into four parts. A brief summary of each is provided below.

Part 1: New Ideas in Portfolio Management

The three chapters in Part 1 challenge many of today's most widely accepted investment beliefs and introduce a better alternative. In Chapter 1, we take a look back at the markets over the last few years and overview some of the problems investors have encountered. In Chapter 2, the most popular investment strategies and tools used today, such as buy-and-hold investing and traditional mutual funds, are examined. In Chapter 3, the key elements of Strategic Index Investing are introduced and a comparison is made between Strategic Index Investing and buy-and-hold investing.

Part 2: Exchange-Traded Index Funds —
A Powerful New Portfolio Management Tool

Part 2 is devoted entirely to the examination of exchange-traded index funds. In Chapter 4, the benefits associated with exchange-traded index funds are discussed. In Chapter 5, exchange-traded index funds are compared to traditional mutual funds, both actively managed and index-based. In Chapter 6, we examine the internal workings of exchange-traded index funds. The benefits associated with indexing are discussed in Chapter 7 while Chapter 8 focuses on those companies responsible for creating most of the currently available exchange-traded index funds.

Part 3: Strategic Index Investing — Unlocking the
Power of Exchange-Traded Index Funds

In Part 3, the focus shifts to the strategies used in Strategic Index Investing. Chapter 9 introduces and explains asset allocation. In Chapter 10, strategic asset allocation is examined. Chapter 11 shows the benefits associated with making tactical changes to the overall asset allocation. In Chapter 12, the importance of using exit strategies is discussed. Advanced portfolio management strategies, including the use of options, selling short, and margin are discussed in Chapters 13 and 14.

Part 4: Building a Better Portfolio

Part 4 explains the key elements of portfolio construction and management. Chapter 15 shows the steps necessary to construct a portfolio following the principles of Strategic Index Investing. In Chapter

16, investment advisory fees and services are discussed. Finally, Chapter 17 provides a list of important investment rules, which should be followed at all times.

An Important Distinction

In this book, the term "Exchange-Traded Index Funds" or "ETIFs" is used when describing this remarkable new investment product. This stands in contrast to the vast majority of those in the financial media, investment professionals, and investors who refer to them as "Exchange-Traded Funds" or "ETFs."

There are several reasons why I believe "Exchange-Traded Index Funds" is a better name. Currently a wide range of very dissimilar products are commonly referred to as "Exchange-Traded Funds." This includes closed-end equity mutual funds, closed-end bond mutual funds, Holding Company Depositary Receipts (HOLDERs), open-end unit investment trusts, and open-end index-based exchange-traded mutual funds. This can and does lead to a great deal of confusion.

I believe a more appropriate name, and one that emphasizes the importance of indexing, is exchange-traded "index" funds. This should prove especially important when actively managed exchange-traded funds are introduced, which will likely happen sometime in the near future. Therefore, throughout this book, the term exchange-traded index fund(s) or the abbreviation ETIF(s) is used.

Part One

New Ideas
in
Portfolio
Management

Chapter 1

THEN AND NOW

A Look Back

On March 12, 1999, a financial milestone occurred at the New York Stock Exchange — the Dow Jones Industrial Average traded above the 10,000-point mark for the first time in its history. The event captured the attention and imagination of virtually every investor from Wall Street to Main Street and put an exclamation point on one of the longest running bull markets ever.

As the Dow crossed the 10,000-point mark in early morning trading, a roar of excitement erupted from the floor of the New York Stock Exchange that reverberated through brokerage firms, corporate boardrooms, and homes across the country. Millions of investors watched the event unfold live on CNBC or one of the many other financial news programs, which seemed to spring up overnight. They watched as brokers and traders bounced about the trading floor like excited children on the last day of school, giving energetic "high-fives" to anyone within reach.

To mark the occasion Exchange Members passed-out hats with the number 10,000 printed boldly across the front to everyone present, reminiscent of the hats given to players on the winning team at the Super Bowl or World Series. Politicians, dignitaries, portfolio managers, and market experts from across the country and around the globe joined in the celebration with glorious speeches and optimistic predictions. As one could imagine, it was truly a joyous day on Wall Street.

For awhile it appeared that the experts had it right. Day after day the Dow climbed higher passing milestones along the way. In May of 1999, the 11,000-point barrier fell. Next came 11,500 in December of that same year. By January of 2000, the 12,000-point mark was clearly in sight for the famous market average. The Dow's performance was the main topic of conversation across America. Investors were in a state of euphoria and everyone was getting rich!

Unfortunately, the Dow never reached 12,000. Instead, as the new millennium began a long and volatile downward spiral that would last years gripped the market. By May 2002, the Dow was back at 10,000. In sharp contrast to the festive mood three years earlier, when the Dow first cracked 10,000, this event didn't generate the same level of excitement among investors. The cheering crowds were gone, as were the politicians, the commemorative hats, the dignitaries, and the market experts with their ambitious predictions.

In May 2004, five years after first hitting 10,000, the Dow Jones Industrial Average was still trading around that same level. Unfortunately for investors, the equity markets didn't just trade sideways during this time period. After hitting a high of 11,908 in January of 2000, the Dow Jones Industrial Average lost 4,540 points, or approximately 40% of its value, by October of 2002. Other market indicators suffered as well. For instance, the Nasdaq Composite Index, an index comprised of companies traded on the Nasdaq market, hit a high of just over 5,000 in March of 2000. By July of 2002, it had lost an unbelievable 80% of its value. The S&P 500 Index, the most recognizable and widely used gauge of market performance in the world, suffered dramatic losses as well. In March of 2000, it registered a high of just over 1,550. By October of 2002 it, too, had lost an incredible 50% of its value.

Mutual funds, the product of choice for millions of investors, provided little protection from the carnage. Hardest hit were the most aggressive funds. For example, the average technology sector mutual fund lost over 70% of its value from the market's peak in January of 2000 through October of 2002, according to Lipper Analytical Services. Even the largest and most conservative broad-based equity mutual funds were not immune to the market's decline. Of the fifty largest mutual funds in the country, based on assets under management, all but a handful posted net losses for the three-year period ending December 31, 2002, leaving few investors unscathed.

What Went Wrong

Recapping the stock market's losses over the last several years is not intended to depress or demoralize anyone, nor is it intended to place blame as others have done. Clearly, the equity markets have experienced an unusually rough time period and many have suffered. It's foolish, however, to act as if this were something new, something that has never happened previously.

As any seasoned investor can attest, the equity markets have experienced similar periods in the past. For instance, in 1968 the Dow Jones Industrial Average traded above the 1,000-point mark for the first time in its history. It didn't close above that level again until 1984, some sixteen years later. After the 1929 market crash, which caused the Dow Jones Industrial Average to lose over 20% of its value in two days, it needed twenty-five years to rise to pre-crash levels. More recently, the S&P 500 Index lost over 35% of its value from August of 1987 through October of that same year. After the steep decline, the S&P 500 Index needed almost four years to move permanently above its previous high.

In other words, the dramatic losses witnessed in the equity markets over the last several years are by no means unprecedented. In fact, bear markets are a normal and necessary part of the market's cycle. Unfortunately, many investors thought it would be different this time. After all, the experts agreed that buying stocks and holding them indefinitely offered incredible rewards. If the market did happen to drop, it was a buying opportunity. "Buy the dips," became Wall Street's battle cry, as everyone knows the market always goes higher.

Just as countless investors before them, investors today are discovering that stocks are risky. Regardless of how many people say that it's different this time, one rule never changes: at some point, sooner or later, the laws of gravity take over and when they do those who are not prepared will lose money. More importantly, investors have learned that those who don't remember the past are destined to repeat it.

Opportunities Abound

The information above may cause some to reach the conclusion that it was impossible to make money in the stock market over the last several years. Nothing could be further from the truth. Opportunities to make money in the market abound, even during the worst bear markets.

For example, during the five-year period ending March 31, 2004, the Dow Jones Industrial Average experienced six rallies of greater than 15%. In fact, from September of 2001 to January of 2002, the Dow increased by over 2,000 points, or about 25% in only four months. Over this same five-year period, the Nasdaq Composite Index and S&P 500 Index saw similar price movements. For instance, the Nasdaq experienced six major rallies of 25%, 32%, 53%, 59%, 18%, and 45% respectively. Keep in mind, these rallies occurred in the midst of a brutal bear market, which caused the Nasdaq to lose some 80% of its total value. Similarly, the S&P 500 Index saw no fewer than seven moves, on an absolute basis, of greater than 25% over this same time period.

It is also common to see certain asset classes, industry segments, or economic sectors shine during even the worst bear market. The most recent bear market was no exception. For instance, in the year 2000 the S&P 500 Index declined by 9.1%. The Russell 2000 Value Index, in contrast, was the top-performing asset class that year posting a total return of 22.8%. In 2001, this same index produced a total return of 14.1% while the broad market, as measured by the S&P

500 Index, lost 11.9%. In 2002, the Lehman 20+ Year Treasury Index was the top-performing asset class with a total return of 17.0%. In contrast, the S&P 500 Index posted a loss of 22.1% that same year.

Then, in 2003, a broad-based rally pushed equity prices dramatically higher. The Nasdaq gained over 40% while the S&P 500 Index and the Dow Jones Industrial Average saw gains of 25.7% and 25.3% respectively. These dramatic gains, however, did little to help most investors recover. Over the five-year period ending May 31, 2004, a buy-and-hold investor using a mutual fund tracking the S&P 500 Index, the Dow Jones Industrial Average, or the Nasdaq lost money. Even though a number of significant profit opportunities occurred, as we have seen.

Why were so many investors caught off guard, seemingly unprepared to cope with something as normal as a bear market? Why did so many investors do nothing as their portfolios were decimated, even though a number of significant profit opportunities existed?

The reason is simple. During the 1990s buy-and-hold investing was touted as the only smart way to invest. Mutual fund executives, Wall Street big shots, and other industry "experts" continually hyped the merits of buy-and-hold, typically in conjunction with a portfolio of traditional mutual funds. If someone in the financial media or a position of power on Wall Street questioned the soundness of this approach they were quickly dismissed as being naïve or out of touch. To go against the prevailing wisdom of buy-and-hold was the equivalent of committing career suicide for Wall Street insiders. Few had the courage to point out that "the emperor had no clothes," even when it became apparent that equities were extremely overvalued and sure to fall.

As the market began to slide, in early 2000, most buy-and-hold investors did nothing to protect their portfolios. Throughout the 1990s, they had been conditioned to approach the market with a fatalistic, "don't question what we say" mindset. As the market dropped, investors were told by brokers, investment professionals, and mutual fund companies to sit tight and wait patiently. It was only a matter of time before their investments would bounce back. At least that is what they were told. Unfortunately, over five years later many are still waiting for their portfolios to bounce back.

Rethink All Assumptions

So what does this mean for us? Perhaps most importantly it points out that investors and financial professionals alike need to rethink how they approach portfolio management. Gone is the notion that a 25% annualized rate of return is easy to achieve or that investing in equities is risk free. Gone too is the notion that all an investor has to do is purchase shares of a mutual fund or common stock, wait patiently, and eventually they will become a millionaire.

There is an old saying on Wall Street, "a bull market hides many problems while a bear market exposes all." In this respect the millennium bear market, as many have called it, was no exception. Over the last several years, investors have witnessed a number of eye opening revelations. Corporate accounting scandals have rocked Wall Street. Mutual fund trading schemes costing shareholders billions of dollars were uncovered at some of the largest and most respected mutual fund companies in the country. The majority of Wall Street analysts have been exposed as nothing more than glorified salespeople, saying whatever is necessary to pump-up a stock's price in order to increase potential investment banking opportunities for his or her firm.

The shortcomings of traditional mutual funds (i.e., lackluster performance, high expenses, tax inefficiencies, and a general lack of liquidity) have been well documented by the financial media, as well. Unfortunately, most investors believe that mutual funds protect them from market risks because a fund manager is watching over the portfolio. If the market turns lower, the fund manager will sell securities thereby limiting losses. At least that's what many shareholders thought.

As millions of investors have discovered, mutual fund portfolio managers do a very poor job of managing risk. The result is billions of dollars in losses each year for fund shareholders.

Investors are disillusioned with Wall Street. Long held beliefs and ideas regarding the equity markets and portfolio management have been washed away in a wave of corruption. Once trusted investment products and strategies are now looked at suspiciously. The answer, however, is not to throw your arms up in defeat and swear off equities. Likewise, continuing to use the same old portfolio management strategies and products that failed you in the past, such as buy-and-hold investing and traditional mutual funds, is no longer an option.

To succeed today investors must change how they approach portfolio management. They must use strategies based on sound financial principles backed by research and data instead of strategies dependent on the market going up to succeed. The strategies must be implemented using the most advanced portfolio management tools available instead of products designed to meet the needs of investors from a different era. Most importantly, investors today must use "all market" strategies that will allow them to achieve their objectives regardless of prevailing market conditions, economic cycle, or political uncertainty.

Strategic Index Investing Is the Answer

It's easy to find fault. Being a critic, however, will not make you a better investor or help you reach your financial goals. Likewise, to simply point out the shortcomings associated with the most popular investment strategies and products is meaningless, unless a better alternative is suggested. In this book, a better portfolio management approach is put forth, which I call Strategic Index Investing.

Strategic Index Investing is a comprehensive portfolio management methodology that combines active investment management strategies with passive (index-based) investment vehicles allowing

9

investors to easily and effectively adapt to changing market conditions. It is a scientific, proactive approach to index fund management designed to maximize portfolio performance while minimizing risk. This "active index" approach is the driving force behind fundamental changes occurring in the area of portfolio construction that are transforming the way individuals think and act about portfolio management.

Proven Portfolio Management Strategies
The first component of Strategic Index Investing is the use of proven investment strategies based on sound financial principles, research, and data. Strategic Index Investing does not rely on strategies predicated on being able to predict the future direction of a stock or mutual fund to succeed. Instead, Strategic Index Investing is based on the use of:

- **Asset Allocation** – Asset allocation is a Nobel Prize winning strategy rooted in Modern Portfolio Theory. It is a scientific approach to portfolio diversification that explains over 90% of the variation in a portfolio's returns making it an important component of successful, long-term portfolio management.

- **Indexing** – Indexing is an investment strategy that attempts to mimic or track the performance of a given market index or benchmark. Index-based investments allow the investor to focus on the key determinants of investment performance such as asset size, style, geographic region, or industry sector instead of trying to predict which actively managed mutual fund or common stock will do best.

- **Active Portfolio Management** – Active investment management provides the flexibility necessary to succeed regardless of prevailing market conditions. It allows the investor to systematically limit losses, protect profits, and preserve capital.

Additionally, active portfolio management provides a way to take advantage of market opportunities in order to enhance return.

Exchange-Traded Index Funds

In Strategic Index Investing we use exchange-traded index funds to implement the strategies discussed above. Exchange-traded index funds are extremely cost-effective, tax-efficient, technologically advanced portfolio management tools. They allow the investor to easily combine elements of active and passive portfolio management because all exchange-traded index funds are actively traded throughout the day and have passively managed (indexed) portfolios. As we will see in Part 2, exchange-traded index funds offer significant portfolio management advantages over traditional mutual funds and common stocks.

Advantages of Strategic Index Investing

Investment fads come and go. The market moves from bull market to bear market and back again. Certain fundamental investment principles endure — diversification, discipline, risk management, consistency, flexibility, efficiency, and the value of planning. Strategic Index Investing is a portfolio management methodology based on these time-honored principles.

Strategic Index Investing is not a pre-packaged product or a one-size-fits-all solution but rather a disciplined approach to portfolio management that represents a superior alternative to the most popular investment strategies and products used today. Most importantly, it is easily customized to meet the unique needs of every investor, regardless of risk tolerance, performance goals, or investment objectives.

Strategic Index Investing is for investors:

- Seeking an alternative to buy-and-hold investing.
- Seeking to avoid the risks and pitfalls associated with tradi-

tional mutual funds or common stocks.

- Seeking to improve investment performance, diversification, and discipline.
- Seeking to minimize overall investment related costs – both seen and unseen.
- Seeking greater control over their financial future.
- Seeking a comprehensive, personalized portfolio management strategy.
- Seeking a practical "active index" all-weather approach to portfolio management.

In addition, Strategic Index Investing is relatively simple to implement and track using the rules put forth in this book. This is not to imply that it does not take a certain amount of time and work. Like any worthwhile endeavor, Strategic Index Investing requires a commitment of both time and energy. Fortunately, for those willing to make the commitment, it offers unlimited rewards.

Combining Active and Passive Investment Strategies

At the heart of Strategic Index Investing is the idea that active and passive investment strategies don't have to exist at polar extremes. Active investment management refers to the use of different strategies, tools, research, trading, or other techniques designed to beat the market. Passive investment management, commonly referred to as index investing, is a portfolio management approach designed to simply match the performance of the market or a specific benchmark.

Since the introduction of the first index mutual fund, in the early 1970s, a tremendous debate has raged. The debate is which type of mutual fund is better: actively managed or index-based. With over thirty years of data, it's now possible to say conclusively that index mutual funds represent the most efficient, cost-effective way to access the true risk and return characteristics of a given asset class, sector, or the entire market. The reasons why are discussed in Chapter 7.

Indexing alone, however, is not enough. Index-based investment products, such as exchange-traded index funds, are simply tools that represent the most efficient way to access the true performance of a given segment of the equity or bond market. How an investor chooses to use that tool will ultimately determine success or failure.

While not as common, the same question — active or passive — can be addressed at the investor's portfolio level. For example, an "active investor" is an investor who incorporates the use of strategies, tools, research, trading, or other techniques designed to maximize return and minimize risk. In contrast, a "passive investor" simply rides the market up or down engaging in few portfolio reviews or changes, thus representing a buy-and-hold approach. As we will see in Chapter 2, buy-and-hold investing is actually a very risky investment strategy. Exhibit 1-1 shows the various ways investors interact with different types of investment products.

In this book, active management of passive investments, or Strategic Index Investing, is shown to be a superior portfolio management strategy. Passive investment vehicles avoid the costs, risks, and inefficiencies associated with traditional mutual funds and common stocks. Active portfolio management adds flexibility, control, and the ability to manage risk. As we will see, Strategic Index Investing is a powerful approach to portfolio management that is helping millions of investors dramatically improve their investment results.

Summary

Today, every investor has a choice. They can choose to succeed or they can choose to follow the herd. This book is designed for those investors who wish to succeed by exploring new portfolio management strategies and tools instead of simply following the herd.

Exhibit 1-1: Comparing Investor Types and Investments

Investment Product	Investor Type	
	Active	**Passive**
Common Stocks	**Active Stock Investor** Very labor intensive, high risk, and potentially costly portfolio strategy. Not practical for most investors.	**Passive Stock Investor** Very high risk because investor does not use a risk management strategy. Individual stocks require active management at all times.
Traditional Mutual Funds	**Active Mutual Fund Investor** The active mutual fund investor usually tries to time the market. Because mutual funds can only be bought or sold at the end of the day, the investor is trading "blind." Some fund companies restrict how often you can buy or sell shares.	**Passive Mutual Fund Investor** The most common investment strategy used today is buy-and-hold using mutual funds. It provides very limited protection from market declines. Also, this strategy can be costly, tax inefficient, and result in sub-par performance.
Exchange-Traded Index Funds	**Active/Passive Investor** The future of portfolio management! Combines the benefits of passive (indexed) investments with the flexibility of active investment strategies. A comprehensive approach to portfolio management offering investors a number of significant benefits.	**Passive/Passive Investor** The ultimate buy-and-hold investor. They use index funds to implement a buy-and-hold strategy. This is a potentially risky strategy that should only be used by investors with an extremely long-term time horizon.

I believe the following quote, credited to Warren Buffett, is an appropriate way to get started: *"To invest successfully over a lifetime does not require a stratospheric IQ, nor does it require unusual business insights, or inside information. What's needed is a sound intellectual framework for making decisions and the ability to keep emotions from corroding that framework."* The goal of this book is to provide just that — a sound intellectual framework by which to make portfolio management decisions. It's up to the reader to provide the emotional discipline and determination necessary to succeed.

Chapter 2

BUY-AND-HOLD INVESTING AND OTHER FAILED PORTFOLIO MANAGEMENT STRATEGIES

The Problems with Buy-and-Hold Investing

When evaluating the merits of a new investment strategy, as we do in this book, it's important to know and understand the most common investment strategies used, if for no other reason than for comparative analysis. For millions of investors, this means evaluating the effectiveness of buy-and-hold investing.

Buy-and-hold investing is based on the observation that over time equity prices, and therefore the equity markets, have tended to move higher. Even if a significant decline does occur, eventually the market will seek new highs meaning you need not panic. Furthermore, since it's impossible to predict when markets will advance or decline, the best strategy is to buy-and-hold. Sounds simple enough, doesn't it?

While it may sound simple there are three fundamental problems associated with buy-and-hold investing. First of all, the investor is at the mercy of the market. Next is the problem of deciding which investment or investments to actually buy and hold. Finally, there is the question of when to sell.

The Unpredictable Market

Buy-and-hold investing is based on the observation that over time equity prices, in general, have tended to move higher. For example, over the last fifty years the S&P 500 Index has produced an average annual return of about 10% per year. Therefore, an investor holding shares of a mutual fund designed to track the S&P 500 Index would have earned about 10% per year, over the last fifty years, by simply following a buy-and-hold approach.

Do these numbers accurately reflect the results achieved by most buy-and-hold investors? Fifty years, after all, is an extremely long holding period. From my experience few, if any, investors will realistically stick with one strategy for such a long time period. Each of us will go through numerous financial changes over the course of our lifetime. As we do our goals, objectives, and investment time horizons change. Given this, a more realistic holding period for most investors is probably in the range of fifteen to twenty years, at most, not fifty. Therefore, to accurately judge the effectiveness of buy-and-hold investing we must evaluate the strategy over a shorter, more realistic holding period, such as twenty years.

Most investors probably realize Wall Street experienced one of its longest and most prolific bull markets during the 1980s and 1990s. For example, in the decade of the 1980s the S&P 500 Index produced an annualized average return of 17.5% per year. Likewise, in the decade of the 1990s the S&P 500 Index produced an annualized average return of 18.2% per year. The performance of the S&P 500 Index over these two decades was not just remarkable; it was the best twenty-year period on record!

Not as well-known, however, is that during the decade of the 1960s the S&P 500 Index could only muster an annualized average return of 7.8%. Furthermore, during the 1970s the S&P 500 Index did even worse, producing a scant 5.8% annualized average return for the entire decade.

What does this mean for the typical buy-and-hold investor? To better understand we will examine the results of two hypothetical investors. Both are forty years old, intend to invest $25,000 in a mutual fund tracking the S&P 500 Index, and have a twenty-year time horizon. In fact, the two investors are virtually identical with one small exception: *when* they start their investment plan. Investor L (Lucky) starts his buy-and-hold investment plan on 12/31/1979 while investor U (Unlucky) starts his buy-and-hold investment plan on 12/31/1959.

So how did our two investors fare? From 12/31/1979 through 12/31/1999, investor L earned an annualized average return of 17.87% meaning his initial investment of $25,000 grew to a very nice sum of $670,781. Because his investment strategy did so well, investor L is looking forward to a comfortable retirement playing golf, traveling with his wife, and fishing.

Now, let's see how the other investor fared. From 12/31/1959 through 12/31/1979, investor U earned an annualized average return of 6.77% meaning his initial investment of $25,000 grew to a dismal $92,700. This represents a difference of over $578,000 compared to investor L. Because his investment strategy did so poorly, investor U must keep working for at least another ten years, which is not exactly how he intended to spend his golden years. Exhibit 2-1 shows the year by year performance results and cumulative difference between the two portfolios.

As the exhibit shows, our two investors experienced dramatically different results even though both followed the exact same strategy: buy-and-hold using an S&P 500 Index fund with a twenty-year holding period. What could account for the dramatic differences between the two portfolios, which allowed one to retire in comfort while the other was left scrambling to make ends meet? Did investor U do something wrong?

The only difference was *when* they invested. Investor L was lucky enough to invest during a remarkably good market environment while investor U wasn't as fortunate. Therefore, a factor beyond the control of either investor determined who would retire comfortably at age sixty and who had to keep working.

Exhibit 2-1:

Year-by-Year Portfolio Analysis of Investor U and Investor L

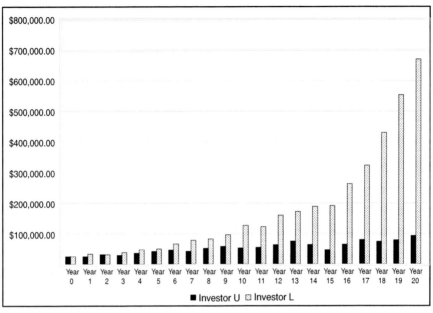

Which investor would you like to be? Unfortunately, when following a buy-and-hold approach you don't get to choose. You're at the mercy of the market, whether you like it or not. The investor fortunate enough to use the strategy during a long-term bull market will do well, as we have seen, while the investor, who happens to use the strategy during a slow growth market environment, will not.

What To Buy and Hold

The next problem associated with buy-and-hold is determining what to buy. Proponents of the strategy emphasize time in the market, not how to pick the best investments. With literally thousands of different stocks, bonds, and mutual funds to choose from, how can any investor know which investments will perform well over the long run? This is particularly important because the performance of the investments used will determine if the strategy succeeds or fails.

For instance, the long-term buy-and-hold investor who purchased shares of Microsoft when it first went public is probably very happy today. A $10,000 investment in Microsoft in 1986 was worth over $3 million as of June 2002. The buy-and-hold investor who purchased shares of Microsoft hit a major league "homerun," but what about the investor who didn't have the foresight, or luck, to buy shares of Microsoft? How did their buy-and-hold strategy work?

Exhibit 2-2 provides a glimpse of how following a buy-and-hold strategy might have fared investing in common stocks of well-known companies over the last seventy-five years. The exhibit shows the growth of $10,000 from March 1, 1928 through March 1, 2003.

As Exhibit 2-2 shows, not all stocks produce great returns over the long-term. How would you feel if your $10,000 investment only grew to $25,725 after seventy-five years? That's exactly what hap-

Exhibit 2-2:
Could You Have Picked the Winners?

Company Name	Amount Invested 3/1/1928	Value 3/2003	Annualized Return*
Chevron	$10,000.00	$ 803,987.00	6.19%
Union Carbide	$10,000.00	$ 798,294.00	6.18%
Texaco	$10,000.00	$ 504,786.00	5.52%
DuPont	$10,000.00	$ 468,627.00	5.26%
Eastman Kodak	$10,000.00	$ 427,125.00	5.13%
Sears Roebuck	$10,000.00	$ 427,800.00	5.13%
Fortune Brands	$10,000.00	$ 204,721.00	4.22%
General Motors	$10,000.00	$ 103,407.00	3.16%
Goodyear Tire	$10,000.00	$ 45,086.00	2.02%
Venator Group	$10,000.00	$ 25,725.00	1.30%

*Annualized yearly return from 3/1/1928-3/1/2003
Source: RCM Financial Data

pened if you owned shares of Venator Group. The reality is most buy-and-hold investors will not own shares of the next Microsoft. They will own companies that produce mediocre results, similar to those shown in the exhibit.

Not only is it difficult to pick stocks, finding the winning actively managed mutual fund can be just as hard. When using actively managed mutual funds, in conjunction with a buy-and-hold strategy, it's very likely that you will end up with a few lemons along the way. In fact, as we will see in later chapters, actively managed mutual funds typically underperform most market averages, often by very sizable amounts for extremely long periods of time. Exhibit 2-3 shows how a long-term buy-and-hold strategy might have fared using actively managed mutual funds.

After reviewing Exhibits 2-2 and 2-3, one point is clear: it's wrong to assume that all investments perform well over the long run. There is nothing magical about time that will suddenly transform a bad investment into a good investment. Some investments are simply dogs

Exhibit 2-3:
Twenty-Year Performance Record of
Select Actively Managed Mutual Funds

Fund Name	Balance 9/30/1983	Balance 9/30/2003	20-year Annualized Return
American Heritage Fund	$25,000.00	$ 1,258.00	-13.88%
U.S. Global Investors Gold Shares	$25,000.00	$ 4,125.00	- 8.62%
Ameritor Investment	$25,000.00	$ 5,290.00	- 8.23%
Ameritor Security Trust	$25,000.00	$17,712.00	- 1.71%
Matterhorn Growth Fund	$25,000.00	$31,702.00	1.19%
Rainbow Fund	$25,000.00	$32,016.00	1.24%
American Growth Fund D	$25,000.00	$37,036.00	2.29%

Source: Morningstar

and will never do well regardless of how long you hold them. If you don't believe this, ask the shareholders of Enron, Waste Management, Sunbeam, Exodus Communications or WorldCom Group, just to name a few.

When To Sell

At the heart of buy-and-hold investing is this simple rule: be patient and wait. As we have seen, however, some investments are just plain bad and no amount of time will change that. Without a clear, concise sell or exit strategy investors are prone to make decisions emotionally, rather than logically. When they do, it usually is the wrong decision.

The tendency of investors to make decisions emotionally is seen by examining net mutual fund cash inflows and outflows. Historically, record amounts of money typically flow into equity-based mutual funds at major market tops while record amounts of money typically flow out of equity-based mutual funds at major market bottoms. This is the exact opposite of what we would expect to see if investors were making buy and sell decisions based on a logical plan or strategy.

A recent study by the Leuthold Group, a financial market research company, provided examples of emotional investing. According to the study, when the S&P 500 Index was at 1,500 in the spring of 2000, equity-based mutual funds were averaging $42 billion per month in new money received. In the fall of 2002, after the index had dropped by almost 50% and was trading at a five-year low, the study found that on average over $22 billion was being pulled out of equity-based mutual funds on a monthly basis. Why would any investor wait until the market had dropped 50% to sell?

While there is no way to be absolutely sure, it's likely that the liquidations were long-term buy-and-hold investors who simply could not handle any more pain. Without a sell strategy in place, providing clear and unemotional parameters, most investors make decisions at exactly the wrong time, as the study indicates.

Like it or not, all investors must do some pruning at some point and sell their losers. The only question is, will you have a plan in place to do so or will you make the decision emotionally? If you follow a buy-and-hold approach, when to sell is never a consideration. Losing investments are often held for years, or the investment is sold only after all hope is lost and utter desperation takes over.

Can You Count on the Market?

Buy-and-hold investing has not always been a popular strategy. It's a by-product of the extremely long bull market Wall Street enjoyed for most of the 1980s and 1990s. Historically, investors haven't always been so eager to simply buy-and-hold. This is illustrated by the following quote, from *U.S. News & World Report,* October 21, 1974: *"Thousands of people who had planned to retire on stock market profits have had to postpone retirement or resign themselves to a lower-than-expected standard of living."*

When studying the history of the market we find that whether one believes it is best to buy-and-hold or to actively manage their portfolio depends primarily on how the market has performed over the preceding couple of years. To highlight this, we need go no further than the May 1999 cover of *Money* magazine. In bold letters the headline proclaimed: "TECH STOCKS — Everyone's Getting Rich! Here's how to get your share." The article suggested that buying and holding technology stocks was a surefire way to achieve wealth.

Contrast this with a January 2002 headline from *Business Week:* "The Betrayed Investor." The article addressed the massive losses many investors experienced from March 2000 through March 2002. The primary reason for the losses, according to the article, was the overwhelming confidence they had in buy-and-hold. Countless investors refused to sell because they were conditioned to believe that the market always goes higher. Instead of selling, they watched and did nothing as profits disappeared, according to the article.

The way the market's performance can influence the buy-and-hold mindset is even more obvious in the following survey. As the decade of the '90s came to a close, Liberty Financial, a large financial services company, surveyed 1,014 mutual fund investors. The survey found that an incredible 85% of those polled expected the market's performance over the next ten years to meet or beat the performance over the previous ten years. Bear in mind, this survey took place shortly after the Dow Jones Industrial Average had recorded its best twenty-year performance ever! Even more amazing, 78% of respondents expected no declines in the market greater than 20% over the next decade. Finally, almost half of those surveyed expected no declines of 10% or greater over the next decade. Wow, now that's irrational exuberance!

The Impact of a Bear Market

The answers given in the survey above are even more remarkable when we consider that since 1900 there have been twenty-nine market corrections of at least 20% or greater. Statistics show that on average, a new bear market begins every five years, lasts eighteen months, causes losses of 39%, and requires five and a half years to return to break-even. Exhibit 2-4 provides a statistical overview of bear markets during the twentieth century.

Exhibit 2-4:
Bear Market Facts, 1900-2000

Extent of Decline	Number of Declines	Average Length	Frequency
5% or Greater	328	40 days	3.3 per year
10% or Greater	108	3.33 months	1.1 per year
15% or Greater	51	7 months	every 2 years
20% or Greater	29	1 year	every 3 years

One of my strongest beliefs is that it's easy to be a long-term buy-and-hold investor as long as the market is going up, as it did through most of the 1980s and all of the 1990s. The struggle comes when the market goes through a prolonged decline and the buy-and-hold investor discovers they don't have the stomach to hold equities. Inevitably, when the pain becomes too great, they sell. Unfortunately, it's usually just as the market is about to go back up.

This is not to suggest that some investors are not able to remain calm as the market decimates their portfolio. If you are young it is much easier to do, than if you are nearing retirement. With the possible exception of Rip Van Winkle, most investors find it very difficult to sleep soundly during market declines. Yet the reality is, if you're in the market for at least ten years there is a good probability you will experience a severe market decline. Is your portfolio prepared? Exhibit 2-5 provides an example of the severe market de-

Exhibit 2-5:
S&P 500 Index Bear Market Study

Time Period	Duration (in months)	% Decline S&P 500 Index	Time Needed to Break-Even
July 1933-March 1935	20	-33.93%	2.25 years
March 1937-March 1938	12	-54.47%	8.83 years
November 1938-April 1942	41	-45.80%	6.42 years
May 1946-March 1948	22	-28.10%	4.08 years
August 1956-October 1957	14	-21.63%	2.08 years
December 1961-June 1962	6	-27.97%	1.75 years
February 1966-October 1966	8	-22.18%	1.42 years
November 1968-May 1970	18	-36.06%	3.33 years
January 1973-October 1974	21	-48.20%	7.58 years
November 1980-August 1982	21	-27.11%	2.08 years
August 1987-December 1987	4	-33.51%	1.92 years
July 1990-October 1990	3	-19.92%	.58 years
July 1998-August 1998	1.5	-19.34%	.25 years
March 2000-October 2002	31	-50.05%	????

clines that have occurred over the last seventy years.

The actual dollar impact of a bear market on a buy-and-hold investor's portfolio is staggering. Just how damaging depends in large part on what point in the investor's time horizon the correction occurs. Consider the following. If an investor saved $5,000 per year for fifteen years, earning 15.0% per year, they would end up with $237,902. If this same investor experienced a bear market decline of 35% in year one of their investment strategy, then earned 15.0% per year for the next fourteen years, their portfolio would grow to $225,520. However, if this same investor earned 15% per year for fourteen years, then experienced a decline of 35% in year fifteen, their portfolio would be worth $131,640, or just half as much as in the first example.

Do You Feel Lucky?

After reviewing the dangers associated with buy-and-hold investing, I'm reminded of a line from one of my favorite Clint Eastwood movies "Dirty Harry." In the movie, Clint's character Harry Calahan asks the bad guy, "Do you feel lucky?" as he points a loaded gun at his head.

Every long-term buy-and-hold investor must ask himself or herself this same question because luck, and nothing else, is going to determine success or failure. Will the market do well or will you suffer the same fate as millions of other investors who depended on the equity markets in an earlier time period; only to see their portfolio values cut in half, or worse. In other words, "Do you feel lucky?"

Other Portfolio Management Mistakes To Avoid

In addition to following a rigid buy-and-hold investment approach, there are other portfolio management mistakes we have all probably made at one time or another. Some of the most common are listed below to help the reader recognize and avoid them in the future.

Mistake # 1: Not Having a Written Investment Plan

Be honest. Do you have a written plan outlining your investment strategy? Could you go to a desk drawer and take out a detailed investment plan that includes your goals, risk tolerance, performance objectives, strategic asset allocation model, and policy for reviewing and monitoring your portfolio? Before adding a new investment to your portfolio, do you take time to review your written investment plan to fully understand how the new investment will impact the overall portfolio?

If you don't, you're not alone. Most investors employ a patchwork portfolio management approach. They gather investment ideas from a number of sources including friends, co-workers, magazines, or television shows without rhyme or reason. Instead of focusing on the overall portfolio, via a comprehensive portfolio plan, they focus on the individual components. The result is often a portfolio loaded with mismatched investments, none of which fit together in a cohesive way.

A detailed, written investment plan is critical to achieving your goals. It will also decrease the stress and anxiety related to investing. A written plan provides guidance during tough markets and forces you to make the hard decisions when necessary, instead of avoiding them.

Mistake # 2: Chasing Last Year's Hot Investment

Year after year one of the most common mistakes investors make is to chase the previous year's hot mutual fund. It's hard to avoid. After all, everyone wants to own a winner. Unfortunately, more often than not last year's hot mutual fund turns out to be next year's dog. Then, in what's almost inevitable timing, disappointed investors sell the former top-performing fund and buy the new top-performing fund, starting the cycle all over again.

Successful investing means avoiding the "I want to own the best performer" mindset. I refer to this phenomenon as newsstand investing because almost every financial publication routinely publishes a list of "The Best Funds To Buy Right Now" or a list ranking the "Top Mutual Funds in the Country." The problem with these "best of the best" lists is that the funds are usually chosen based on past performance. What every investor must understand is that past performance is just that. It represents what has already happened, not what is going to happen.

I challenge anyone to prove a consistent correlation between past performance and predictable future results. Some studies, in fact, suggest that mutual funds, which outperform market averages one year, are more likely to underperform the market at some point in the future, a statistical concept known as regressing to the mean. Yet, everyday mutual funds are sold to investors based on past performance alone.

Finally, simply because a mutual fund has a good track record does not mean it's the best fund for you. To invest in a mutual fund because it earned 45% the previous year and was one of the top-performing mutual funds in the country is foolish. Many factors, in addition to performance, are important when choosing an investment.

Mistake # 3: Relying on Get-Rich-Quick Schemes or Hot Tips
I'm sure everyone reading this book has taken the time to read one of those crazy get-rich-quick letters that show up in the mail. They typically have headlines that make incredible claims, such as "How I Made $500,000 in Only Five Weeks," or, "How to Safely Turn $5,000 into $1,000,000." These advertisements are usually filled with testimonials from average people who used the system being touted and their lives were forever changed. Now, instead of taking the bus, they fly on their private jet to exotic locations.

Even though we know deep down that these claims are too good to be true, we still want to believe. We want to believe that there is an easy, safe way to turn small amounts of money into huge Bill Gates type fortunes. From my experience, most investors are optimistic. Otherwise they wouldn't be investing. The people pushing these systems understand this and they prey on that optimism.

Always remember — the only people who make money from get-rich-quick investment systems are the ones selling them. The simple truth is they don't work. If they did, why on earth would anyone be willing to sell the system to you at any price? A foolproof system for making money in the stock market is worth far more than anyone could ever make selling such a system to investors.

I include hot stock tips with get-rich-quick schemes because they are very similar in that they usually promise quick profits with little risk. The only difference is the person providing you with the "sure thing." Instead of someone trying to sell you something, it's typically a friend, co-worker, or relative doing you a "favor." The best advice I can give you is to listen politely, nod appreciatively, and then forget what they tell you.

The common thread between all quick and easy profit ideas is the potential for high returns with limited risk. Some tout 50%, 75%, 150% returns or greater. We are led to believe that the way to financial freedom lies in achieving huge returns on our investment dollars. Greed takes over and common sense goes out the window.

Perhaps the greatest investment myth is that high investment returns are necessary to succeed. Contrary to what most investors have read, this is not true. Consistent returns are more important. For instance, if a stock increases by 50% a year for two years, then drops by 50% in year three the investor will actually end up earning less than if they had simply earned a consist 9% return in each of the three years. An example of this is shown in Exhibit 2-6.

I'm sure we have all heard the story about the tortoise and the hare. It's also true when investing, as the exhibit points out. Investors often get lost in the bells and whistles surrounding the investment management process. Falling prey to the belief that they must find an investment that produces a big return. In reality, it's not necessary to

Exhibit 2-6:
The Tortoise and the Hare

	Value	Return	Ending Value
Portfolio 1:			
Year 1	$10,000.00	50%	$15,000.00
Year 2	$15,000.00	50%	$22,500.00
Year 3	$22,500.00	-50%	$11,250.00
Three Year Average Return: 4.00%			
Portfolio 2:			
Year 1	$10,000.00	9.0%	$10,900.00
Year 2	$10,900.00	9.0%	$11,881.00
Year 3	$11,881.00	9.0%	$12,950.29
Three Year Average Return: 9.00%			

chase last year's hot mutual fund or follow every hot stock tip to be successful. Instead, the focus must be to build a portfolio that produces consistent returns over time.

Mistake # 4: Lack of Proper Diversification

Whenever the topic of portfolio diversification is discussed you can almost be certain that someone will give the following warning: "Do not put all of your eggs in one basket." This very simple statement clearly captures the essence of portfolio diversification. For centuries people have practiced diversification as a way of reducing risk in their daily lives. The above quote actually dates back to 1605 when Miguel de Cervantes wrote, "Tis the part of a wise man to keep himself today for tomorrow, and not venture all his eggs in one basket," in *Don Quixote de la Mancha*.

When discussing portfolio management, diversification refers to the practice of reducing investment risks by allocating dollars among several different types of investments, in essence putting your eggs in different baskets. Proper diversification allows the investor to re-duce portfolio risk without reducing expected returns or increase expected returns without increasing expected risk.

Systematic portfolio diversification is an important component of investing. Likewise, the lack of diversification is a recipe for fail-ure. Exhibit 2-7 shows the dangers associated with failing to prop-erly diversify.

As we can see in the exhibit, concentrated portfolios are risky. Even though all three investments produced the same results, portfo-lio A, the better diversified portfolio, had a higher overall return com-pared to portfolio B. The reason for this is simple; since each invest-ment is equally weighted the poor performing investment cannot impact the performance of the entire portfolio to the same degree, as it can in portfolio B. Therefore, diversification must be a central component of any sound portfolio management strategy.

Exhibit 2-7:
The Risk of Not Diversifying

	Amount Invested	1-year % Return	Ending Value
Portfolio A:			
Investment A	$ 33,333.00	12.0%	$ 37,332.96
Investment B	$ 33,333.00	15.5%	$ 38,499.62
Investment C	$ 33,334.00	-25.0%	$ 25.000.50
Total	**$100,000.00**		**$100,833.08**
Portfolio B:			
Investment A	$ 25,000.00	12.0%	$ 28,000.00
Investment B	$ 25,000.00	15.5%	$ 28,875.00
Investment C	$ 50,000.00	-25.0%	$ 37,500.00
Total	**$100,000.00**		**$ 94,375.00**

Mistake # 5: Blindly Following the Advice of Stock Analysts

While the risks associated with blindly following the advice of Wall Street analysts is rarely discussed, I believe it represents a major problem. Stock analysts, as a whole, wield tremendous power in the market. This is primarily due to the growth in popularity of financial news programs and the Internet.

In the past, an analyst's recommendations might only reach the clients of the firm for which they worked. Now, analysts have been propelled to a new level of notoriety where they can reach millions of investors in seconds through an appearance on one of a number of financial news programs. A popular market analyst can easily move the price of a stock in a positive or negative way by simply changing his or her opinion of the company.

Investors must realize that the vast majority of these analysts are not overly accurate at predicting the future. Most of them are also somewhat reluctant to issue any type of sell recommendation on the stocks that they follow, for a variety of reasons. For example, of 6,000 recommendations made by Wall Street firms during 1999, according to one study, only eight were sell recommendations. What makes this even more amazing is that the market was on the verge of one of the greatest declines in history, yet the majority of analysts were extremely bullish. They completely missed all signs pointing to the pending market debacle.

Another example of how wrong analysts can be was seen at the height of the technology bubble. Most analysts continued to recommend stocks with little or no earnings. Even as share prices began to plummet, they continued to recommend companies that were virtually worthless on paper, boldly touting outlandish price targets based on questionable valuation models. In the end, many investors who followed the recommendations were financially devastated.

An example of how wrong analysts often are is seen by examining WorldCom Corporation. When WorldCom stock was trading at $60 per share over thirty different analysts had its stock rated as a buy or strong buy. As the price dropped from $60 per share to $20

33

per share not one analyst changed their rating to a sell. Not only did the analysts, like the company, they predicted it would flourish. Remarkably, fifteen stock analysts maintained their buy ratings on the shares of WorldCom right up to when they filed for Chapter 11 protection. At that point, however, the stock was virtually worthless. For the investors following the opinions of these Wall Street analysts it was too late, they had already lost billions of dollars.

It should be noted that sometimes a stock analyst will get it right. When this occurs it's more likely the result of the entire market going up or the specific industry they follow, rather than some great insight they may or may not possess. For example, when technology stocks were hot, all an analyst had to do was issue a buy rating on a technology stock and it would go up. Once the bubble burst, however, the geniuses suddenly became very average indeed.

Mistake # 6: Fear of...

Fear is one of the greatest obstacles standing between investors and the successful completion of their goals. As investors we experience all sorts of fears. Fear of taking action. Fear of losing money. Fear of buying at the top. Fear of selling at the bottom. Fear of failing. Fear of succeeding. Fear of going against prevailing wisdom. The fears that investors can and do experience are virtually limitless.

Fear can be an all consuming emotion, many times disguising itself as lack of action, or at other times as over action. As investors, we will never overcome all of our fears. I'm not sure we should want to. The day we lose fear of the awesome power and destructive capabilities of the markets is the day we may live to regret. Fear helps keep our minds sharp and our senses keen. However, unchecked fear can wreck havoc on an investment portfolio.

The best way I have found to keep fear in check is to have an investment plan based on sound financial principles. Not surprisingly, this takes us full circle, back to Mistake #1: Failing To Plan. If you have ever driven through an unfamiliar city in the middle of the night without a road map, then you probably understand what it is like to feel a certain level of anxiety. Investing is no different. It's amazing how comforting a road map is when you are lost, especially when you are able to pinpoint your exact location on the map and then develop a strategy for finding your way back to familiar territory. An investment road map provides similar comforts, calming fears during even the worst markets. While fear can be disastrous, we should never let it stop us from succeeding; at least not after reading this book.

Summary

Buy-and-hold investing is a popular portfolio management strategy based on the premise that the market always moves higher. However, whether or not the strategy works for you is based more on luck than anything else. When examined closely, many problems are soon discovered that can dramatically alter an investor's performance. These problems include the time period over which you invest, the investments used, and knowing when to sell a losing investment.

Investors fall into many other traps as well, such as chasing last year's hot investment or blindly following the advice of stock analysts. Some investors base investment decisions on hot tips or follow get-rich-quick schemes. Unfortunately, these strategies rarely, if ever, work on a consistent basis.

Chapter 3

STRATEGIC INDEX INVESTING

A Superior Approach to Portfolio Management

What is an investor to do? After the overview provided in Chapter 2, which highlighted the problems associated with today's most popular portfolio management strategies, you may be ready to give up. Sell everything and put your money under the mattress as so many did after the great stock market crash of 1929.

Hiding your money under the mattress is not the answer. Nor does it make sense to continue with the ineffective strategies and products discussed in the previous chapter. The solution is to change the way you approach portfolio management. To achieve success today, investors must discard failed strategies and products, such as buy-and-hold investing and traditional mutual funds and embrace a superior portfolio management alternative: *Strategic Index Investing.*

In this chapter, the final chapter of Part 1, we introduce and explain the key elements of Strategic Index Investing. Next, a detailed comparison between Strategic Index Investing and buy-and-hold investing is provided. Finally, the important role active risk management plays in portfolio management is discussed.

Key Elements of Strategic Index Investing

Portfolio management should be viewed as a science, no different than medicine, engineering, aeronautics, or physics. Portfolio management after all, like other areas of scientific study, is based on certain fundamental principles or rules. The principles of sound portfolio management are found in academic research, portfolio management textbooks, and industry publications. The *Journal of Finance* is one such publication. It is the investor's equivalent to the *New England Journal of Medicine*, yet few investors or stockbrokers have ever read it.

Even though an incredible body of research and data relevant to portfolio management is readily available, most investors and financial professionals tend to shoot from the hip and fail. They never consider following basic financial principles that have been proven successful many times over. Instead, they feast on the equivalent of investment junk food, relying on late night infomercials, trading systems, or get-rich-quick schemes to get investment ideas. Unfortunately, these approaches generally focus on finding winning investments and not sound financial principles. It's like playing the lottery, guess the correct numbers and you win.

Strategic Index Investing, in contrast, is a scientific approach to investing based on proven financial principles. The behavior of the portfolio as a whole, and not the individual investments in it, is what matters most. For example, instead of worrying about what to buy, the focus is on constructing the most efficient portfolio possible to achieve the intended goals. This is often referred to as "portfolio theory" and is at the heart of Strategic Index Investing.

Strategic Index Investing is based on:

1. The use of **exchange-traded index funds**.
2. The diversification benefits of **asset allocation**.
3. The efficiency of **indexing**.
4. The flexibility of **active portfolio management**.

An overview of each aspect of Strategic Index Investing follows. Then, in Part 2, a detailed analysis of exchange-traded index funds is provided while Part 3 focuses on the strategies associated with Strategic Index Investing (asset allocation, indexing, and active portfolio management).

Exchange-Traded Index Funds

Exchange-traded index funds make Strategic Index Investing possible. They are scientifically engineered investment vehicles designed to meet the needs of investors today and in the future. Exchange-traded index funds allow the investor to easily and efficiently combine the benefits associated with asset allocation, indexing, and active portfolio management into a single, comprehensive strategy.

Why is it important to use the most up-to-date investment products? Imagine this. You hire a contractor to remodel your kitchen and he shows up with tools circa 1750. No power drill, power screwdriver, or nail gun. Or, you walk into your local electronics store and they try to sell you an 8-track tape player. For those of you who don't remember, 8-track tapes were popular in the 1970s along with mood rings and pet rocks. Would you buy an 8-track tape player or let the eighteenth century throwback remodel your kitchen? Of course not! Why then, do millions of investors rely on ancient technology when it comes to investing?

Traditional mutual funds were created over seventy years ago to meet the needs of investors from a very different time and place. They were created when the markets moved a little bit slower. Stock prices were quoted on ticker tape machines and most Americans did not own a television set. Before the advent of the Internet or online investing, discount brokers, money market accounts, or computers. Exchange-traded index funds, in contrast, are designed to meet the needs of investors in the twenty-first century. They are powerful investment tools that offer intraday liquidity, index-based advantages, low-costs, and tax efficiency.

While exchange-traded index funds represent the future of portfolio management, traditional mutual funds and common stocks fall short. When used to build and manage a portfolio they present several problems.

- Individual stocks do not present an attractive risk/return relationship. They subject the investor to company specific risks, which include the potential to "blow-up."
- It's difficult and often expensive to achieve the appropriate diversification using individual common stocks.
- It's impossible to know if a given stock or actively managed mutual fund will accurately track the asset class targeted.
- It's too time consuming to research hundreds, if not thousands, of individual stocks or mutual fund managers.
- Actively managed mutual funds are expensive, tax inefficient, and rarely beat the performance of market indexes or benchmarks.
- Mutual funds do not offer intraday liquidity, which drastically limits the risk management strategies available.

Exchange-traded index funds avoid each of the pitfalls listed above commonly associated with traditional mutual funds and common stocks. Most importantly, exchange-traded index funds make Strategic Index Investing possible by allowing investors to easily combine the benefits of asset allocation, indexing, and active portfolio management into a single, comprehensive strategy.

Asset Allocation

When constructing a portfolio it is essential that we start with a solid foundation. Why is a solid foundation important, you may ask? The markets change constantly. The performance of any given investment is influenced by events occurring around the globe twenty-four hours a day seven days a week. The "hot" investment today will most certainly be out of favor tomorrow. As investors, we must routinely deal with future events which, by definition, are unknown. Therefore, it's imperative that we build our portfolio on solid principles backed by proven research, and not guesswork. Otherwise, the portfolio will be wrecked by the inevitable ups and downs of the market.

No one in their right mind would build a house on sand. Every time a hard wind blows, the sand under the house will shift and cause its foundation to crack, eventually causing it to tumble down. Portfolio management is the same. If you follow every new investment gimmick that comes along, or follow strategies that only work in certain types of markets, your portfolio will lack a solid foundation. Every time the investment climate changes and a new wind blows, your portfolio will suffer. Eventually, it will come crashing down.

Diversification is the key to constructing a solid foundation for your portfolio. Asset allocation, or how dollars are allocated among different types of investments, represents the most fundamentally sound way to diversify a portfolio. According to one well-known study, how dollars are allocated among different types of assets explains over 90% of the variation in total returns between portfolios. Over the years, the results of this study have been reaffirmed in countless others. There is no reason to believe that it does not hold true today.

Asset allocation is a scientific approach to investing based on statistical research, proven models, historical performance data and comparisons. It's derived from a Nobel Prize winning portfolio management theory known as Modern Portfolio Theory (MPT). The theory explains, in mathematical terms, how the mix of assets within a portfolio will alter that portfolio's overall risk and return. Asset allocation is a highly customizable approach to portfolio management that allows each investor to build a portfolio that best fits their specific performance objectives, risk tolerance, and time horizon. In fact, asset allocation is the only portfolio diversification strategy that allows every investor to build his or her "optimal" portfolio, as we will see in Chapter 9.

In Strategic Index Investing, a top-down approach to asset allocation is followed. First, the investor's optimal asset allocation is determined between three broad financial asset categories: stocks, bonds, and cash. Next, the overall allocation is "fine-tuned" by making strategic changes among different types of stocks and bonds. A process commonly referred to as *strategic asset allocation.*

For example, instead of allocating the equity portion of a portfolio to a single broad-based market index, like the S&P 500 Index, multiple equity asset categories are used. These could include equity asset categories based on company size, investment style, industry or economic sector, and geographic location. Likewise, the bond portion of the portfolio is allocated among various bond asset classes.

As we will see in Part 3, strategic asset allocation is a strategy that encourages the investor to view the portfolio as a whole instead of concerning themselves with the parts. By doing this, it's possible to create a portfolio that will maximize expected return and minimize risk regardless of prevailing market conditions. Therefore, strategic asset allocation is an important aspect of building a solid portfolio foundation and an integral part of Strategic Index Investing.

The Efficiency of Indexing

The goal of an index-based investment product is to match the performance of a specific market index or benchmark in both advancing and declining markets. Indexing allows the investor to focus on the key drivers of investment performance, such as asset size, style, economic sector, or geographic region instead of trying to guess which actively managed mutual fund or individual stock will be the best performer.

Index-based investments, like exchange-traded index funds, are central to Strategic Index Investing because they represent the most accurate way to implement a strategic asset allocation plan. As we discussed above, strategic asset allocation is a scientific approach to portfolio diversification based on statistical models and proven research. For strategic asset allocation to provide any meaningful benefits, each investment used must accurately reflect the true risk and reward of the underlying index being tracked. The only way to ensure that an investment accurately tracks a specific index or market segment is with an index-based investment product.

As we will see in Chapter 7, indexing offers additional portfolio management benefits, as well. These benefits include superior performance compared to most actively managed mutual funds, lower internal operating expenses, greater tax efficiency, and portfolio transparency.

Active Portfolio Management Strategies

At the beginning of this chapter we said that portfolio management must be approached as a science. Creating a strategic asset allocation plan, implementing the plan using an index-based investment product like exchange-traded index funds, and then rebalancing the portfolio on a regular basis represents an extremely scientific approach to portfolio management. In a logical world where the past is a good indicator of the future and all assets act as they are expected, this approach will produce extremely effective portfolios.

Unfortunately, the markets do not always act in a logical and scientific manner. It is a fact that, from time to time, investors act very irrationally. The markets are comprised of millions of investors around the globe buying or selling securities based on billions of bits of information. Investors experience both fear and greed which can cause them to react emotionally to market news and information. This can cause the market to move to extremes on both the up and down side. When this occurs, asset allocation may not be enough to protect you. At times, every investor must take specific actions to protect their portfolio from the irrational actions of others. In Strategic Index Investing we rely on active portfolio management strategies for this purpose.

There are clearly times when it's beneficial to use active portfolio management strategies. In today's fast-paced markets, active risk management is not only a good idea, it's a necessity. Even the most dedicated practitioners of buy-and-hold cannot, in good conscious,

43

deny this statement. Like it or not, there are times when all investors must act. The only question is, "Will you have a plan in place or will you react emotionally?"

The active portfolio management strategies used in Strategic Index Investing are designed to help limit losses, protect unrealized gains, preserve capital during market corrections, and enhance return. They are based on sound financial principles and applied in a systematic way using predetermined entry and exit points. This includes the use of dynamic stop-loss orders, tactical asset allocation, covered call writing, protective puts, and selling short. These and other active portfolio management strategies are discussed in Part 3.

Unfortunately, whenever active portfolio management is mentioned many investors immediately become fearful. They envision a high risk, volatile portfolio where money is whipped around faster than eggs in a blender. Because of their fear, they never explore the benefits associated with active portfolio management. In reality, when done properly, active portfolio management allows the investor to create a more stable portfolio, not a riskier one. It allows an investor to take specific steps to protect their portfolio instead of simply watching it drop in value when the market falls, as is the case when using a buy-and-hold strategy. Therefore, the proper implementation of active portfolio management strategies can mean the difference between long-term success or failure.

Active Investing within an Index Framework

Strategic Index Investing presents a practical compromise between the flexibility of active portfolio management and the rigidness of passive portfolio management. Asset allocation combined with indexing provides a framework solidly rooted in proven financial principles and research. Active portfolio management strategies provide the necessary flexibility to navigate changing market cycles. In essence, it allows the portfolio to bend rather than break.

Strategic Index Investing is designed to work regardless of market conditions, economic cycle, or political turmoil. It is highly customizable and places an incredible level of control in the hands of the investor. Most importantly, Strategic Index Investing will revolutionize the way every investor thinks and acts regarding portfolio management.

Comparing Strategic Index Investing to Buy-and-Hold

With an understanding of the key elements of Strategic Index Investing it's now possible to compare it to buy-and-hold investing. In Chapter 2, the logic behind buy-and-hold investing was discussed. As we saw, buy-and-hold is based on two basic beliefs: markets tend to go higher over time and it's impossible to predict, with any degree of consistency, exactly when the markets will move up or down. Therefore, the best approach is to simply buy an investment and hold it. Eventually, as the strategy goes, the market will move higher and so will the investment.

As for the first premise of buy-and-hold investing, that equity markets tend to move higher over time, I'm in complete agreement. It goes without saying that the equity markets have historically trended higher. All that one needs to do is examine a long-term chart of the S&P 500 Index, Dow Jones Industrial Average, or any other equity-based index to be convinced of this truth. The tendency of equity prices to trend higher over time is shown in Exhibit 3-1.

The second premise of buy-and-hold investing, that it's impossible to correctly predict when various markets will move up or down, is sound as well. Predicting the direction of the markets, with any degree of accuracy, is virtually impossible. Countless investment experts have proven, by their inability to do so, just how difficult it can be.

Given the fact that equity markets tend to move higher over time and that it's futile to try to predict exactly when markets will advance or decline, Strategic Index Investing and buy-and-hold investing reach

Exhibit 3-1:
Tendency of Equity Prices to Move Higher Over Time*

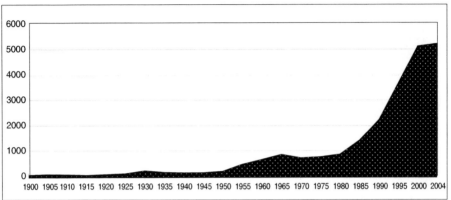

* Benchmark based on composite stock index created by RCM

two very different conclusions. The buy-and-hold proponents take a fatalistic hands-off approach. Basically telling the investor they must accept the inevitable ups and downs of the market and simply have faith that eventually everything will work out for the best. This, of course, is easier said than done, especially during times of severe market turbulence or uncertainty.

Strategic Index Investing, in contrast, is a systematic approach to portfolio management that provides the investor with a framework for making decisions. Like buy-and-hold, Strategic Index Investing is designed to keep the investor in the market the majority of the time. This is important given the fact that markets tend to move higher over time. Instead of simply riding the market down during periods of weakness, however, specific strategies are used that are designed to limit risk, protect profits, and preserve capital.

In other words, Strategic Index Investing is a proactive approach to investing that allows the investor to actively navigate the market while buy-and-hold forces the investor to ride the market up and down like an out of control rollercoaster. Exhibit 3-2 highlights the primary differences between buy-and-hold investing and Strategic Index Investing.

46

As the exhibit shows, there are several important differences between Strategic Index Investing and buy-and-hold investing. One difference is the use of active portfolio management strategies designed to limit losses and protect profits, also referred to as *active risk management*. Unlike buy-and-hold investing, active risk management is an important aspect of Strategic Index Investing. Unfortunately, many investors fail to understand just how important risk management is to the overall portfolio management process.

Exhibit 3-2:
Differences Between Strategic Index Investing and Buy-and-Hold Investing

	SII	Buy-and-Hold
Easy to implement	Yes	Yes
Based on proven financial principles	Yes	No
Utilizes strategies specifically designed to limit losses	Yes	No
Utilizes strategies specifically designed to protect profits	Yes	No
Changes as market changes	Yes	No
Provides flexibility	Yes	No
Decreases overall portfolio volatility	Yes	No
Allows investor to profit in both advancing and declining markets	Yes	No
Incorporates the many benefits of exchange-traded index funds	Yes	Maybe

Active Risk Management –
A Key Aspect of Strategic Index Investing

The ability to properly manage market related risks is a key predictor of long-term portfolio management success. In fact, no other single action will add as much value to the portfolio management process, over the long run as active risk management. Therefore, before concluding our overview of Strategic Index Investing we will discuss how investors typically view market risk and what they do to limit its influence on their portfolios.

Even though professional investors would never dream of putting money in the market without a risk management strategy in place to protect them, the vast majority of individual investors today think nothing of it. Instead, they tend to focus on the question of what to buy or when to buy it, often disregarding risk management altogether. This happens because investors are told that superior research will always produce winning investments. Therefore, risk management is not necessary. Unfortunately, believing that every investment you make will be a winner is akin to living in la-la land. It's not reality.

Another reason investors struggle with the question of how best to manage risk is because investment risk is such a hard thing to define in the first place. It has a different meaning for virtually every investor. What one investor considers a high risk investment could be thoroughly boring to another. To invest successfully, it's crucial that you not only understand and recognize risk, but also take clear and definitive steps to lessen its effect on your portfolio.

Throughout most of the 1990s, risk management was not a popular subject. The prevailing wisdom was that a new market paradigm existed where sustained market corrections were a thing of the past. If a market correction were to occur, all one had to do was wait patiently and eventually everything would be fine.

If you get nothing else from this book, please remember this. If you have money invested in the equity or bond markets you are subject to risk. The actual amount of risk depends on the investments and strategies you are using. Therefore, the question is not if investment risk will affect you, because it will. The question is, "How will you react to it and what will you do to protect your portfolio?"

How Investors Respond to Risk

When confronted with risk, investors have several choices. They can avoid it altogether, ignore it and hope it won't affect them, or they can try to manage it. For anyone seeking equity market rates of return, avoiding risk altogether is not an option. Risk is an unavoidable aspect of investing in equities. This is an absolute certainty and should never be forgotten.

Unfortunately, what typically happens is that most investors will pay too little attention to risk during good market environments and give it too much weight after prolonged market corrections. Both of these actions, being too conservative or too aggressive, can have long-term devastating results on a portfolio's performance. The aggressive investor will inevitably be over-weighted in equities when the market peaks, thereby exposing himself or herself to undo risk. Similarly, the conservative investor will be under-weighted in equities at major market bottoms. When the market does make a substantial advance they will miss out on potentially spectacular returns.

I experienced this type of investor psychology firsthand in early 1999 when speaking to a group of about fifty investors. After a short presentation, I asked the group how many had a risk management strategy in place. I was amazed to discover that not one of them did. In fact, most considered risk management completely unnecessary. They believed that any market correction would be short lived and easily weathered.

Even though this occurred at the tail end of one of the longest bull markets in history, I was still shocked at the nonchalant, almost cavalier attitude this group of investors displayed regarding market related risk. The encounter reinforced a basic belief of mine, which I have held since first entering the investment management industry.

I believe the vast majority of investors have absolutely no idea how destructive the equity markets can be. From my experience, the group mentioned above is by no means an exception to the rule; they are the rule. Unfortunately, many of the same investors, who thought risk management was unnecessary just a few years ago, have recently learned about market risk the hard way.

To succeed going forward, investors must acknowledge that risk is ever present in the markets, accept it as a necessary part of investing, and incorporate strategies designed to manage and consequently minimize its effect. In other words, investors should follow the active risk management strategies used in Strategic Index Investing.

I Don't Need To Worry — My Mutual Fund Manager Is Watching Over My Investments

A common myth associated with traditional actively managed mutual funds is that the fund manager will protect shareholders from market related risks. I've got news for you, they won't. To effectively manage risk you must do it yourself or hire someone to do it for you. Mutual funds are not the answer.

Mutual funds are managed for the masses. Fund managers are not rewarded for protecting shareholders from market risks; they are rewarded based on the amount of money they attract to the fund. Simply put, the more money they bring in, the more they earn in fees. In the mutual fund industry, the best way to attract money is to generate high annual returns, regardless of how much risk must be taken to achieve the returns.

This means mutual fund managers are always under the gun. They must perform or risk being fired. The pressure can cause some fund managers to take on far greater risk than the shareholders of the fund may realize. One tactic is to overload the portfolio in a handful of stocks or a few sectors in an attempt to enhance return. Another popular tactic is to increase trading, sometimes turning the portfolio over

200% to 300% a year in an attempt to increase return. This often leads to higher internal costs and greater tax liability for the fund's shareholders.

The never ending battle to produce superior returns leads mutual fund companies to pay hefty bonuses to attract good fund managers from other fund companies. It is common to see fund managers change companies as often as professional athletes change teams. This hurts shareholders because frequent management change can lead to lower performance. Ironically, even though financial experts suggest knowing a fund manager's tenure before purchasing a specific mutual fund most shareholders never know when one fund manager has left and another has taken over.

Another common misconception is that mutual funds are long-term, dependable investment vehicles. Consider that almost 25% of the mutual funds in business in 1986 are no longer in operation. In 2002 alone, according to several widely published industry studies, over 200 mutual funds were either closed altogether or merged with other funds. It is probably safe to assume that these funds were closed due to poor performance.

On top of all the other problems associated with traditional actively managed mutual funds, by some estimates only 20% are able to beat the S&P 500 Index in any given year. How ironic. You pay a mutual fund manager to produce superior returns and help reduce investment risks, and they typically can't do either one very well.

In spite of the problems and inefficiencies associated with actively managed mutual funds, they continue to be the most popular type of investment product today among individual investors. However, as we will see in Part 2, exchange-traded index funds are making significant inroads. As a result of the advantages they offer and the favorable coverage from the financial media, exchange-traded index funds are quickly becoming the investment of choice for millions of former mutual fund investors.

Summary

Strategic Index Investing is a comprehensive portfolio management approach that blends the benefits of active and passive investing. Exchange-traded index funds are used to construct portfolios based on the diversification benefits of asset allocation, the efficiency of indexing, and the flexibility of active portfolio management strategies. Active risk management is also an important part of successful portfolio management and an important part of Strategic Index Investing.

Part Two

Exchange-Traded Index Funds

A Powerful New Portfolio Management Tool

Chapter 4

EXCHANGE-TRADED INDEX FUNDS — AN IDEA WHOSE TIME HAS COME

An Unprecedented Announcement

The nineteenth century French novelist Victor Hugo once wrote: "An invasion of armies can be resisted but not an idea whose time has come." The New York Stock Exchange (NYSE), the most respected and powerful stock exchange in the world, affirmed the validity of this statement when they issued the following press release:

> *New York, July 12, 2001 – The New York Stock Exchange will extend Unlisted Trading Privileges (UTP) to the three most-active exchange-traded funds on Tuesday, July 31. They include the Nasdaq 100 Index Tracking Stock (QQQ), Standard & Poor's Depositary Receipts (SPY), and the Dow Industrial DIAMONDS (DIA).*

Why was this announcement so unusual? It was the first time in its history that the NYSE had extended Unlisted Trading Privileges to a security. What are Unlisted Trading Privileges? An Unlisted Trading Privilege is a right, provided by the Securities Act of 1934, that permits securities listed on any national exchange to be traded by other such exchanges. For example, if shares of XYZ common stock are listed and traded exclusively on Exchange A, Members of Exchange B can trade shares of XYZ by extending Unlisted Trading Privileges. In essence, Unlisted Trading Privileges allow competing exchanges to gain access to the most popular securities listed on other exchanges.

Ironically, over the years the NYSE had been a very vocal critic of Unlisted Trading Privileges. However, by August of 2003 they had extended such privileges to over forty exchange-traded index funds, even though each fund was already listed and traded on the American Stock Exchange (AMEX), a long time rival.

The decision by the NYSE to extend Unlisted Trading Privileges to some of the most actively traded exchange-traded index funds was undoubtedly intended to increase trading revenue, not make a bold statement. However, by taking an "if you can't beat'em, join'em" approach, the NYSE did make a very bold statement, whether they intended to or not. For millions of investors from Main Street to Wall Street their actions pointed out:

- The growing popularity and importance of exchange-traded index funds.

- The need for a more efficient portfolio management tool.

- Traditional mutual funds, long the investment of choice for millions of individuals, had a major new competitor.

In other words, by their actions the New York Stock Exchange declared to the world that exchange-traded index funds are an idea whose time has come.

The Best of Both Worlds

First introduced in 1993, exchange-traded index funds bridge the gap between the control and versatility of direct stock ownership and the simplicity and diversification of mutual funds. Basically, exchange-traded index funds are index mutual funds that look, feel, and act like common stocks, offering investors the best of both worlds.

Like common stocks, exchange-traded index funds trade on organized stock exchanges providing continuous intraday pricing, order entry flexibility, and liquidity. Shares are easily bought or sold through any brokerage account using a wide range of different types of orders. Exchange-traded index funds can be purchased on margin, sold short, and some funds have underlying option contracts, similar to common stocks.

Like index mutual funds, each exchange-traded index fund share represents a fractional ownership in an underlying portfolio of securities designed to track a specific market index or benchmark. Indexing provides a number of significant portfolio management benefits, such as tax efficiency, low internal operating costs, consistent market level performance, diversification, and portfolio transparency.

Similar to traditional mutual funds, exchange-traded index funds are open-ended investment vehicles. New shares can be created or existing shares redeemed at the fund's net asset value, on any day the exchange is open. Unlike traditional mutual funds, shares of exchange-traded index funds are created and redeemed through a unique "in-kind" transfer of securities, adding an additional layer of tax efficiency and cost savings compared to traditional mutual funds. The unique in-kind creation/redemption mechanism associated with exchange-traded index funds is explained in Chapter 6.

Net asset value pricing solves a major problem most often associated with another type of exchange-traded mutual fund, commonly referred to as closed-end mutual funds. Unlike exchange-traded index funds, closed-end mutual funds can only be bought or sold on an exchange. They don't offer the protection of net asset value pricing. As a result, closed-end mutual funds are notorious for their propensity to trade at prolonged discounts or premiums to their actual net asset value per share, making them a less than desirable investment vehicle. In contrast, exchange-traded index funds are a hybrid investment vehicle offering both net asset value pricing and secondary market trading. As a result, they avoid the discount/premium problems commonly associated with closed-end mutual funds.

Exhibit 4-1 provides an overview of the similarities and differences between exchange-traded index funds, index-based mutual funds, actively managed mutual funds, and closed-end mutual funds.

Exhibit 4-1:
Comparison of Different Types of Investment Products

	Exchange-Traded Index Funds	Index Mutual Funds	Actively Managed Mutual Funds	Closed-End Mutual Funds
Tax-efficient	Yes	Yes	Varies	Varies
Cost-effective	Yes	Yes	Varies	Varies
Intraday liquidity	Yes	No	No	Yes
NAV pricing	Yes	Yes	Yes	No
Limit negative consequences of other shareholders' actions	Yes	No	No	Varies
Transparent portfolio	Yes	Yes	No	Varies
Can be sold short	Yes	No	No	Yes
Offer underlying option contracts	Yes	No	No	No
Can be purchased on margin	Yes	No	No	Yes

Exhibit 4-2:
Assets Under Management for All Exchange-Traded Index Funds,
1993-2003*

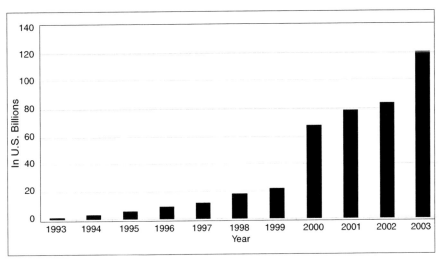

Source: BGI Analysis
* Through 12/31/2003

Exchange-Traded Index Funds Experience Remarkable Growth

By any measurement standard, exchange-traded index funds are one of the most successful investment products ever created. In the competitive environment of Wall Street, a common measurement of success is assets under management. According to the Investment Company Institute, a national association of the U.S. investment company industry, total exchange-traded index fund assets under management grew from $36.8 billion in March of 2000 to $120 billion by the end of 2003, an increase of over 220% in less than three years.

Amazingly, this remarkable growth occurred within the confines of one of the worst bear markets in decades, which caused many managed products to suffer dramatic net outflows of capital. Exhibit 4-2 shows the growth in assets under management enjoyed by all domestic exchange-traded index funds from 1993 through 2003.

The spectacular growth detailed in Exhibit 4-2 shows no signs of slowing down. In fact, the Financial Research Corporation, a well respected market analysis firm, projects total assets invested in all domestic exchange-traded index funds will reach $500 billion to $1 trillion by the year 2010.

Exchange-Traded Index Fund Benefits

Why have so many investors shifted billions of dollars out of traditional mutual funds, opting instead for exchange-traded index funds? The reason is simple: exchange-traded index funds combine a number of significant benefits not found together in any other single investment product. They offer: 1) a cost-effective way to access the equity and fixed income markets, 2) intraday liquidity, flexibility, and control, 3) tremendous tax efficiency, 4) index-based performance, diversification, and transparency, 5) access to a wide array of market indexes, and 6) the ability to easily implement a wide range of portfolio management strategies.

The benefits associated with exchange-traded index funds are briefly summarized below with a more detailed analysis provided over the next several chapters.

Low Internal Operating Expenses — The internal operating fees and expenses associated with exchange-traded index funds are significantly lower than even the lowest cost mutual funds. Because expenses directly decrease net investment performance, all else being equal, the low-cost alternative is the superior choice. More often than not, exchange-traded index funds are the low-cost alternative when compared with other investment products.

Intraday Liquidity, Flexibility, and Control — Shares of exchange-traded index funds are actively traded on all major exchanges, providing the investor with a high level of liquidity, flexibility, and control. For example, when purchasing or selling shares investors can use market orders, limit orders, stop-loss orders, day orders, or good-till-canceled orders, to name a few.

Tax Efficiency — Exchange-traded index funds are one of the most tax-efficient investment vehicles ever created. Unlike mutual funds, which often pass-through significant amounts of taxable capital gains to shareholders, exchange-traded index funds limit the pass-through of unwanted capital gains. As we will see, pass-through capital gains dramatically decrease net after-tax performance and need to be avoided whenever possible.

Index-Based Performance, Diversification, and Portfolio Transparency — Most actively managed mutual funds cannot beat the market on a consistent basis. By some estimates approximately 70% of all actively managed mutual funds fail to beat the S&P 500 Index in any given year. In addition to superior performance, indexing offers a number of other significant portfolio management benefits, such as broad diversification, performance consistency, portfolio transparency, tax efficiency, and cost savings.

Access to a Wide Range of Market Indexes — Exchange-traded index funds provide access to over 125 well-known and respected market indexes and benchmarks. This includes indexes based on specific investment styles (growth or value), market capitalization (large cap, mid cap, and small cap), broad-based indexes covering the entire market, country specific indexes, industry segments, economic sectors, and various regions of the world. More recently, exchange-traded index funds tracking fixed income indexes have been introduced.

Portfolio Management Benefits — Exchange-traded index funds allow investors to easily implement a wide range of portfolio management solutions. This includes strategic asset allocation, active sector rotation strategies, covered call writing, selling short, margin transactions, protective put buying and a number of other strategies, as we will see in Part 3.

When we consider the benefits offered by exchange-traded index funds, it's easy to see why they are such powerful portfolio management tools. More so than any other financial product created in the last fifty years, exchange-traded index funds have the potential to dramatically and forever change the way investors access the equity and bond markets.

A Brief History of Exchange-Traded Index Funds

Ironically, the first exchange-traded index fund was created out of sheer necessity. By the mid 1990s, the survival of the American Stock Exchange was in doubt. Trading volume, the lifeblood of any exchange, had declined dramatically over the previous decade. Many companies which traditionally moved from the Nasdaq Market to the AMEX were staying put. A relentless bear market in the shares of gold and silver mining companies, long a mainstay at the AMEX, caused trading in these issues to dwindle.

For the AMEX to survive and remain relevant they needed to increase trading volume and revenue. In an attempt to do both, they teamed up with State Street Global Advisors to create a new type of index-based investment product specifically designed for institutional investors. The objective was to offer a way for institutional investors to gain quick, easy, and efficient access to the entire market with a single transaction. The result of the collaboration was the first ever domestic exchange-traded index fund: Standard & Poor's Depositary Receipts (SPDRs), or "Spiders."

Spiders began trading in January 1993 with barely $1 billion in total assets under management. Within ten years, assets under management had grown to well over $30 billion, an increase of more than 1,900%. When compared head-to-head against all mutual funds Spiders ranked in the top five, based on total assets under management, as of December 2003. Today, Spiders are one of the most popular and actively traded securities on the American Stock Exchange with average daily trading volume routinely surpassing five million shares. Exhibits 4-3 and 4-4 show the remarkable increase in trading volume and assets under management which the Spiders have experienced, over the last ten years.

Exhibit 4-3:
Change in Monthly Trading Volume of Spiders, 1996 to 2001

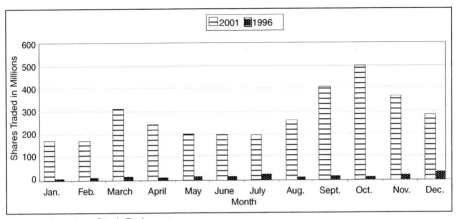

Source: American Stock Exchange

Exhibit 4-4:
Growth in Assets Under Management Experienced by
S&P 500 Index Spiders

Period Ended	Assets Under Management
12/31/1993	$ 461,270,700.00
12/31/1994	$ 419,173,362.00
12/31/1995	$ 999,182,578.00
12/31/1996	$ 2,001,756,375.00
12/31/1997	$ 5,514,411,813.00
12/31/1998	$12,203,868,188.00
12/31/1999	$19,806,669,709.00
12/31/2000	$25,480,978,991.00
12/31/2001	$30,089,990,098.00
12/31/2002	$35,080,102,001.00
12/31/2003	$40,368,204,230.00

Source: American Stock Exchange

Based on the success of Spiders, the American Stock Exchange introduced Standard & Poor's MidCap 400 Depositary Receipts in May 1995. The MidCap Spiders, as they were dubbed, are structured identically to the original Spiders, with one exception. They track the performance of the S&P MidCap 400 Index while the original Spiders are based on the S&P 500 Index. Otherwise, from a structural point of view, the two are identical.

In early 1996, Barclays Global Investors, an indexing heavyweight, entered the exchange-traded index fund arena. They teamed up with Morgan Stanley to create World Equity Benchmark Shares (WEBS). WEBS are a family of seventeen separate exchange-traded index funds. Each fund represents ownership in a basket of stocks designed to track the equity market of a specific country based on a Morgan Stanley Capital International (MSCI) index, long considered the international equity performance standard.

The most innovative aspect of WEBS is the way they are structured. Unlike Spiders and MidCap Spiders, which are structured as unit investment trusts, WEBS are structured as mutual funds. As we will see in Chapter 5, exchange-traded index funds structured as mutual funds offer advantages over those structured as unit investment trusts. By structuring WEBS as mutual funds, Barclays changed the direction of the exchange-traded index funds marketplace and laid the foundation for bigger and better offerings to come.

After several quiet years, 1998 saw two major exchange-traded index fund offerings. The first, which came in January, was the DIAMONDS Trust. DIAMONDS are designed to closely track the price performance and dividend yield of the Dow Jones Industrial Average. For the first time investors could buy shares of a security tracking one of the oldest and best known barometers of U.S. stock market performance. DIAMONDS are listed and traded on the American Stock Exchange.

The second exchange-traded index fund offering of 1998 came in December when nine Select Sector Standard & Poor's Depository Receipts were introduced. Select Sector Spiders, as they are called, "unbundled" the S&P 500 Index. Each of the nine funds track the price performance and dividend yield, before fees and expenses, of a given Select Sector Index. In essence, Select Sector Spiders were the first "sector" or "industry" specific exchange-traded index funds.

The Nasdaq-100 Index Tracking Stock or Cubes were introduced in March 1999. Cubes track the Nasdaq-100 Index, an index comprised of the one hundred largest non-financial companies listed on the National Market tier of The Nasdaq Stock Market. Remarkably, in less than two years Cubes surpassed $15 billion in assets under management. In contrast, S&P 500 Index Spiders needed five years to reach this same mark. Cubes are currently one of the most popular and actively traded securities on the AMEX, routinely trading over ten million shares per day.

Throughout the second half of the 1990s, exchange-traded index funds continued to grow in popularity at both the retail and institutional level. Investors had discovered the many advantages they offered and were using them to meet a wide range of portfolio management needs. This popularity helped set the stage for the largest launch of new exchange-traded index funds to date. It was an event that would mark a turning point for this remarkable new investment tool and forever change the face of portfolio management.

In the summer of 2000, Barclays Global Investors introduced a total of thirty-five new exchange-traded index funds, which they dubbed "iShares." On the first official day of trading, the initial four iShares attracted more assets, about a quarter of a billion dollars, than any previous exchange-traded index fund offering. The iShares tracked a wide range of market indexes and benchmarks based on investment style, company size, and industry sector. As of July 2004, the iShares family consisted of over eighty funds. This included the previously existing WEBS, which Barclays renamed and added to the iShares family. Exhibit 4-5 shows the wide range of indexes tracked by the various iShares.

Not to be left out State Street Global Advisors, the Investment Advisor to the original Spiders, quickly followed with their own family

Exhibit 4-5:
Range of Indexes Tracked by Various iShares

Index Type/Classification	Number of iShares Available*
Market Capitalization (Large Cap, Mid Cap, Small Cap)	8
Investment Style (Growth or Value)	14
Domestic Broad-Based	6
Domestic Sector/Industry	20
Global Sector/Industry	5
Global Broad-Based	2
Country Specific/Regional	30
Fixed Income	6

Source: Barclays Global Investors
* As of 7/1/04

of exchange-traded index funds, which they named streetTRACKS. While somewhat involved with the creation and management of several of the earliest exchange-traded index funds (Spiders, MidCap Spiders, and Select Sector Spiders), streetTRACKS represented State Street Global Advisors first attempt at creating their own family of exchange-traded index funds.

The streetTRACKS family is a group of ten distinct exchange-traded index funds designed to track indexes as diverse as the Wilshire REIT Index to the Fortune e-50 Index. Like the majority of exchange-traded index funds, streetTRACKS are structured as mutual funds and trade primarily on the American Stock Exchange.

It has been said that imitation is the highest form of flattery. Since first introduced in 1993, as a way for the American Stock Exchange to boost trading revenue, the original S&P 500 Index Spiders have been copied many times over. The strongest validation of this powerful new investment tool occurred in March of 2001 when the Vanguard Group created their own family of exchange-traded index funds, which they named Vanguard Index Participation Equity Receipts (VIPERs).

The Vanguard Group is the largest and best known provider of traditional index-based mutual funds in the country. In the early 1970s, the company's founder, John Bogle, took over a small mutual fund company that had been struggling for years. His first major decision was to change the investment strategy of one of the mutual funds in the group. The mutual fund was changed from being actively managed to an unproven academic concept, which some referred to as indexing. It was a radical departure for his day and generated unprecedented criticism from Wall Street. He stuck to his guns and persevered. Today, the Vanguard 500 Index fund is one of the largest mutual funds in the country and Vanguard Group is considered the undisputed leader in traditional index-based mutual funds.

Therefore, when Vanguard Group announced their intentions to create up to twenty exchange-traded index funds under the VIPERs name it was more than just a small ripple in the mutual fund pond. It was the strongest signal yet that exchange-traded index funds are a portfolio management tool whose time has come.

Exhibit 4-6 lists all currently available exchange-traded index funds.

Summary

Exchange-traded index funds are a unique new portfolio management tool that combines the best structural features of open-end mutual funds, closed-end mutual funds, and common stocks. Exchange-traded index funds are passively managed offering the same benefits associated with index-based mutual funds such as low operating expenses, tax-efficiency, diversification, and transparency. As a result, exchange-traded index funds are one of the most popular, powerful, and fastest growing portfolio management tools ever created.

Exhibit 4-6:
Overview of Exchange-Traded Index Funds by Category*

Category/Fund Name	Symbol
Broad-Based Exchange-Traded Index Funds:	
iShares S&P 500 Index Fund	IVV
iShares S&P 500 BARRA Growth Index Fund	IVW
iShares S&P 500 BARRA Value Index Fund	IVE
iShares Russell 1000 Growth Index Fund	IWF
iShares Russell 1000 Value Index Fund	IWD
iShares Russell 1000 Index Fund	IWB
iShares Russell 2000 Growth Index Fund	IWO
iShares Russell 2000 Value Index Fund	IWN
iShares Russell 2000 Index Fund	IWM
iShares Russell 3000 Growth Index Fund	IWZ
iShares Russell 3000 Value Index Fund	IWW
iShares Russell 3000 Index Fund	IWV
iShares Russell MidCap Growth Index Fund	IWP
iShares Russell MidCap Index Fund	IWR
iShares Russell MidCap Value Index Fund	IWS
iShares S&P 100 Index Fund	OEF
iShares S&P 1500 Index Fund	ISI
iShares S&P MidCap 400 Index Fund	IJH
iShares S&P MidCap 400/BARRA Growth Index Fund	IJK
iShares S&P MidCap 400/BARRA Value Index Fund	IJJ
iShares S&P SmallCap 600 BARRA Growth Index Fund	IJT
iShares S&P SmallCap 600 BARRA Value Index Fund	IJS
iShares S&P SmallCap 600 Index Fund	IJR
DIAMONDS Trust	DIA
FORTUNE 500 Index Tracking Stock	FFF
MidCap SPDRS Trust	MDY
Nasdaq-100 Index Tracking Stock	QQQ
S&P 500 Index Trust "Spiders"	SPY
Vanguard Extended Market VIPERs	VXF
Vanguard Large-Cap VIPERs	VV
Vanguard Mid-Cap VIPERs	VO
Vanguard Small-Cap Growth VIPERs	VBK
Vanguard Small-Cap VIPERs	VB
Vanguard Small-Cap Value VIPERs	VBR
Vanguard Total Stock Market VIPERs	VTI
PowerShares Dynamic Market Portfolio	PWC
PowerShares Dynamic OTC Portfolio	PWO

* As of 7/31/2004. Source: AMEX

Exhibit 4-6: (continued)
Overview of Exchange-Traded Index Funds by Category*

Category/Fund Name	Symbol
Broad-Based Exchange-Traded Index Funds:	
streetTRACKS Dow Jones Global Titans 50 Index	DGT
streetTRACKS Dow Jones US LargeCap Growth Index Fund	ELG
streetTRACKS Dow Jones US LargeCap Value Index Fund	ELV
streetTRACKS Dow Jones US SmallCap Growth Index Fund	DSG
streetTRACKS Dow Jones US SmallCap Value Index Fund	DSV
iShares Morningstar Large Core Index Fund	JKD
iShares Morningstar Large Growth Index Fund	JKE
iShares Morningstar Large Value Index Fund	JKF
iShares Morningstar Mid Core Index Fund	JKG
iShares Morningstar Mid Growth Index Fund	JKH
iShares Morningstar Mid Value Index Fund	JKI
iShares Morningstar Small Core Index Fund	JKJ
iShares Morningstar Small Growth Index Fund	JKK
iShares Morningstar Small Value Index Fund	JKL
Rydex S&P Equal Weight ETF	RSP
Sector Exchange-Traded Index Funds:	
iShares Dow Jones Transportation Average Index Fund	IYT
iShares Dow Jones US Basic Materials Index Fund	IYM
iShares Dow Jones US Consumer Cyclical Index Fund	IYC
iShares Dow Jones US Consumer Non-Cyclical Index Fund	IYK
iShares Dow Jones US Energy Index Fund	IYE
iShares Dow Jones US Financial Sector Index Fund	IYF
iShares Dow Jones US Financial Services Index Fund	IYG
iShares Dow Jones US Healthcare Index Fund	IYH
iShares Dow Jones US Industrial Index Fund	IYJ
iShares Dow Jones US Real Estate Index Fund	IYR
iShares Dow Jones US Technology Index Fund	IYW
iShares Dow Jones US Telecommunications Index Fund	IYZ
iShares Dow Jones US Total Market Index Fund	IYY
iShares Dow Jones US Utilities Index Fund	IDU
iShares Goldman Sachs Natural Resources Index Fund	IGE
iShares Goldman Sachs Networking Index Fund	IGN
iShares Goldman Sachs Semiconductor Index Fund	IGW
iShares Goldman Sachs Software Index Fund	IGV
iShares Goldman Sachs Technology Index Fund	IGM
Select Sector SPDR-Consumer Discretionary Index Fund	XLY

* As of 7/31/2004. Source: AMEX

Exhibit 4-6: (continued)
Overview of Exchange-Traded Index Funds by Category*

Category/Fund Name	Symbol
Sector Exchange-Traded Index Funds:	
Select Sector SPDR-Consumer Staples Index Fund	XLP
Select Sector SPDR-Energy Index Fund	XLE
Select Sector SPDR-Financial Index Fund	XLF
Select Sector SPDR Healthcare Index Fund	XLV
Select Sector SPDR-Industrial Index Fund	XLI
Select Sector SPDR-Materials Index Fund	XLB
Select Sector SPDR-Technology Index Fund	XLK
Select Sector SPDR-Utilities Index Fund	XLU
iShares Cohen & Steers Realty Majors Index Fund	ICF
iShares Nasdaq Biotechnology Index Fund	IBB
Vanguard Consumer Discretionary VIPERs	VCR
Vanguard Consumer Staples VIPERs	VDC
Vanguard Financial VIPERs	VFH
Vanguard Growth VIPERs	VUG
Vanguard Healthcare VIPERs	VHT
Vanguard Information Technology VIPERs	VGT
Vanguard Materials VIPERs	VAW
Vanguard Utilities VIPERs	VPU
Vanguard Value VIPERs	VTV
streetTRACKS Morgan Stanley Technology Index Fund	MTK
streetTRACKS Wilshire REIT Index Funds	RWR
Country/Regional Exchange-Traded Index Funds:	
iShares MSCI-Australia Index Fund	EWA
iShares MSCI-Austria Index Fund	EWO
iShares MSCI-Belgium Index Fund	EWK
iShares MSCI-Brazil Index Fund	EWZ
iShares MSCI-Canada Index Fund	EWC
iShares MSCI-France Index Fund	EWQ
iShares MSCI-Germany Index Fund	EWG
iShares MSCI-Hong Kong Index Fund	EWH
iShares MSCI-Italy Index Fund	EWI
iShares MSCI-Japan Index Fund	EWJ
iShares MSCI-Malaysia Index Fund	EWM
iShares MSCI-Mexico Index Fund	EWW
iShares MSCI-Netherlands Index Fund	EWN
iShares MSCI-Pacific Ex-Japan Index Fund	EPP

* As of 7/31/2004. Source: AMEX

Exhibit 4-6: (continued)
Overview of Exchange-Traded Index Funds by Category*

Category/Fund Name	Symbol
Country/Regional Exchange-Traded Index Funds:	
iShares MSCI-Singapore Index Fund	EWS
iShares MSCI-South Africa Index Fund	EZA
iShares MSCI-South Korea Index Fund	EWY
iShares MSCI-Spain Index Fund	EWP
iShares MSCI-Sweden Index Fund	EWD
iShares MSCI-Switzerland Index Fund	EWL
iShares MSCI-Taiwan Index Fund	EWT
iShares MSCI-U.K. Index Fund	EWU
iShares S&P Europe 350 Index Fund	IEV
iShares S&P Latin America 40 Index Fund	ILF
iShares MSCI-EAFE Index Fund	EFA
iShares MSCI-EMU Index Fund	EZU
iShares S&P/TOPIX 150 Index Fund	ITF
iShares MSCI Emerging Markets Index Fund	EEM
Global Sector Exchange-Traded Index Funds:	
iShares S&P Global Energy Sector Index Fund	IXC
iShares S&P Global Financial Sector Index Fund	IXG
iShares S&P Global Healthcare Sector Index Fund	IXJ
iShares S&P Global Information Technology Sector Index Fund	IXN
iShares S&P Global Telecommunications Sector Index Fund	IXP
Fixed Income Exchange-Traded Index Funds:	
iShares Lehman 1-3 Year Treasury Bond Fund	SHY
iShares Lehman 7-10 Year Treasury Bond Fund	IEF
iShares Lehman 20+ Year Treasury Bond Fund	TLT
iShares Lehman Aggregate Bond Fund	AGG
iShares Lehman TIPS Bond Fund	TIP
iShares Goldman Sachs Corporate Bond Fund	LQD

* As of 7/31/2004. Source: AMEX

Chapter 5

COMPARING EXCHANGE-TRADED INDEX FUNDS TO MUTUAL FUNDS

A Better Investment Alternative

Today, millions of individuals routinely depend on traditional mutual funds to fill a variety of investment needs. They are used to fund Individual Retirement Accounts, 401(k) plans, and pension plans. Mutual funds are used to implement asset allocation strategies, in market timing strategies, or simply as an easy way to access the equity and bond markets.

With over $7 trillion in total assets under management and an estimated 90 million individual shareholders, mutual funds are far and away the most popular investment product ever created. But, does this mean they are the *best* investment product available?

As we will see, despite their enormous popularity mutual funds are not the best available investment product. That distinction belongs to exchange-traded index funds, which offer substantial advantages over traditional mutual funds, both actively managed and index-based. These advantages include:

- Greater portfolio management flexibility and choice.
- Lower internal operating expenses.
- Greater tax efficiency.
- Protection for existing shareholders from the actions of other investors.
- Access to a wider range of market indexes.

In addition to the advantages listed above, exchange-traded index funds are passively managed investment vehicles meaning they provide investors with the same benefits as traditional index-based mutual funds. As we will see in Chapter 7, index-based mutual funds offer important portfolio management advantages over actively managed mutual funds such as pure market level performance, diversification, portfolio transparency, and superior performance.

Portfolio Management Flexibility and Choices

The first major advantage we will address, which exchange-traded index funds offer compared to traditional mutual funds, is flexibility. Portfolio management flexibility refers to the number of ways an investment vehicle can be used when constructing and managing a portfolio. In virtually every instance, the investment product that offers the greatest amount of flexibility is desirable.

The benefits associated with flexibility apply to many situations, not just portfolio management. For example, if lost in the wilderness which would you rather have. A Swiss Army Knife that can perform multiple functions or a single-blade pocketknife that can only perform one or two basic functions.

Portfolio management is the same. The investment product that provides the greatest number of solutions is preferable. Exchange-traded index funds are like a Swiss Army Knife, easily adaptable to a number of different situations. Traditional mutual funds, in contrast, are like a basic pocket knife, they are not easily adaptable to changing portfolio management situations.

Because they are traded throughout the day on organized stock exchanges, exchange-traded index funds offer investors the same level of flexibility and choice as shares of common stocks. This includes 1) intraday liquidity, 2) access to a wide range of orders, 3) access to a wide range of strategies, and 4) unlimited trading.

Intraday Liquidity

Unlike traditional mutual funds, shares of exchange-traded index funds can be bought or sold throughout the day. They are actively traded on all major exchanges offering investors the same high level of liquidity as common stocks. Investment liquidity refers to how quickly and easily a security can be bought or sold with the least amount of disruption to its price.

There are many advantages associated with intraday liquidity in today's fast-paced information based markets. For example, if the Federal Reserve unexpectedly increases the Fed Funds rate, causing the equity market to turn lower, what alternatives do investors have?

The mutual fund shareholder can call their broker or the mutual fund company and place an order to sell his or her shares. The sell order, however, will not be executed in a timely fashion. Mutual funds can only be bought or sold at the closing price on the day the order is entered. Therefore, the shareholder receives the fund's closing net asset value per share and not the value of the fund's portfolio when the order was entered. If the market drops considerably, after the sell order is entered but before the market closes, the shareholder loses money due to a lack of liquidity.

The exchange-traded index fund shareholder, in contrast, can react immediately to the news. They can place a sell order with their broker or directly online. In a matter of minutes, if not seconds, the order is executed. Regardless of how much the market drops, after the shares are sold, they are not affected. As we can see, traditional mutual fund shareholders are locked-out of the market and often forced to ride it lower. Exchange-traded index fund shareholders, in contrast, can take specific steps to immediately limit their losses.

The costs associated with end-of-day pricing are potentially staggering for the average mutual fund investor. While it's difficult to place a quantitative value on the ability to trade throughout the day, we can examine market volatility to determine if there are times when

Exhibit 5-1:
Percentage of Trading Days with Intraday Movements of Greater than 1%

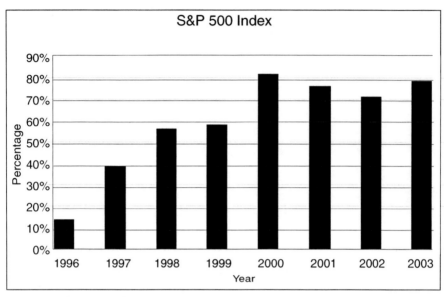

Source: FactSet Research Systems, Inc.

it's advantageous. Exhibit 5-1 shows that opportunities do exist, over the course of a normal trading day, to benefit from intraday pricing.

As the exhibit shows, the market, as measured by the S&P 500 Index, routinely moves in excess of 1% per day. When discussing volatile sector funds, the ability to trade shares intraday is even more beneficial.

For example, assume an investor decides to sell shares of their technology sector mutual fund because of a negative news report. Depending on the severity of the news, it would not be unusual for this type of asset to drop by 5%, or more, over the course of the day. The mutual fund investor is helpless, unable to sell their shares until the end of the day. The exchange-traded index fund shareholder, however, can react immediately; selling their shares and limiting further losses. When investing in volatile sector funds, the intraday liquidity of exchange-traded index funds makes them a far superior alternative compared to traditional mutual funds.

One criticism often voiced about intraday pricing is that it promotes too much trading. Mutual funds are made for long-term investors, these same critics like to point out, and therefore intraday trading isn't necessary. From my experience, it's not a question of trading but rather a question of control. More importantly, who is in control? Is it the mutual fund company or the investor? Exchange-traded index funds place a tremendous amount of control and decision making flexibility in the hands of the investor while mutual fund companies restrict the investor at every turn.

Access to a Wide Range of Orders

Exchange-traded index funds can be bought or sold using a wide range of orders. Investors can use market orders, limit orders, at-the-close or at-the-open orders, stop orders, or stop limit orders, just to name a few. Various time constraints, such as "day" or "good-till-canceled" are also available. And, just like common stocks the investor can cancel any order prior to it being filled by the broker.

Exhibit 5-2 provides a quick overview of the most commonly used orders when buying or selling shares of exchange-traded index funds.

Exhibit 5-2:
Summary of Orders Available with Exchange-Traded Index Funds

Type of Order	Description
Market Order	A market order must be executed immediately at the best available price. It is the most common order used today.
Limit Order	A limit order specifies the maximum price an investor is willing to buy shares at, or the minimum price they are willing to accept when selling.
Stop Order	A stop order (either buy-stop or sell-stop) becomes a market order when the current trading price of the underlying security trades at the stop price.
GTC	GTC stands for good-till-canceled. The order remains effective until it is filled or cancelled by the investor.
AON	An "all or nothing" order indicates that the order is to be executed in its entirety or not at all.

As the exhibit shows, exchange-traded index funds provide many choices. Mutual funds, in contrast, provide only one way for investors to buy or sell shares. Millions of investors with vastly different goals, objectives, and needs are all forced to buy or sell shares the same way, at the end of the day.

Mutual fund companies argue that it's not necessary to have access to different types of orders. It's too confusing for the investor, they say. However, according to most professional money managers, the most powerful risk management tool ever created is the stop-loss order. It allows the investor to protect his or her investment by setting a predetermined sell point. When using exchange-traded index funds investors have access to this important risk management tool. Traditional mutual fund investors, in contrast, don't have access to this powerful tool.

I can't think of any other industry that limits the choices of consumers as much as the mutual fund industry does. How long would a car company survive if they only offered one color or make of car? How about an ice cream parlor that only offered one flavor of ice cream? It seems as if consumers demand choice in everything except the investments they use. When managing an investment portfolio, flexibility and choice is so important it is reason enough to use exchange-traded index funds instead of traditional mutual funds.

Access to a Wide Range of Strategies

Exchange-traded index funds make it possible to take advantage of the same strategies common stock investors have used for years to reduce risk and enhance return. This includes buying on margin, selling short, and the use of option contracts.

- *Margin* allows an investor to make purchases using borrowed capital. It's a way to increase potential returns through the use of leverage. Exchange-traded index funds can be purchased on margin while traditional mutual funds cannot.

- *Selling short* allows the investor to profit from a decrease in prices or hedge an existing position. Exchange-traded index funds can be sold short on either an up-tick or down-tick in price. This represents an advantage not only compared to traditional mutual funds, which cannot be sold short under any circumstance, but also compared to common stocks, which can only be sold short on an up-tick or no change up-tick in price.

- With the introduction of *option contracts* based directly on some exchange-traded index fund shares investors are able to use strategies such as covered call writing, buying protective puts, and writing naked puts. Traditional mutual funds, once again, don't offer underlying option contracts and therefore are not eligible for option-related strategies.

Each of the three strategies summarized above are explained in greater detail in Part 3.

Unlimited Trading

Most mutual fund companies limit the number of times an investor can move in or out of a particular fund or impose fees to switch between funds. The stated reason for this is to discourage market timers. Why should a mutual fund company dictate what type of investment strategy you can implement? Although I'm not an advocate of market timing, I believe individual investors should be able to decide which strategies are best for them. The decision shouldn't be made for them by a mutual fund company.

Not only are active traders hurt by restrictive trading rules, investors using momentum trading strategies, or active risk management strategies are affected as well. Exchange-traded index funds don't limit investor buying or selling in any way because the investor is interacting directly with other like-minded investors through the exchange. While I wouldn't recommend it, you could literally make hundreds of trades per day and no one would care.

It Comes Down to Choice

Does every mutual fund investor want to use margin? Will every investor take advantage of the benefits offered by options or stop-loss orders? Probably not, but it's nice to know these choices are available should you wish to use them.

As we've seen, mutual funds offer investors very little in the way of portfolio management flexibility and choice. Exchange-traded index funds, on the other hand, provide a tremendous amount of flexibility and choice because they are actively traded throughout the day on various exchanges. Exhibit 5-3 summarizes the advantages exchange-traded index funds offer over traditional mutual funds as a direct result of being exchange-traded.

To succeed today investors need every possible edge. Access to portfolio management tools that provide flexibility and choice is an absolute necessity. It's not a question of whether or not you want to use every strategy listed in Exhibit 5-3. The question is whether or not you should be able to implement whatever strategy you deem appropriate, regardless of what that strategy entails. When using exchange-traded index funds, the investor decides which strategies to use. When using traditional mutual funds, the mutual fund company decides for them by limiting the choices available.

Exhibit 5-3:
Advantages Derived from Being Traded on an Exchange

Advantages	Exchange-Traded Index Funds	Traditional Mutual Funds
Intraday Liquidity	Yes	No
Order Flexibility	Yes	No
Able to Buy on Margin	Yes	No
Underlying Option Contracts	Yes	No
Able to Sell Short	Yes	No
Unlimited Trading	Yes	No

Comparing Expenses

The second major area where exchange-traded index funds offer significant advantages over traditional mutual funds is operating expenses. It's easy to compare traditional mutual funds and exchange-traded index funds on a total cost or expense basis because every mutual fund (including exchange-traded index funds) is required to report all expenses necessary for the operation of the fund in the prospectus. Mutual fund expenses are usually quoted as a percentage of the fund's portfolio and referred to as the "total expense ratio" or "expense ratio." The expense ratio represents the ongoing costs of ownership, as compared to acquisition costs, which are commonly referred to as sales charges or loads.

Items typically included in a fund's expense ratio include investment advisory fees (sometimes called management fees), administrative expenses, and a third category usually referred to as other expenses. The other expense category includes charges incurred directly by the fund itself for such items as custodial fees, state and local taxes, legal expenses, and directors' fees. Additionally, all mutual funds incur transaction-related expenses, which vary based on the amount of trading within the fund's portfolio. Unlike the other costs necessary to run a mutual fund, transaction-related fees do not show up in the prospectus. Instead we must estimate them based on the amount of trading within a given fund's portfolio.

Exhibit 5-4 compares the median expense ratio of various types of actively managed mutual funds, traditional index-based mutual funds, and exchange-traded index funds. As the exhibit shows, exchange-traded index funds, in general, represent a very cost-efficient alternative to traditional mutual funds. Compared against most actively managed mutual funds, exchange-traded index funds offer cost savings of at least 1.00% per year, and in some instances significantly greater.

Investors often fail to appreciate just how important it is to use the lowest cost investment vehicle. Over time the compounding ef-

Exhibit 5-4:
Comparison of Average Annual Expense Ratios

Fund Category	Avg.Actively Managed Fund	Avg.Traditional Index Fund	Representative ETIFs
U.S. Taxable Bond	1.08%	0.52%	0.15%
Large Cap Blend	1.29%	0.76%	0.20%
Large Cap Value	1.40%	1.19%	0.18%
Small Cap Blend	1.64%	0.86%	0.20%
Mid Cap Blend	1.51%	0.88%	0.20%
Foreign Stock	1.72%	0.99%	0.35%
Emerging Markets	2.13%	0.53%	0.50%
Specialty Technology	1.90%	1.49%	0.60%

Source: BGI analysis, 6/02

fect of saving 1% per year in fees is quite remarkable. To show the difference 1% can make we will examine two hypothetical mutual funds. Fund A has a total expense ratio of 0.50% while fund B has a total expense ratio of 1.5%. For this example we will assume a twenty-year holding period, an initial investment of $100,000, and a growth rate of 9.0% before expenses. Based on these assumptions, fund A, the lower cost fund, is worth $86,418 more than fund B at the end of the time period. The savings almost equals the initial investment of $100,000. This means an extra $86,418 in your portfolio instead of lining the pockets of some mutual fund company.

As if paying an extra 100 to 200 basis points in annual expenses every year isn't bad enough, according to many published reports the fees mutual funds charge investors have steadily increased throughout the 1990s. According to an August 2000 *Investor's Business Daily* article, mutual fund expenses are up almost 40% over the last five years. Even worse, most experts predict traditional mutual fund fees will continue to increase as they have to "make-up" for assets lost to exchange-traded index funds.

Not only do exchange-traded index funds do well when compared against average mutual fund expenses, as we saw in Exhibit 5-4, they also tend to beat the traditional mutual funds with the lowest expense ratios. For years, the lowest cost mutual fund available was the Vanguard Trust 500 Index fund, the brainchild of John Bogle, retired Chairman of the Vanguard Group. His rallying cry is that the mutual fund industry needs to lower the fees it charges shareholders.

It now appears the shoe is on the other foot. With total annual expenses of 0.18% the Vanguard Trust 500 Index fund is no longer the lowest cost fund available. That proud distinction is held by an exchange-traded index fund, iShares S&P 500 Index fund with stated expenses of 0.09% or half that of the Vanguard Fund. Even the lowest cost traditional index mutual fund in the country is no match for the low cost exchange-traded index fund structure.

How Much Does Your Mutual Fund Really Cost?

By some estimates, mutual fund companies collected over $1 billion in fees from investors, in 2003. Yes, that is billion with a "B." "Oh, but my fund is a no-load," I can hear many of you say. It doesn't matter. All mutual funds, and I emphasize all, pass various portfolio management related expenses on to shareholders. Some charge more than others do, but every mutual fund, regardless of whether they are a load or no-load, charge fees. How else do you think they can afford to install those high technology phone answering systems? You know, the ones where you spend twenty minutes trying to push enough buttons to reach a live person only to be disconnected.

The reason investors are confused about how much they're actually paying each year in fees is that most mutual fund companies make it very difficult to find out. Anyone who has ever tried to read a mutual fund prospectus knows exactly what I'm talking about. If you have a magnifying glass and the time, hidden in the fine print you will find a laundry list of charges.

In early 2001, the U.S. Congress and the Securities and Exchange Commission (SEC) held hearings to address the issue of mutual fund expenses. They decided that mutual fund companies should clearly list all fees and charges, in dollars, on the investor's annual statement. By doing this, the investor would know exactly how much they are paying the mutual fund company to manage their money. It sounds like a good idea, right.

Not surprisingly, the mutual fund and brokerage industry are fighting hard to keep this proposal from being implemented. Industry lobbyists are waging fierce battles with the SEC to keep the information from the investor. After we examine how much most investors are actually paying for their mutual funds, you will understand why the industry doesn't want the information easily obtainable.

Exhibit 5-5 provides an example of how much more expensive, in dollars, traditional mutual funds are compared to exchange-traded index funds. The fees are based on a $100,000 initial investment and a gross return (before fees) of 10%. The mutual fund's expense ratio is 2% while the exchange-traded index fund's expense ratio is 0.20%.

As the exhibit shows, the mutual fund investor ends up paying almost $200,000 more in fees over the course of twenty years, compared to the investor using low-cost exchange-traded index funds. That amounts to almost $10,000 per year ($200,000/20years) in unnecessary fees and charges.

Of course, the response from the mutual fund industry is that you are paying for professional portfolio management. Therefore, the

Exhibit 5-5:
Cost Analysis ETIFs vs. Traditional Mutual Funds*
Based on Initial Investment of $100,000

	Value After 5 Years	Value After 10 Years	Value After 15 Years	Value After 20 Years
Exchange-traded Index Fund	$159,592.00	$254,696.00	$406,476.00	$648,704.00
Mututal Fund	$146,932.00	$215,892.00	$317,216.00	$466,095.00
Savings	**$ 12,660.00**	**$ 38,804.00**	**$89,260.00**	**$182,609.00**

* Based on gross return (before fees) of 10%. Total expenses for ETIF = 0.20%. Mutual fund = 2.0%.

higher fees are justified. I find it amazing that they can make this argument with a straight face. As we will see in Chapter 7, in any given year only about 20% to 25% of all actively managed mutual funds are able to beat the S&P 500 Index. As an investor you must ask yourself one simple question, "Am I getting my money's worth?" If answered candidly my guess is you are not.

The Mutual Fund Costs You Do Not See

In addition to the fees and expenses that comprise a fund's expense ratio, all mutual funds have "invisible costs" as well. Invisible costs are those costs incurred by the fund as a result of executing portfolio transactions. Buying and selling stocks is expensive whether you are an individual investor or large mutual fund company. Trading related costs typically incurred by mutual funds include commissions, the dealer's bid/ask spreads, and market impact costs, meaning large buy orders tend to push prices higher while large sell orders tend to push prices lower.

The invisible costs incurred by a mutual fund are difficult to calculate with any degree of accuracy. They vary widely depending on the type and liquidity of the securities held in the fund's portfolio, the frequency of trading, and the skill of the trader handling the transactions. While it's impossible to know the full impact of invisible costs, various experts suggest a fair estimate is 0.5% to 2% of a fund's assets per year, based on the fund's portfolio turnover. Mutual funds with a high portfolio turnover, like most actively managed mutual funds, would tend to have higher invisible costs. Funds with a lower portfolio turnover, such as index-based funds, would have lower invisible costs.

We can measure the amount of trading activity in a fund's portfolio, and therefore the likelihood of incurring invisible costs, using something called the portfolio turnover ratio. The portfolio turnover ratio measures how much trading a fund does, on average, in a given year. Very roughly, 100% turnover implies that the fund's assets are sold and replaced once a year on average, 200% turnover means that the fund's assets are replaced every six months on average.

A simple rule of thumb is the following: more trading means higher expenses, less trading means lower expenses. Exchange-traded index funds are designed to limit unnecessary portfolio trading, as we will see in Chapter 6. This, in turn, lowers trading related expenses. Traditional actively managed mutual funds, in contrast, trade frequently. In fact, a recent study found that the average actively managed mutual fund has a turnover ratio of about 115%. Traditional sector mutual funds and aggressive growth mutual funds often exceed 250% in portfolio turnover. In contrast, most exchange-traded index funds have portfolio turnover ratios of less than 50%. The result is higher invisible trading costs for traditional actively managed mutual fund shareholders and lower invisible trading costs for exchange-traded index fund shareholders.

Tax Advantages

Not only are exchange-traded index funds more cost-effective than mutual funds, they are also more tax-efficient. The negative effect taxes have on the wealth creation process is astronomical. By some estimates, investors pay over $1 billion each year in unnecessary taxes because of the tax inefficiencies inherent with mutual funds. In fact, mutual funds are so tax inefficient I've often wondered if the mutual fund industry has some type of secret deal with the IRS. Maybe for every extra dollar they generate in taxable distributions the mutual fund industry gets a small percentage back from the IRS.

All registered investment management companies, including mutual funds and exchange-traded index funds, are considered passthrough vehicles for tax purposes. As such, they are required to distribute most types of income to shareholders to avoid being taxed at the fund level. For example, dividend and interest income, net of fund expenses must be passed through to shareholders in the year it is received. Capital gains resulting from the sale of a security at a profit must also be passed through to shareholders. Ironically, even if an investor buys shares of the fund *after* the gain has been realized, but before the proceeds have been distributed, they are still liable for any applicable taxes resulting from the gain.

Regardless of the reasons why, when a stock is sold at a profit it creates a capital gain for the fund's portfolio. The mutual fund is then required to pass the gain through to the shareholders. Therefore, a direct correlation exists between portfolio trading and taxes. Knowing this, we can make the following generalized statements regarding mutual funds. High portfolio trading or turnover means a greater chance of pass-through capital gains. Low portfolio trading or turnover means less of a chance of pass-through capital gains.

As we saw in the previous section, exchange-traded index funds tend to have lower portfolio turnover compared to traditional mutual funds. There are two reasons why. First, they are index-based and indexing tends to be a lower portfolio turnover strategy. Second, the unique way exchange-traded index funds are structured tends to limit portfolio trading. This will be discussed in Chapter 6. The net result is exchange-traded index funds tend to be far more tax-efficient compared to traditional mutual funds.

The Financial Impact of Taxes

Countless investors have found out the hard way just how devastating taxes are on performance and how little most traditional mutual funds do to limit the damage. For example, by December 1999 a majority of mutual funds had accumulated large amounts of unrealized capital gains as a result of the long running bull market — unrealized capital gains just waiting to wreck havoc on unsuspecting investors.

When the bear market of 2000 hit, many investors liquidated mutual fund holdings. This, in turn, forced fund managers to sell stocks to meet the avalanche of redemption requests. In most cases, the securities being sold had been purchased years earlier at dramatically lower prices generating huge capital gains that were then passed through to the remaining shareholders.

Long-term buy-and-hold investors who decided not to sell paid a heavy price for their loyalty. They were hit with large, and in many instances completely unexpected, capital gains distributions. This was especially difficult to accept since most mutual funds saw their share price drop dramatically over this same time period.

Exhibit 5-6 shows several examples of just how hard the combination of market losses and taxable capital gains hit some investors. The total taxable distributions and performance numbers shown in the exhibit are from the prospectuses of several widely held mutual funds. The examples are based on a $100,000 initial investment made on December 31, 1999.

Shareholders of fund A, from the exhibit, not only lost $11,000, they were also hit with a $3,088 tax bill, assuming a tax rate of 32%. Even worse, fund C investors lost $21,000 and were hit with a $2,918 tax bill. While it may be hard to believe, the funds shown in the exhibit do not represent the extreme. Over the last few years, they represent the norm.

In contrast, exchange-traded index funds are very tax-efficient. In fact, of the over eighty funds that currently comprise the iShares family of exchange-traded index funds, not one made a taxable capi-

Exhibit 5-6:
The Negative Impact of Capital Gains

Fund Name	Initial Investment 12/31/1999	Ending Value 12/31/2000*	Capital Gains Distribution	Taxes Due 32% Tax Rate
Fund A	$100,000.00	$89,000.00	$9,653.00	$3,088.96
Fund B	$100,000.00	$85,000.00	$8,857.00	$2,834.24
Fund C	$100,000.00	$79,000.00	$9,120.00	$2,918.40
Fund D	$100,000.00	$84,000.00	$8,176.00	$2,616.32

* Includes the reinvestment of all capital gains and dividends.

tal gains distribution for the tax year 2001, 2002, or 2003. It's hard to imagine how an investor, in a taxable account, could justify owning any of the traditional mutual funds listed in Exhibit 5-6. However, each year millions of investors continue to hold on to their tax inefficient mutual funds, paying a hefty penalty when April 15th rolls around.

Shielding Shareholders from the Activity of Others

The next advantage exchange-traded index funds offer over traditional mutual funds is the way they protect existing shareholders from the actions of other investors. Most traditional mutual fund shareholders believe that if they are long-term, buy-and-hold investors the actions of other investors will not impact them. They are wrong.

Investors buying or selling shares of traditional mutual funds inflict major damage on the fund's portfolio. The reasons why are found by examining how mutual funds are structured. As their name implies, they are "mutual" investment pools. They grow or shrink in the following ways:

1. An investor deposits cash with the mutual fund company and receives shares of the fund in return.
2. The mutual fund portfolio manager takes the new cash and purchases securities for the portfolio.
3. An investor redeems shares by returning their shares to the mutual fund company. The mutual fund portfolio manager sells securities in the portfolio to generate cash to meet the liquidation request.
4. The fund company sends the shareholder his or her cash in the form of a check.

As we can see, shareholders interact directly with the fund's portfolio whenever they purchase or redeem shares. Therefore, the fund's portfolio can be adversely affected by the actions of investors.

Exchange-traded index funds, in contrast, separate the actions of investors from the fund's portfolio in two ways. First, investors buy or sell shares on an exchange and not directly through the fund company. The exchange, and not the fund's portfolio, provides the necessary liquidity. Second, when new shares are created or existing shares redeemed it is through a unique in-kind transfer of securities, which does not create taxable capital gains for the portfolio.

As a result of their hybrid structure, exchange-traded index funds shield existing shareholders from the actions of other investors. This provides three advantages over traditional mutual funds. It makes exchange-traded index funds more cost-effective, more tax-efficient, and it keeps the actions of irrational investors from undermining the fund's performance. Since we have already discussed cost and tax advantages of exchange-traded index funds, the focus here is performance.

Undermining Performance

History shows that mutual funds, in general, will experience their highest net inflows of new money at market peaks. Likewise, mutual funds typically experience their highest net outflows of cash after the market has declined dramatically. This means mutual fund managers are often forced to put new money to work when stock prices are high and sell when prices are low, often to the detriment of long-term shareholders. In essence, the mutual fund manager is forced to buy high and sell low. The tendency for investors to add money to mutual funds at market peaks and pull money out at market bottoms is shown in Exhibit 5-7.

Early in my career, while working at Fidelity Investments, I learned first hand how fund shareholders can sabotage a portfolio manager. At the time Peter Lynch, arguably one of the most successful fund managers ever, was in charge of the Fidelity Magellan fund. As I was about to learn, not even Mr. Lynch's reputation as a superb portfolio manager could change the way investors react to bad news.

On October 19, 1987, a date that subsequently became known as

Exhibit 5-7:
Tendency of Investors to "Buy High" and "Sell Low"

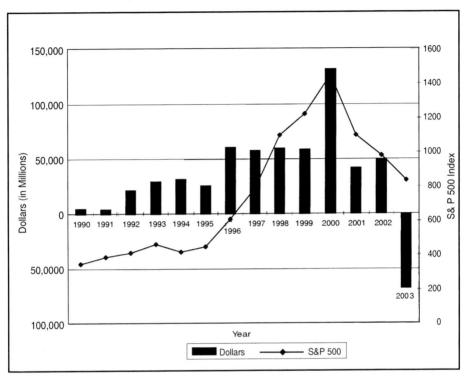

Source: RCM

"Black Monday," the Dow Jones Industrial Average lost 508 points or almost 23% of its value. The following day, the brokers at Fidelity were deluged with redemption requests, including requests to sell shares of the Magellan fund. Investors were selling out as fast as possible and there was nothing any of us could do about it. As a result of the way mutual funds are structured, when shareholders sell cash must be generated from the fund's portfolio. Fidelity mutual fund managers, including Peter Lynch, were forced to liquidate stocks at panic level prices to meet the large number of sell requests.

A few months later I was in the audience as Mr. Lynch was speaking about the frustration he felt in the days immediately following the market's crash. He described it as one of the greatest buying opportunities of his lifetime. Blue chip stocks were trading at levels they hadn't seen in over a decade. However, because of the way mutual funds are structured, the actions of irrational investors forced Mr. Lynch to sell securities at ridiculously low prices. He clearly wanted to be a buyer but was forced to sell. One of the best portfolio managers of all time was unable to take advantage of what he believed was the greatest buying opportunity of his lifetime because of the way traditional mutual funds are structured.

Who ultimately suffered? The long-term shareholders of the Magellan fund suffered. Ironically, the shareholders that showed the most faith in Mr. Lynch's abilities and held tight were punished for their loyalty. As we all know, it did turn out to be a spectacular buying opportunity, yet the long-term buy-and-hold shareholders who stuck with the Magellan fund missed out on this great opportunity because of the outdated structure of traditional mutual funds.

Exchange-traded index funds, as we have seen, shield existing shareholders from the actions of other investors. Therefore, irrational shareholders will not influence portfolio management decisions or force the fund manager to raise cash to meet liquidation requests, as is the case with mutual funds. This allows each investor to make the decision that is right for them (i.e., buy more, sell, or hold tight) instead of having other shareholders make the decision.

Access to a Wide Number of Market Indexes

The final area we will examine where exchange-traded index funds offer significant advantages over traditional mutual funds is in the availability of indexes to track. While it's difficult to believe, a little over ten years ago investors had few choices when it came to indexing. At that time, over 90% of all index-based mutual funds tracked the same index: the S&P 500. As late as 1995, 82% of all traditional index-based mutual funds tracked that same index. Even today, a remarkable 75% of all traditional index-based mutual funds still track the same index, the S&P 500 Index. Consequently, many investors believe indexing simply entails buying shares of a mutual fund that tracks the S&P 500 Index and holding it.

Exchange-traded index funds, on the other hand, track over eighty of the most respected and followed market indexes. When creating and managing a portfolio based on the theories of asset allocation, as we do in Part 3, it's important to have access to a wide array of different types of asset categories. Exchange-traded index funds provide access to an unparalleled number of indexes ranging from broad-based indexes tracking the entire market to indexes tracking industry groups, economic sectors, and geographic regions of the world. The wide range of choices available, when building an index-based portfolio, make exchange-traded index funds the better investment vehicle compared to traditional mutual funds.

Summary

Throughout this chapter, one recurring theme is clear: exchange-traded index funds provide the investor with far more choices than traditional mutual funds. I'm always amazed when so-called financial experts can only come up with intraday pricing when asked about the advantages offered by exchange-traded index funds. While this is clearly an important advantage it's just one of many advantages they offer investors.

Compared to traditional mutual funds, exchange-traded index funds provide greater portfolio management flexibility, they are more tax-efficient, have lower operating expenses, and provide access to a far greater number of indexes. Additionally, because of their unique structure, exchange-traded index funds separate portfolio management decisions from shareholder activity. This greatly reduces the risk of unwanted taxable distributions, reduces overall portfolio related expenses, and keeps the irrational actions of investors from hurting performance.

Chapter 6

HOW EXCHANGE-TRADED
INDEX FUNDS WORK

Unique Hybrid Structure

While it's not necessary to understand how the internal combustion engine works prior to operating a car, it doesn't hurt to know the basics (i.e., where to add gas, how to start the engine, which pedal is the accelerator and which is the brake). Exchange-traded index funds are similar, in this respect: it's not necessary to understand their inner workings to benefit from them. However, understanding the unique way they are structured will clarify why exchange-traded index funds are such powerful portfolio management tools and explain how they can offer so many advantages over traditional mutual funds.

Exchange-traded index funds are considered "hybrid" investment vehicles because they combine the structural characteristics of common stocks and traditional open-end mutual funds. Like common stocks, they offer the benefits associated with secondary market trading. Like traditional open-end mutual funds, shares can be created or redeemed at the fund's net asset value on any day the market is open. In this chapter, we examine how secondary market trading and net asset value pricing combine to make exchange-traded index funds a better portfolio management vehicle compared to traditional mutual funds and common stocks.

Secondary Market Trading

Exchange-traded index funds are actively traded throughout the day on every major stock exchange with the American Stock Exchange being home to the vast majority. Similar to other exchange-traded securities, shares of exchange-traded index funds must be bought or sold through a broker. The broker could be a traditional full service broker, a discount broker, or an online broker. Regardless of the type of broker used, a commission is typically charged to complete the transaction. The size of the commission will vary greatly among brokers based on factors such as how much or how little help is needed, the type of broker used (full service or discount), and the number of shares traded.

Instead of charging a commission on each trade, some brokerage firms now offer a "wrap" fee alternative. With a wrap account the investor is charged an asset management fee, based on the size of their account, instead of a commission on each separate transaction. The fee is typically quoted as a percentage of total assets and deducted from the account on a quarterly basis. Given the many alternatives available, it's the responsibility of the investor to know and understand all applicable fees and/or commissions prior to opening an account with a brokerage firm.

While exchange-traded index funds typically trade in "round lots" of 100 shares, an investor can purchase shares in any quantity they wish. Keep in mind, if buying shares through a brokerage account where a commission is charged on each transaction purchasing one share, two shares, or other small share amounts is probably not the most economical way to invest. For example, dollar-cost averaging (buying small amounts in equal and regular intervals) is probably not the most cost-effective way to purchase shares of an exchange-traded index fund.

How Your Order Is Processed

To purchase or sell shares of a given exchange-traded index fund the investor places an order with their broker. After the broker receives the order, they forward it to a floor broker who in turn will take the order to the floor specialist assigned to that specific security. The floor specialist has the responsibility of maintaining a fair, competitive, orderly, and efficient market in the shares they're assigned. This means the specialist will act as a principal, buying shares when no one else wants to buy and selling shares from their own inventory when no one else wants to sell, thereby providing the necessary liquidity to the marketplace. The floor specialist is required to make sure that every investor receives the best available price, regardless of the size of his or her order.

All exchange-traded index fund transactions settle on the third business day after the trade date, often referred to as T+3 where "T" stands for the trade date and "3" is the number of days until settlement. When buying shares, the purchase amount is not due until the third business day after the transaction. When selling shares, the proceeds due the seller are not disbursed until the third business day after the trade date. Although T+3 is the current standard, most experts agree a same-day or one-day settlement period is not far away.

All exchange-traded index funds are book-entry, meaning an actual paper certificate is not issued to the shareholder as proof of ownership. The shareholder is simply noted as the owner of record with the fund company. The position is also shown on their brokerage statement. This helps reduce the costs associated with issuing certificates. Other book-entry securities include traditional mutual funds, U.S. Treasury bonds, Government Agency bonds, and many municipal bonds.

Pricing Information

Daily pricing information for exchange-traded index funds is widely accessible and easy to locate. A large number of Internet sites provide current price information by simply entering the trading symbol of the desired security. Many of these sites also provide additional data, including historic prices, volume, and charts. Pricing information is also available in the business section of most daily newspapers and in financial publications such as *The Wall Street Journal* or *Investors Business Daily.*

Typically, most newspapers list the previous day's closing price, the daily high and low price, the opening price, and trading volume. Exhibit 6-1 provides an example of how exchange-traded index funds are commonly quoted in the financial section of most newspapers.

The Bid/Ask Spread

Like all exchange-traded securities, exchange-traded index funds trade subject to a bid/ask spread. The bid price of a security represents the highest price a buyer is currently willing to pay while the ask price represents the lowest price a seller is willing to accept. The buyer or seller could be an individual investor, an institutional investor, or the floor specialist. The difference between the bid and ask price is referred to as the spread, or the bid/ask spread.

For example, if the Nasdaq 100 Index Tracking Shares (QQQ) were quoted $45 to $45.20, it would mean that a buyer is currently willing to pay $45 per share and that a seller is currently willing to accept $45.20 per share. The bid price is quoted first and the ask price is quoted second. The spread, or the difference between the bid

Exhibit 6-1:
Pricing Information Provided by Most Financial Newspapers

Name	Symbol	Closing Price	Net Change	High	Low	Volume
iShares S&P 500	IVV	$95.27	$.046	$95.57	$93.50	237,000
iShares Russ 3000	IWV	$52.95	$0.28	$53.07	$52.00	51,600
iShares S&P 400	IJH	$97.00	$0.88	$97.16	$95.00	80,900
iShares Russ 1000	IWB	$50.56	$0.31	$50.56	$49.60	297,500
iShares DJ US R/E	IYR	$82.32	$0.91	$82.45	$81.12	11,500
iShares DJ Basic Ind.	IYM	$37.19	$0.22	$37.43	$36.08	44,500

and the ask price, is $0.20, which is calculated by subtracting the bid price of $45 from the ask price of $45.20 ($45.20-$45.00).

Based on the information above, we can anticipate that a market order to buy 100 shares of QQQ will be filled at $45.20 per share while a market sell order will be filled at $45.00 per share. If an investor placed an order to buy 100 shares, with a limit price of $45.10, the bid price shown by the specialist should change to $45.10 reflecting a new buyer's willingness to pay a higher price per share.

Several factors that may influence the bid/ask spread of a given exchange-traded index fund include:

- Daily trading volume of the underlying index components.
- Execution related costs.
- The type of underlying index the fund is tracking.
- Overall market volatility.
- Whether a corresponding futures contract is available on the underlying index the fund is tracking.
- Whether option contracts are available on the shares of the exchange-traded index fund.

The bid/ask spread represents a cost associated with investing. As spreads tighten (become narrower), it becomes more cost-effective for the investor to trade. Several factors that should help reduce the spreads on exchange-traded index funds in the future include: increasing popularity and use, the recent conversion to decimal pricing by most major exchanges, and improved liquidity of underlying index components. Regardless of the reasons why, when the bid/ask spread narrows all investors benefit.

Trading Volume and Liquidity
Whenever exchange-traded securities are discussed one question is inevitably always asked: "What's the daily trading volume?" The answer to this question, when discussing exchange-traded index funds, is not as important as one might imagine. In fact, there is actually

little correlation between trading volume and liquidity as it relates to exchange-traded index funds.

Investment liquidity refers to the ease of buying or selling a security without disrupting the market. When discussing common stocks, trading volume and liquidity are usually considered one in the same: the greater the trading volume the greater the liquidity. In regards to exchange-traded index funds, however, trading volume and liquidity are two very different things.

The reason for this is simple. Unlike common stocks, which have a finite number of shares, exchange-traded index funds are open-ended. That is, additional shares can be created at any time through a unique in-kind exchange of securities, as we will see later in this chapter. Since a virtually unlimited number of shares can be created, liquidity and volume are not interrelated. Therefore, traditional supply and demand constraints, which will influence the price per share of common stocks, will not have the same influence on the price per share of exchange-traded index funds.

For instance, if an investor tried to purchase 10,000 shares of a common stock that averaged 5,000 shares traded per day, he is likely to move the market dramatically higher. Because new shares cannot be created, all 10,000 shares must be purchased from existing shareholders. To entice shareholders to sell, the price will have to go up. In the case of common stocks, low supply combined with high demand means higher prices. Therefore, a direct correlation exists between daily trading volume and liquidity when discussing common stocks.

If this same investor tried to purchase 10,000 shares of an exchange-traded index fund that averaged 5,000 shares traded per day, the result would be very different. Unlike common stocks, if the shares are not available to meet demand they can be created. The trading price of the exchange-traded index fund does not have to move higher to entice someone to sell. New shares would simply be created at the fund's net asset value. Therefore, when discussing exchange-traded index funds there is no correlation between daily trading volume and liquidity.

The Creation/Redemption Process

The second major structural innovation associated with every exchange-traded index fund is the unique mechanism for creating new shares and redeeming existing shares. As we have discussed, unlike most exchange-traded securities, exchange-traded index funds are open-ended meaning additional shares can be created at any time.

New exchange-traded index fund shares are created and existing shares redeemed, at the fund's net asset value, in large block aggregations known as "creation units." A creation unit is simply a large block of shares, usually 50,000, of a specific exchange-traded index fund. For example, a DIAMONDS creation unit consists of 50,000 shares of the DIAMONDS Trust. Three DIAMONDS creation units would consist of 150,000 shares of the DIAMONDS Trust (3 units x 50,000).

Exhibit 6-2 provides an example of the number of shares per creation unit for several widely held exchange-traded index funds, along with the approximate dollar value of each creation unit.

Exhibit 6-2:
Number of Shares and Market Value of Selected Creation Units

Fund Name	Number of Shares per Creation Unit	Market Value of Creation Unit*	Creation Transaction Fee**
iShares S&P 500 Index Fund	50,000	$4,695,500.00	$2,000.00
iShares MidCap 400 Index Fund	50,000	$4,518,000.00	$1,500.00
iShares S&P Global Energy Fund	50,000	$2,487,000.00	$ 600.00
iShares MSCI Australia Fund	100,000	$ 827,000.00	$1,200.00
iShares MSCI Spain Fund	75,000	$1,391,250.00	$2,300.00

* Approximate market value as of 08/02
** Charged to Authorized Participant

The Role of the Authorized Participant (AP)

Given the dollar value of each creation unit, as shown in Exhibit 6-2, most individual investors would never create or redeem shares. Instead, the vast majority of investors will simply buy or sell shares through secondary market transactions. The ability to create new shares or redeem existing shares is reserved for pre-approved individuals and institutions known as Authorized Participants.

An Authorized Participant is typically a large investor, an institution, or an exchange specialist. They are able to turn baskets of equity securities, comprising the underlying index, into blocks of new exchange-traded index funds. Conversely, Authorized Participants redeem blocks of exchange-traded fund shares, in creation unit size aggregations, and convert them into shares of the securities comprising the underlying index the fund is tracking. By standing ready to buy or sell large blocks of exchange-traded index fund shares, Authorized Participants perform a vital function, which benefits all shareholders. They help maintain intraday trading prices at values close to the fund's actual net asset value and provide liquidity to the market.

To create new shares of an existing exchange-traded index fund, the Authorized Participant places an order with the National Securities Clearing Corporation (NSCC) for one or more creation units of a specific fund. Payment for the creation unit order is made through the in-kind deposit of a predetermined basket of securities that comprise the underlying index and a set amount of cash, directly with the fund. This in-kind deposit of securities and cash is sometimes referred to as the "creation unit deposit." In return for each creation unit deposit, the Authorized Participant receives 50,000 newly created shares of the fund (creation unit), which they can hold or sell in the open market.

For instance, if shares of the S&P 500 Index Spiders were trading at $100 per share a creation unit aggregation for the Spiders would have an approximate market value of $5,000,000 (50,000 shares x $100 per share). The creation unit deposit includes the securities that comprise the S&P 500 Index, in the exact same percentages, along with a smaller cash portion and a creation fee. The cash portion of the deposit represents accumulated dividends, referred to as the Dividend Equivalent Payment, and a smaller portion referred to as the "balancing cash." The balancing cash portion ensures that the total value of the creation unit deposit exactly equals the net asset value of one creation unit aggregation of the fund's shares. The creation fee is designed to offset the costs associated with the transaction and is paid by the firm creating the new shares. An example of a creation unit deposit is shown in Exhibit 6-3. In the exhibit, the components of the iShares Dow Jones US Telecommunications Index Fund (IYZ) creation unit deposit are shown.

In return for the creation unit deposit, as shown in the exhibit, the Authorized Participant receives the creation unit number of shares, in this example 50,000 shares of the iShares Dow Jones US Telecommunications Index Fund. The Authorized Participant can sell all or a portion of the new shares or hold them indefinitely. Once created, the new exchange-traded index fund shares are no different than the shares of the fund that are already in existence.

If the Authorized Participant wanted to redeem shares of the iShares Dow Jones US Telecommunications Fund, the process is simply reversed. They first deliver 50,000 shares of IYZ to the fund and in return receive the individual components comprising the underlying index in the form of the creation unit deposit. Similar to the previous example, after the Authorized Participant receives the individual components that comprise the underlying index they can hold them indefinitely or sell them in the open market.

Under certain circumstances, such as a restriction on an Authorized Participant from dealing in a component stock in the underlying index, they can receive cash in lieu of the security in question. Otherwise, all securities that comprise the underlying index are delivered to the Authorized Participant in-kind when shares of an exchange-traded index fund are redeemed.

To offset transfer related fees and other costs, each exchange-

Exhibit 6-3:

Components of a Creation Unit Deposit for Shares of IYZ (as of 07/30/2002)

Component Companies of the iShares Dow Jones US Telecom.Sector Index Fund	# of Shares per Creation Unit Deposit	Market Price (7/30/2002)	Total Value
Verizon Communications	6,047	$ 33.00	$199,554.00
SBC Communications	6,640	$27.66	$183,675.00
Centurytel Inc.	1,455	$26.60	$ 38,710.00
Bellsouth Corp.	1,406	$26.85	$ 37,762.00
Alltel Corp.	928	$40.52	$ 37,604.00
AT&T Corp.	3,492	$10.18	$ 35,550.00
Telephone & Data Systems	621	$56.95	$ 35,392.00
Sprint Corp.	3,650	$ 9.35	$ 34,128.00
AT&T Wireless	6,771	$ 4.69	$ 31,758.00
Citizens Communications	5,406	$ 5.48	$ 29,625.00
BCE Inc.	1,448	$16.53	$ 23,937.00
Vodafone Group	1,099	$15.17	$ 16,669.00
Broadwing Inc.	7,044	$ 2.03	$ 14,299.00
Nextel Communications	2,413	$ 5.73	$ 13,825.00
United States Cellular	493	$26.10	$ 12,877.00
Sprint PCS Group	1,696	$ 4.10	$ 6,952.00
Metro One Telecom	415	$14.85	$ 6,162.00
Qwest Communications	4,135	$ 1.28	$ 5,293.00
Surewest Communications	117	$45.42	$ 5,293.00
Allegiance Telecom Inc.	2,184	$ 1.23	$ 2,686.00
Time Warner Telecom	2,209	$ 1.18	$ 2,607.00
IDT Corp. Class B	136	$16.31	$ 2,212.00
Touch America Holdings	2,096	$ 0.98	$ 2,054.00
Nextel Partners Inc.	485	$ 3.91	$ 1,896.00
IDT Corp.	87	$18.10	$ 1,580.00
Western Wireless Corp.	255	$ 3.10	$ 790.00
Aether Systems Inc.	80	$ 2.98	$ 237.00
Triton PCS Holdings	113	$ 2.10	$ 237.00
Wireless Facilities Inc.	35	$ 4.50	$ 158.00
Airgate PCS Inc.	61	$ 1.29	$ 79.00
Leap Wireless Inc.	87	$ 0.91	$ 79.00
Cash Component			$ 6,320.00
Total Value of Creation Unit Deposit			**$790,000.00**

traded index fund may impose a purchase transaction fee and a redemption transaction fee. The Authorized Participant that is either creating or redeeming shares is responsible for paying the fee. The fee typically ranges from $1,500 to $3,500 per creation unit. Unlike traditional mutual funds, which indirectly charge the cost associated with purchases or redemptions to all shareholders, exchange-traded index funds assess the fee to the institutions actually responsible for creating or redeeming the shares.

The National Securities Clearing Corporation or a Depository Trust Company participant is responsible for actually processing the in-kind transfers between a given exchange-traded fund and the Authorized Participant. It is also the responsibility of the NSCC to ensure that all required pricing information pertaining to the creation/redemption process is disseminated throughout the day in a timely manner.

For example, every fifteen seconds the intraday portfolio value for every available exchange-traded index fund is calculated and disseminated making it easy for both retail investors and Authorized Participants to determine if a particular fund is trading at a premium or discount to its actual net asset value. Typically, investors will compare the midpoint between the fund's current bid/ask price against the actual portfolio value. If at any time a sufficient premium or discount is observed, then an arbitrage opportunity may exist.

Arbitrage in Action: A Hypothetical Example

As we have seen, Authorized Participants provide a vital function necessary for the overall success of the exchange-traded index funds marketplace. Without the ability of Authorized Participants to create and redeem shares, exchange-traded index funds would be no different than traditional closed-end mutual funds, subject to trading at prolonged premiums or discounts to their actual net asset value per share.

Some of you may be wondering why an Authorized Participant would go through the trouble of creating or redeeming shares of a given exchange-traded index fund. Is it the result of some deep seeded feeling of Wall Street civic pride? Probably not, as with everyone else on Wall Street, Authorized Participants are motivated by the potential to make a profit.

Perhaps the easiest way to understand why an Authorized Participant would undertake the risks and costs associated with creating or redeeming shares of exchange-traded index funds is to work through a hypothetical transaction. In our example, we will use the iShares S&P 500 Index Fund (IVV), which allows for creations/redemptions in creation unit size aggregations of 50,000 shares.

At 11:00 a.m. our Authorized Participant observed the following price differential, shown in Exhibit 6-4, between the current market price per share of IVV and the fund's actual net asset value per share. Because shares of IVV and the component stocks, which make up the portfolio, are in essence interchangeable through the creation and redemption process, this price differential provides the potential to make a profit through arbitrage. Accordingly, we would expect an Authorized Participant to implement the following transactions in an attempt to take advantage of this price discrepancy.

1. Sell short 50,000 shares of IVV in the open market at $90.00 per share, receiving proceeds of $4,500,000. The shares are sold short since the Authorized Participant does not hold a position in the fund at the time of the transaction.

2. Simultaneously buy the underlying securities necessary to fully replicate the S&P 500 Index with a market value equal to 50,000 shares of IVV. The cost to purchase all of the issues comprising the index, in our example, is $4,425,000.

3. As soon as the above two transactions take place, the Authorized Participant places an order for one creation unit of IVV

Exhibit 6-4:
Hypothetical Example Showing Arbitrage Profit Potential

Security	Current Market Price	Shares	Total Market Value
iShares S&P 500 Fund (IVV)	$90.00	50,000*	$4,500,000.00
Total value of all 500 securities in S&P 500 Index			$4,425,000.00
Potential Arbitrage Profit ($4,500,000 - $4,425,000)			**$ 75,000.00**

* 50,000 shares per creation unit
Source: Barclays Global Advisors

shares with the National Security Clearing Corporation. This is done to cover the shares sold short in step one.

On the third business day after the above transactions are made, the NSCC would take delivery of the creation unit deposit from the Authorized Participant. The creation unit deposit includes the securities comprising the underlying index purchased in step two plus a cash equalization portion. In return for the deposit, the NSCC delivers 50,000 newly created shares of IVV to the Authorized Participant, who in turn delivers the newly created shares to their broker to cover the short sale from step one.

The net effect of the above transactions is the following: first, 50,000 new shares of IVV are created and made available to trade in the open market. Second, and most important from the Authorized Participant's perspective, an arbitrage profit of $75,000 is realized. This represents the difference between what they paid for the securities that comprise the S&P 500 Index and the proceeds received for selling 50,000 shares of IVV short. Third, and most important for the shareholders, the price differential between the market price per share of IVV and the fund's actual net asset value per share should dissipate.

If the price differential doesn't disappear, we would expect other Authorized Participants to enter the market and perform the same transactions, in an attempt to make a profit. Eventually, the action of various Authorized Participants should cause the market price of IVV to trade in-line with its actual net asset value per share.

In the above example, the impact of commissions and transaction costs were omitted. This does not mean to imply that they are not relevant in the decision making process. In the end, all costs are important and must be considered when making any investment decision. In this example, the intent was to show the arbitrage process with as few distractions as possible.

Does It Work?

Like any subjective analysis, it's impossible to know, with any degree of certainty, the extent to which the action or the potential action by Authorized Participants has in reducing premiums or discounts between an exchange-traded index fund's trading price and net asset value per share. However, one thing is clear: when presented with a profit opportunity most market participants will take advantage of it. The unique creation/redemption mechanism associated with exchange-traded index funds allow Authorized Participants to profit whenever a significant premium or discount is present. Hopefully, this incentive will be strong enough to keep the market price per share of any given exchange-traded index fund in-line with its actual net asset value per share.

To see how well the mechanism works we can review Exhibit 6-5. The exhibit shows how closely the market price of two different exchange-traded index funds tracked their actual net asset value per share during a recent one month period. While it's impossible to say with complete certainty why the funds in Exhibit 6-5 have traded so close to their actual net asset value per share, one can conclude the primary reason is the creation/redemption mechanism inherent in all exchange-traded index funds.

In addition to the relatively short-term analysis presented in Exhibit 6-5, information regarding discounts and premiums is readily available for longer time periods as well. For instance, on the iShares Web page (www.ishares.com) it's easy to quickly research the average premium or discount of a given iShare over the last six to eight months. This same information is also provided in the prospectus of every exchange-traded index fund.

While the unique way exchange-traded index funds are structured will minimize the occurrence of premiums and discounts, it's unrealistic to expect such differences to disappear completely. The markets are fluid. Investors continually change their opinions about the future. Each new piece of data brings changes in attitudes. These changes take place twenty-four hours a day 365 days a year, whether the market is open or not. However, by providing a built in profit incentive (arbitrage) for large investors, exchange-traded index funds offer a unique solution to the problem of discounts and premiums.

Beneficial Tax Treatment

The unique way shares of exchange-traded index funds are created and redeemed adds to their tax efficiency. As we have seen, shares are created and redeemed through the in-kind exchange of securities. The Internal Revenue Service (IRS) considers the in-kind exchange of securities a non-taxable transaction. Therefore, when shares of exchange-traded index funds are redeemed, the fund's portfolio does not realize capital gains. In fact, when exchanging securities held in the fund's portfolio for a creation unit block of fund shares, the fund can deliver the lowest cost basis securities. This process, known as "stepping-up," makes exchange-traded index funds extremely tax-efficient for existing shareholders.

To explain how "stepping-up" benefits shareholders, we will refer to the hypothetical exchange-traded index fund portfolio shown in

Exhibit 6-5:
Premium/Discount of Closing Price to Net Asset Value

iShares Russell 1000 Index Fund (IWB)				iShares Russell 3000 Index Fund (IWV)			
Date	Closing Price	Closing NAV	Premium/ (Discount)	Date	Closing Price	Closing NAV	Premium/ (Discount)
4/1/2002	$60.71	$60.79	-0.132%	4/1/2002	$63.79	$63.85	-0.094%
4/2/2002	$60.34	$60.23	0.182%	4/2/2002	$63.42	$63.28	0.221%
4/3/2002	$59.54	$59.64	-0.168%	4/3/2002	$62.57	$62.66	-0.144%
4/4/2002	$59.72	$59.69	0.050%	4/4/2002	$62.66	$62.73	-0.112%
4/5/2002	$59.57	$59.51	0.101%	4/5/2002	$62.63	$62.55	0.128%
4/8/2002	$59.64	$59.68	-0.067%	4/8/2002	$62.67	$62.76	-0.144%
4/9/2002	$59.36	$59.27	0.152%	4/9/2002	$62.40	$62.37	0.048%
4/10/2002	$60.04	$59.96	0.133%	4/10/2002	$63.17	$63.11	0.095%
4/11/2002	$58.60	$58.57	0.051%	4/11/2002	$61.65	$61.69	-0.065%
4/12/2002	$58.92	$58.98	-0.102%	4/12/2002	$62.21	$62.19	0.032%
4/15/2002	$58.69	$58.56	0.222%	4/15/2002	$61.80	$61.76	0.065%
4/16/2002	$59.93	$59.91	0.033%	4/16/2002	$63.13	$63.17	-0.063%
4/17/2002	$59.84	$59.79	0.084%	4/17/2002	$63.00	$63.02	-0.032%
4/18/2002	$59.82	$59.73	0.150%	4/18/2002	$62.96	$62.95	0.016%
4/19/2002	$59.77	$59.75	0.033%	4/19/2002	$62.95	$62.97	-0.032%
4/22/2002	$58.88	$58.84	0.068%	4/22/2002	$62.05	$62.02	0.048%
4/23/2002	$58.41	$58.49	-0.137%	4/23/2002	$61.68	$61.67	0.016%
4/24/2002	$58.16	$58.11	0.086%	4/24/2002	$61.28	$61.27	0.016%
4/25/2002	$58.14	$58.05	0.155%	4/25/2002	$61.28	$61.23	0.082%
4/26/2002	$57.41	$57.25	0.279%	4/26/2002	$60.51	$60.38	0.215%
4/29/2002	$56.60	$56.68	-0.141%	4/29/2002	$59.85	$59.82	0.050%
4/30/2002	$57.29	$57.32	-0.052%	4/30/2002	$60.52	$60.54	-0.033%
Avg. Absolute Premium/Discount			**0.045%**	**Avg. Absolute Premium/Discount**			**0.014%**

Exhibit 6-6. As we can see, the exchange-traded index fund shown holds shares of XYZ common stock purchased on four separate occasions. For this example, we will assume shares of XYZ are currently trading at $50 per share meaning the fund has an unrealized gain of $12.50 per share. This is calculated by subtracting the current price of $50 per share by the average cost of $37.50 per share.

As we have seen, when an Authorized Participant redeems shares of the fund they do so by delivering a creation unit number of fund shares to the exchange-traded index fund. In return, the fund delivers, on an in-kind basis, shares of the underlying portfolio. Because they can deliver the lowest cost basis shares held, it's safe to assume the fund would deliver lot 1 and lot 2 to the redeeming Authorized Participant. The cost basis on the remaining shares (lot 3 and lot 4) will change to $52.50 (($45.00 + $60.00)/2). Therefore, the fund is able to increase the cost basis on shares held in the portfolio without realizing a taxable gain on lower cost basis shares delivered in-kind to the Authorized Participant.

If shares of XYZ are subsequently removed from the underlying index and sold from the fund's portfolio a tax-loss is realized. The transaction results in a loss for tax purposes even though the fund

Exhibit 6-6:
Hypothetical Exchange-Traded Index Fund Portfolio

	Purchase Date	Number of Shares	Purchase Price
Lot 1: Security XYZ	1/1/1985	100	$15.00
Lot 2: Security XYZ	1/1/1990	100	$30.00
Lot 3: Security XYZ	1/1/1995	100	$45.00
Lot 4: Security XYZ	1/1/2000	100	$60.00
Total Number of Shares		**400**	
Average Cost per Share		**$37.50**	

made a net profit on shares of XYZ. This is because the in-kind exchange of securities is not considered a taxable event by the IRS. As a result of the unique creation/redemption mechanism, the exchange-traded index fund is able to step-up the cost basis on securities held in the portfolio without creating a tax liability for shareholders.

Unit Investment Trust or Mutual Fund

Exchange-traded index funds are typically structured as either an investment management company (mutual fund) or unit investment trust. Currently, only four exchange-traded index funds are structured as unit investment trusts. They are SPDR Trust "Spiders," Diamond Trust, Nasdaq-100 Trust, and S&P MidCap 400 Trust. All other available exchange-traded index funds are structured as mutual funds. There are relative advantages and disadvantages associated with each structure.

Exchange-traded index funds structured as mutual funds employ the services of a fund manager, no different than any other type of mutual fund. As such, the fund manager can make strategic decisions regarding the use of futures contracts, whether or not to incorporate various "sampling" or "optimization" strategies, and the use of derivatives. Sampling and optimization are strategies that allow the portfolio manager to track a particular index without holding every security in the underlying index. The fund manager can also lend out securities held in the portfolio to earn additional income to offset some of the fund's operating expenses.

The unit investment trust structure, in contrast, does not have a portfolio manager. A trustee is in charge of overseeing the portfolio. Once the securities are purchased within the trust, changes are rarely, if ever, made precluding the use of futures contracts or other derivatives that allow for more efficient reinvestment of dividends. Therefore, the unit investment trust structure typically holds accumulated dividends in a non-interest bearing account until they are paid to the shareholders.

Because they do not have a portfolio manager running the portfolio, exchange-traded index funds structured as unit investment trusts must fully replicate the underlying index they are tracking. Full replication means all of the stocks in the underlying index must be held in the exact same proportion as the index. Therefore, indexes comprised of a large number of thinly traded issues quickly become difficult to track efficiently using a unit investment trust structure.

With the services of a portfolio manager to oversee fund operations, comes the potential for higher internal expenses. However, the incremental costs are usually not sufficient to offset the many advantages the mutual fund structure has to offer, such as the ability to immediately reinvest dividends, the ability to track a greater number of indexes, and the ability to lend out securities to decrease portfolio expenses.

What's In a Name
Before proceeding to the next chapter, a final point regarding structure needs to be addressed. The name exchange-traded index "fund" is commonly applied to both the unit investment trust and investment management company structures. That is, investors will often refer to exchange-traded index funds structured as unit investment trusts as exchange-traded index "funds," even though, when discussing the unit investment trust structure, the correct name is exchange-traded index "trust." Although technically incorrect, in this book both exchange-traded index "funds" and exchange-traded index "trusts" are referred to as exchange-traded index "funds," since this is by far the most common usage today.

Summary

Exchange-traded index funds are hybrid investment vehicles that combine secondary market trading and net asset value pricing. Shares of exchange-traded index funds are bought and sold just like shares of common stocks. They trade subject to a bid/ask spread, which is influenced by a number of different factors, including the liquidity of the stocks comprising the underlying index. Unlike common stocks, however, trading volume does not necessarily predict liquidity when discussing exchange-traded index funds.

Exchange-traded index funds also allow for the creation and redemption of shares at net asset value through a unique in-kind exchange of securities. This is reserved for large institutional investors known as Authorized Participants. Authorized Participants provide a necessary function that helps the exchange-traded index fund market work by turning large baskets of stocks into shares of exchange-traded index funds or turning shares of exchange-traded index funds into large baskets of stocks that comprise the underlying index.

Chapter 7

THE POWER OF INDEXING

Why Indexing Is Important

Today, there are two competing theories about how best to manage mutual fund portfolios: indexing and active portfolio management. Index mutual funds try to match the performance (dividends plus price appreciation) of a given index or benchmark in both up and down markets. Actively managed mutual funds, in contrast, employ various stock analysis techniques, market research, economic forecasting and other means to outperform a given index, benchmark, or the market in general. While seemingly simple in concept, indexing is actually an extremely powerful portfolio management approach offering significant advantages over actively managed mutual funds.

It is important to understand the advantages index-based investments offer over actively managed mutual funds because every exchange-traded index fund is index-based. Therefore, they offer the same portfolio management advantages associated with other index-based investment products.

In this chapter, we show why index-based investments, like exchange-traded index funds, are such powerful portfolio management tools and why they play such a key role in Strategic Index Investing. We begin our analysis by reviewing the performance advantages indexing has traditionally enjoyed over actively managed mutual funds. Next, we discuss the role performance consistency plays in portfolio construction. Finally, the advantages associated with portfolio transparency are shown.

Two additional advantages index-based investments offer compared to actively managed mutual funds, greater tax efficiency and lower internal expenses, will not be discussed since both were already covered in great detail in Chapters 5 and 6.

Superior Performance

An unwritten goal of every actively managed mutual fund is to beat the market. However, year after year, the vast majority of fund managers fail to achieve this one basic objective. For example, in 2001 almost 70% of all actively managed large cap stock funds failed to beat the Russell 1000 Index, according to Lipper Analytical Services. Over longer time periods the same pattern holds true. Many studies have shown that approximately 75% of all actively managed mutual funds failed to beat the S&P 500 Index over the ten-year period ending December 2003.

When we compare performance within specific investment categories, such as large cap growth stocks or small cap value stocks, the number of active fund managers that beat the underlying index is often worse. For instance, less than 10% of all mid cap growth funds beat the Russell MidCap Growth Index over the five-year period ending May 31, 2002. Exhibit 7-1 provides an overview of the percentage of actively managed funds, by asset category, which underperformed various indexes.

While the percentage of actively managed funds unable to beat underlying indexes is quite high, it's wrong to assume every actively managed mutual fund underperforms the market. Every year a small percentage of funds are able to beat the market, some by significant margins. The problem is trying to predict which funds it will be. It is virtually impossible to know, in advance, which actively managed funds will do well and which will not. Yet, year after year countless investors pay huge sums of money to investment advisors, newsletter writers, and other market analysts to do just that — predict which

Exhibit 7-1:
Percentage of Active Funds Outperformed by Index
Five-Year Period Ending 5/31/2002

	Value	Blended	Growth
Large Cap	56%	67%	61%
Mid Cap	83%	90%	94%
Small Cap	73%	52%	51%

Large Cap Indexes: Russell 1000 Value, Russell 1000, Russell 1000 Growth
Mid Cap Indexes: Russell MidCap Value, Russell MidCap, Russell MidCap Growth
Small Cap Indexes: Russell 2000 Value, Russell 2000, Russell 2000 Growth

Source: RCM Data

actively managed funds will beat the market. A task made even harder given the fact that so few are able to beat the market in any given year, as we have seen.

Survivorship Bias

The performance comparisons, shown in Exhibit 7-1, do not speak highly of the abilities of actively managed mutual fund managers. In actuality the percentage of funds beating the market is even worse than reported due to a phenomenon known as "survivorship bias."

Survivorship bias refers to the fact that most performance comparisons fail to take into account those actively managed mutual funds that have closed or been merged with other funds. For instance, if a habitually poor performing mutual fund closes after five dismal years, its disappointing track record simply disappears. Even though the fund may have dramatically underperformed the market over those five years, once it's closed everything is forgotten. Regardless of how many investors lost money. When we consider all actively managed mutual funds, those closed because of poor performance and those still in operation, the performance advantage swings even further in the direction of indexing.

Consistent Market Level Performance

A common mistake made by both investors and financial professionals is to consider index mutual funds superior to actively managed mutual funds based on performance alone. After seeing the performance differences, shown in Exhibit 7-1, it's easy to understand how someone might reach such a conclusion.

In addition to superior performance, indexing provides the investor with another important benefit: consistent market level performance. This is not to imply that indexing offers predictable returns. There is no such thing as predictable returns when it comes to equities. Consistent market level performance refers to the premise that a properly managed index fund will follow the performance of the underlying index it's tracking, in both up and down markets.

For example, if the S&P 500 Index dropped by 10% over a given time period it's safe to assume that all funds tracking the S&P 500 Index will also drop by approximately 10%. Likewise, if the S&P 500 Index increased by 10% over a given time period we would expect all funds tracking that index to increase by approximately 10%. Remember, the index fund portfolio manager is not trying to outperform the index, they are simply trying to match its performance.

In contrast, it's virtually impossible to know, in advance, if any given actively managed mutual fund will perform in-line with the market, better than the market, or worse than the market. That's because the fund manager relies on educated guesses to determine which stocks to buy or sell. If he or she is wrong, it opens the door to the possibility of the fund underperforming the market, which translates to a lack of market consistency.

The real risk associated with actively managed mutual funds, however, is not owning a fund that slightly underperforms a specific benchmark or index. The greater risk comes from owning the fund that ends up dramatically underperforming the market. For instance, according to Weisenberger Mutual Fund Services, as of

June 2002, there were 339 mutual funds classified as mid cap growth funds, which had been in existence for at least five years. The worst-performing fund in this group lost 60.8% of its value from May 2001 through June 2002. Over this same time period, the S&P Mid Cap 400 Growth Index, an index designed to track the performance of the mid cap growth segment of the market, experienced a loss of only 5.7%.

This is unacceptable at best and borderline financial malpractice at worst. Unfortunately, it is also very common. Exhibit 7-2 shows the range of returns, over various time periods, for several actively managed mutual funds classified as mid cap growth funds by Weisenberger Financial Services.

As we can see from the exhibit, investors in these mid cap growth funds experienced dramatically different results. A $10,000 investment in the top-performing mid cap growth fund grew to $29,498 over the five-year period ending June 30, 2002. A $10,000 investment in the worst-performing mid cap growth fund dropped to $2,832 over this same period of time. This represents a difference of over $15,000 on a $10,000 investment in just five years.

How is this possible? After all, both investors owned actively managed mutual funds classified as mid cap growth funds. Each

Exhibit 7-2:
Range of Returns for Various Actively Managed Mid Cap Mutual Funds (as of 6/30/2002)

	Best-Performing Mid Cap Fund	Worst-Performing Mid Cap Fund	S&P 400 Mid Cap Index
1-Year Return	15.6%	-60.8%	-5.7%
3-Year Average Return	18.7%	-42.5%	5.5%
5-Year Average Return	23.3%	-22.3%	11.3%
10-Year Average Return	16.8%	4.9%	13.4%

Source: Weisenberger Financial Services

fund, however, had a different portfolio manager. Therefore, the performance of a given fund is based on the ability (or lack of ability) of the fund manager and not the overall performance of mid cap growth stocks in general.

In contrast, an index mutual fund tracking the S&P 400 Mid Cap Growth Index can offer investors consistent, market level performance since it's designed to track the performance of the index. Another name for this is asset class consistency, which is critical to the successful implementation of an asset allocation plan. Actively managed mutual funds cannot guarantee asset class consistency while index-based investments, such as exchange-traded index funds can.

Manager Risk

When an actively managed mutual fund dramatically underperforms the market, as we saw above, it's often the result of forecasting errors or mistakes made by the fund manager. This is commonly referred to as "manager risk" or "manager error." Several common mistakes active fund managers make are the following:

- Holding excess cash, also known as "cash drag."
- Allowing the portfolio to drift from its stated objective.
- Improper diversification or concentrated holdings.

Most investors fail to realize the negative impact these three mistakes can have on their portfolio. As we will see, indexing is the only way to entirely eliminate all types of manager risk from the portfolio management process.

Indexing Eliminates "Cash Drag"

Simply stated, cash drag occurs when an equity mutual fund holds cash. Since cash has a lower expected return than stocks any cash held has the potential to drag down the fund's long-term investment performance. This is especially true during periods of strong market appreciation because cash or money market will presumably earn a much lower return than dollars invested in equities.

A mutual fund manager may hold cash for a variety of reasons: in anticipation of a downward move in equity prices, in anticipation of future buying opportunities, or to meet shareholder liquidation requests. Whatever the reason, holding excess cash can and does hurt the fund's shareholders.

In addition to lowering overall performance during good markets, holding excess cash can dramatically alter an investor's asset allocation plan. For example, assume an investor decided to allocate 90% of their portfolio to equities and 10% to cash. To accomplish this goal, they implemented the portfolio shown in Exhibit 7-3 using various actively managed mutual funds.

As we can see from Exhibit 7-3, the investor has successfully implemented their desired asset allocation plan. Or have they? After receiving a year-end report on each fund, our hypothetical investor was shocked to discover that each fund held a sizable cash position, as follows:

Exhibit 7-3:
Hypothetical $100,000 Portfolio
Comprised of Actively Managed Mutual Funds

	Dollars Invested	Percent of Total Portfolio
Actively Managed Fund A	$30,000.00	30.0%
Actively Managed Fund B	$30,000.00	30.0%
Actively Managed Fund C	$30,000.00	30.0%
Total Equities	**$90,000.00**	**90.0%**
Money Market	$10,000.00	10.0%
Total Portfolio	**$100,000.00**	**100.0%**

- Mutual Fund A: 85% invested in equities, 15% in cash.
- Mutual Fund B: 90% invested in equities, 10% in cash.
- Mutual Fund C: 95% invested in equities, 5% in cash.

Based on this new information it's easy to calculate the investor's actual asset allocation. The real asset allocation is shown in Exhibit 7-4.

In reality, the investor's portfolio had almost double the intended cash position, or about 19%, compared to a goal of 10%. This means instead of $10,000 allocated to cash, as was intended, the overall portfolio had $19,000 in cash or $9,000 more than planned. Likewise, instead of 90% or $90,000 allocated to equities, only 81% of the portfolio or $81,000 was actually invested in equities. In essence, the various active mutual fund managers, by holding cash instead of equities, caused the investor to be much more conservative than intended. Worst of all, the investor had no idea his asset allocation strategy was being undermined.

How prevalent is the problem of cash drag? The problem is far more widespread than one might think. Exhibit 7-5 shows five of the most popular actively managed mutual funds today, ranked by assets under management, and the corresponding cash holdings of each.

Exhibit 7-4:
How the Investor Was Actually Allocated

Fund Name	Fund's Portfolio Mix Equities / Cash	Portion of Fund in Equities	Portion of Fund in Cash
Fund A	85% / 15%	$25,500.00	$ 4,500.00
Fund B	90% / 10%	$27,000.00	$ 3,000.00
Fund C	95% / 5%	$28,500.00	$ 1,500.00
Money Market		$ -	$10,000.00
Actual Portfolio Allocation		**$81,000.00**	**$19,000.00**
Percentage Allocation		**81%**	**19%**

Exhibit 7-5:
Cash Holdings of Various Actively Managed Growth Funds

Fund Name	Cash Holdings (%) as of 3/31/02
Fidelity Magellan Fund	7.3%
Janus Adviser Growth Fund	5.8%
American Century Ultra Fund	4.0%
Russell Select Growth Fund	6.5%
Oppenheimer Capital Appreciation Fund	9.7%

Source: Weisenberger

Unlike the mutual funds shown in Exhibit 7-5, equity indexes never include cash as a component. A mutual fund tracking an equity index will never hold cash, avoiding the problems associated with cash drag. During both up and down markets the index fund will be 100% in equities providing the investor with consistent, pure market exposure at all times. Therefore, when index-based funds are used to implement an asset allocation plan, as we do in Strategic Index Investing, the planned allocation is not undermined by a mutual fund manager. Unfortunately, when using actively managed mutual funds to implement an asset allocation plan mistakes made by the fund managers can, and do, damage the intended asset allocation plan.

Indexing Eliminates Portfolio Drift
For asset allocation purposes, individual stocks are often classified or grouped based on common characteristics. For instance, stocks are frequently grouped by size (large cap, mid cap, and small cap) or by style (growth and value). This is important since numerous studies have shown that asset classes perform differently at various points in the economic cycle. By changing the allocation between various asset classes, it is possible to alter the overall volatility and potential

return of a portfolio. This is a central theme of asset allocation, as we will see in Part 3.

When an active portfolio manager deviates from the fund's stated investment objective, whether it is a style or size objective, it's known as portfolio drift. An example of portfolio drift is the manager of a small cap value fund moving a portion of the fund's portfolio from small cap value stocks to small cap growth stocks in an attempt to enhance return. Another example is a large cap growth fund manager moving 30% of the fund's portfolio to small cap value stocks in anticipation of a correction in large cap growth stocks.

Like cash drag, portfolio drift can create significant problems for investors because it distorts asset allocation models, undermines performance, and alters risk calculations. For an asset allocation plan to work effectively, the investment used to represent a given asset category must have the same risk and return profile as the underlying asset class being tracked. When it doesn't, problems can and will develop. For example, portfolio drift might cause an investor to take on far greater risk than planned, or cause their portfolio to dramatically underperform projected models.

Unfortunately, when discussing actively managed mutual funds, portfolio drift is a common occurrence. A recent study by the Association for Investment Management, a non-profit global leader in educating investment professionals, found that approximately 40% of all actively managed funds are classified incorrectly.

An example of this is seen by examining the portfolio of one of the most popular value funds in the country. As of October 31, 1999, the value fund in question listed American Online Inc., Gateway Inc., and Amazon.com as its three largest holdings. This same fund had an average price to earnings ratio (P/E) that was 43% higher than the value category average and its price-to-book ratio was 186% higher than the value category average according to Morningstar. Price to earnings ratio and price-to-book ratio are widely accepted measurements used to determine if a particular stock exhibits growth or value characteristics. To make matters worse, the fund had as part of its name "Value Trust," even though it was clearly not a value fund.

When growth stocks corrected in 2000 and 2001, this so-called value mutual fund dropped as much as most growth mutual funds, even though true value mutual funds were actually moving higher. As a result of the fund's style drift the shareholders were bearing greater risk than they realized and subsequently suffered larger than expected losses.

Any investor using this fund as a means of gaining exposure to value stocks was greatly disappointed. The fund was in fact a closet growth fund. If an investor had allocated 50% of their portfolio to growth stocks and 50% to value stocks using the value fund above, they were taking on far greater risk than anticipated. The portfolio was not balanced between growth and value, as intended, but was heavily weighted to growth, creating a blueprint for disaster.

In contrast, index mutual funds provide pure asset class exposure at all times. An index is unaffected by emotional factors that may cause an active fund manager to drift, moving from one style to the other in an attempt to enhance return. Therefore, since index mutual funds track specific market indexes, comprised of securities based on pre-set qualifications, portfolio drift is not a concern.

Indexing Eliminates Over Concentration and Lack of Diversification

Many actively managed mutual funds live or die by taking large positions in only a handful of securities. Current diversification requirements for regulated mutual funds allow for up to 50% of a fund's portfolio in as few as two securities. Unfortunately, when active mutual fund managers establish large positions in just a few securities the shareholders are the ones who usually end up paying for the mistake.

This problem was prevalent as the bull market of the 1990s continued its long run. As the market moved higher it became more and more acceptable for actively managed funds to hold large, over-concentrated positions in a small number of securities. Many new mutual funds were created with the primary objective of investing in only a handful of companies. A number of mutual fund companies proudly touted these concentrated portfolio funds as a way to maximize return, often failing to mention the added risks. Exhibit 7-6 provides an example of several overly concentrated actively managed mutual funds.

Actively managed funds can be over-concentrated in specific industries as well, exposing the fund's shareholders to the risks associated with owning a sector or industry fund. This is typically seen during periods when one industry or sector substantially outperforms all others. In an attempt to enhance return, many active fund managers will become over-concentrated in the "hot" sector of the day. This can have a devastating effect on the shareholders when the hot industry or sector corrects, as it always does.

An example of this type of activity was seen in late 1999 and early 2000 when many supposedly broad-based growth mutual fund managers moved larger and larger portions of their portfolios into the technology sector. As long as technology stocks continued to climb higher these funds posted remarkable returns. It wasn't until technology stocks corrected that many shareholders learned just how over-

Exhibit 7-6:
Example Showing How Overly Concentrated
Many Actively Managed Mutual Funds Can Be

Fund Name	Top Holding	Percent of Fund's Assets	Date of Report
American Heritage	Senetek ADR	78.00%	Nov-98
Amerindo Technology	Yahoo	43.40%	Dec-98
IAI Value	Pathnet	39.10%	June-99
IAI Emerging Growth	Tut Systems	30.80%	June-99
Legg Mason Value Trust	American Online	18.90%	Mar-99
Rydex OTC	Microsoft	17.50%	Mar-99

Source: Fund Reports, Morningstar

concentrated their mutual funds actually were.

The index fund manager is restricted from over-weighting the portfolio in any given security since they must follow the exact weighting of the underlying index. Investors are protected from a fund manager "loading-up" on a security in an attempt to increase potential return. Likewise, investors are protected from the index fund manager becoming over-weighted in the hot sector or industry group in an attempt to enhance return. In contrast to actively managed mutual funds, indexing offers the investor tremendous diversification and portfolio purity. Two key factors when constructing a portfolio based on the principles of asset allocation.

Portfolio Transparency

Not only does indexing avoid the three major problems most often associated with manager risk (cash drag, portfolio drift, and over-concentrated positions), it also offers investors portfolio transparency. That is, investors can look inside the portfolio of an index fund at any time and know exactly which stocks are owned and in what percentage. There is never any guesswork regarding the composition of the underlying portfolio because it's public information, unlike actively managed mutual funds which often try to hide the stocks they own.

The Index Provider who created the index will routinely list all components of the underlying index, the percentage each security represents within the index, and the criteria for being included in the index. They will also list other relevant factors such as the weighting method used to calculate the index and any reasons for making changes to the index. The net result is that index mutual fund investors will always know exactly what stocks the fund owns simply by looking at the components of the underlying index, which the fund is tracking.

Actively managed mutual fund shareholders, in contrast, will usually have no idea what the portfolio looks like at any one time. Many active funds only publish their holdings semi-annually or annually, often going out of their way to keep the portfolio a secret so competitors cannot duplicate their trades. This cloak and dagger approach leaves the shareholders in the dark and can create potential problems, as we have seen.

As a result, it is very difficult for investors to build well-balanced, diversified portfolios using actively managed mutual funds because the investor never knows exactly what securities are held or in what percentage. This makes it all but impossible to use actively managed mutual funds to effectively implement an asset allocation plan.

Summary

As we have seen, index-based investments provide a number of substantial portfolio management advantages compared to actively managed mutual funds. Since all exchange-traded index funds are index-based investment vehicles they offer investors these same benefits.

Index-based investments represent the best tool to use when implementing an asset allocation plan. Actively managed mutual funds, in contrast, are not a good choice. Indexing avoids problems associated with actively managed mutual funds such as excess cash holdings, portfolio drift, and lack of diversification. Indexing also provides the investor with portfolio transparency allowing them to see inside the portfolio at all times.

Chapter 8

EXCHANGE-TRADED INDEX FUND PROVIDERS

Exchange-Traded Index Fund Families

As we have seen, exchange-traded index funds offer substantial advantages over traditional mutual funds and common stocks. Our examination of this remarkable new product would not be complete, however, without mentioning those companies most responsible for creating the majority of the currently available exchange-traded index funds.

Although several well-known traditional mutual fund companies have recently joined the exchange-traded index fund club, most notably Vanguard in 2002 and Fidelity Investments in 2004, the undisputed leader remains Barclays Global Investors (BGI). Under the iShares family of exchange-traded index funds, BGI offers eighty-four funds that cover every conceivable asset type, class, size, and segment of the market. The iShares family of exchange-traded index funds is the largest family of funds comprising over 70% of all funds in existence, as of June 2004.

In addition to the iShares, there are three other families of exchange-traded index funds that need to be mentioned. They are:

1. **streetTRACKS** — Created and managed by State Street Global Advisors (SSGA).
2. **Select Sector SPDRs** — Created by SSGA in conjunction with

the American Stock Exchange. SSGA serves as investment advisor.

3. **VIPERs** — Created and managed by The Vanguard Group.

Exhibit 8-1 provides an overview of the number of funds in each of the four main families of exchange-traded index funds.

The final company that must be mentioned is the American Stock Exchange. As we have already seen, the AMEX pioneered the concept of exchange-traded index funds in 1993 by introducing SPDRs (Spiders). Today, the AMEX continues to play a major role in the growth and development of new exchange-traded index funds.

Barclays Global Investors

Barclays Global Investors is a business unit of Barclays, a London based money management firm which traces its roots back to the late 1690s. With over $800 billion in assets under management and offices in thirty-six countries Barclays is one of the largest and most respected asset management companies in the world.

BGI is perhaps best known for their innovations in the area of

Exhibit 8-1:
Exchange-Traded Index Funds by Fund Family*

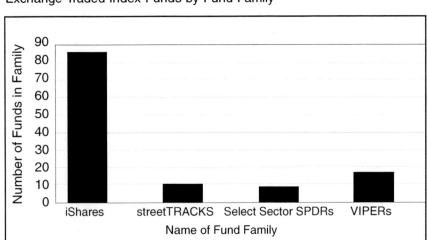

* As of 05/01/2004

Exhibit 8-2:
iShares Available by Index Provider

Index Provider	Number of Indexes Tracked by iShares*
Morgan Stanley	25
Standard & Poor's	20
Dow Jones & Company	15
Russell Company	12
Lehman Brothers	6
Goldman Sachs	5
New York Stock Exchange	2
Cohen & Steers	1
Nasdaq	1

* As of 05/01/2004

portfolio management. For example, in 1971 they created the world's first institutional index strategy. In 1978, they created the first quantitative active strategy. In 2000, BGI rolled out iShares, the first true family of exchange-traded index funds. And, in the fall of 2002 BGI was on the cutting edge once again when they introduced the first exchange-traded index funds based on fixed income indexes.

Today, the iShares are the largest and most diverse family of exchange-traded index funds available. Structured as mutual funds, iShares track indexes created by such well respected Index Providers as Standard & Poor's, Dow Jones & Company, Russell, Lehman Brothers, Morgan Stanely, and Goldman Sachs. Exhibit 8-2 provides an overview of iShares by Index Provider.

In addition to those iShares listed in Exhibit 8-2, on March 8, 2004 BGI announced that it had entered into an agreement with Morningstar, Inc. to license sixteen of their style-based indexes. The Morningstar Indexes track the U. S. equity market by capitalization and investment style and are based on the proprietary methodology of Morningstar Style Box. When the new funds are offered, anticipated to be in the fall of 2004, investors will be able to construct a portfolio based entirely on a targeted asset allocation using Morningstar research.

State Street Bank & Trust
State Street Bank & Trust is one of the largest money management firms in the world. Through their State Street Global Advisors division, State Street Bank & Trust has been instrumental in the development and growth of the exchange-traded index funds marketplace. For instance, SSGA is Trustee for the DIAMONDS and Spiders, two of the most popular exchange-traded index funds, based on assets under management. They also serve as investment advisor to the Select Sector SPDRs. As such, SSGA is responsible for the day-to-day management of fund assets. In return, each Select Sector fund pays them an advisory fee based on the fund's average daily net assets.

State Street Global Advisors also created and manages streetTRACKS, a family of ten diverse exchange-traded index funds. While playing a behind the scenes role in the past, streetTRACKS represented SSGAs first attempt to create their own brand of exchange-traded index funds. Exhibit 8-3 lists the funds in the streetTRACKS family of exchange-traded index funds.

The Vanguard Group
The last family of exchange-traded index funds, which we will review, is Vanguard Index Participation Equity Receipts (VIPERs). Even though a latecomer to the exchange-traded index funds table, Vanguard has the potential to create incredible investor awareness as a result of their well-known and respected name within the indexing arena. It was Vanguard, after all, who created the first index-based mutual fund for retail investors in the early 1970s.

As of June 2004, there were sixteen exchange-traded index funds in the VIPERs family. Most industry observers believe that over the next several years as many as fifteen to twenty-five new funds could be offered under the VIPERs family of funds. Exhibit 8-4 provides a list of the Vanguard VIPERs currently available.

Exhibit 8-3:
streetTRACKS Family of Exchange-Traded Index Funds*

Index Provider	Fund Name	Symbol
Dow Jones	streetTRACKS Dow Jones Global Titans Index Fund	DGT
	streetTRACKS Dow Jones U.S. LargeCap Growth Index Fund	ELG
	streetTRACKS Dow Jones U.S. LargeCap Value Index Fund	ELV
	streetTRACKS Dow Jones U.S. SmallCap Growth Index Fund	DSG
	streetTRACKS Dow Jones U.S. SmallCap Value Index Fund	DSV
Morgan Stanley	streetTRACKS Morgan Stanley Technology Index Fund	MTK
Fortune	streetTRACKS Fortune 500 Index Fund	FFF
Wilshire	streetTRACKS Wilshire REIT Index Fund	RWR

*As of 05/01/2004

The American Stock Exchange

Last, but certainly not least, is the American Stock Exchange. As we saw in Chapter 4, the AMEX single handedly started the exchange-traded index funds revolution in early 1993 when they introduced Spiders. Today, a little over ten years later, they continue to play an important role in the growth of the exchange-traded index funds marketplace.

The AMEX is currently home to over 80% of all exchange-traded index funds. On any given day approximately half of all trading volume at the AMEX is from exchange-traded index funds. Through PDR Services, a wholly owned subsidiary, the AMEX provides portfolio management and advisory services to some of the most popular exchange-traded index funds available today. Safe to say, without

Exhibit 8-4:
VIPERs Family of Exchange-Traded Index Funds*

Fund Type	Fund Name	Symbol
Broad Market	Total Stock Market VIPERs	VTI
Size/Style	Large-Cap VIPERs	VV
	Growth VIPERs	VUG
	Value VIPERs	VPU
	Mid-Cap VIPERs	VO
	Small-Cap VIPERs	VB
	Small-Cap Growth VIPERs	VBK
	Small-Cap Value VIPERs	VBR
	Extended Market VIPERs	VXF
Sector & Industry	Consumer Discretionary VIPERs	VCR
	Consumer Staples VIPERs	VDC
	Healthcare VIPERs	VHT
	Information Technology VIPERs	VGT
	Materials VIPERs	VAW
	Financials VIPERs	VFH
	Utilities VIPERs	VPU

* As of 5/01/2004

the creativity and foresight of the AMEX, the exchange-traded index funds marketplace would not be what it is today.

The Underlying Indexes

Before concluding this section, it's important to understand the wide range of underlying indexes tracked by available exchange-traded index funds. Therefore, an overview of the various indexes is provided, by Index Provider. Each index listed is tracked by at least one exchange-traded index fund and in some cases by several. To find a specific fund that tracks one of the following indexes, refer to the list of exchange-traded index funds provided in Chapter 4. All index descriptions and definitions are taken directly from the prospectuses of the exchange-traded index funds tracking the given index.

The Standard & Poor's Indexes

The S&P 500 Index is a market capitalization weighted index consisting of 500 domestic stocks, but not necessarily the 500 largest. Index components are chosen based on their market size, liquidity, and industry group representation. The S&P 500 Index is widely regarded as the standard for measuring large capitalization U.S. stock market performance. It represents approximately 80% of the total market value of all publicly traded stocks in the United States.

The S&P 500/BARRA Growth Index is a subset of the S&P 500 Index, consisting of those companies with the highest price-to-book (P/B) ratios. Twice a year, the S&P 500 Index is split in half by market capitalization (not by number) and sorted by P/B ratio. Those stocks with the highest relative P/B ratios are then assigned to the Growth Index.

The S&P 500/BARRA Value Index is a subset of the S&P 500 Index consisting of those companies with the lowest price-to-book (P/B) ratios. Twice a year, the S&P 500 Index is split in half by market capitalization (not by number) and sorted by P/B ratio. Those stocks with the lowest relative P/B ratios are then assigned to the Value Index.

The S&P MidCap 400 Index is a market capitalization weighted index consisting of 400 mid cap companies from leading industries in the U.S. economy. It represents approximately 6% of the market capitalization of all U.S. equity securities. Index components will typically have a total market capitalization of between $1 billion and $5 billion.

The S&P MidCap 400/BARRA Growth Index is a subset of the S&P MidCap 400 Index consisting of those companies with the highest price-to-book (P/B) ratios. Twice a year, the S&P MidCap 400 is split in half by market capitalization (not by number) and sorted by P/B ratio. Those stocks with the highest relative P/B ratios are then assigned to the Growth Index.

The S&P MidCap 400/BARRA Value Index is a subset of the S&P MidCap 400 Index consisting of those companies with the lowest price-to-book (P/B) ratios. Twice a year, the S&P MidCap 400 is split in half by market capitalization (not by number) and sorted by P/B ratio. Those stocks with the lowest relative P/B ratios are then assigned to the Value Index.

The S&P SmallCap 600 Index measures the performance of publicly traded securities in the small cap sector of the U.S. equity market. It is a market capitalization weighted index of 600 companies chosen based on their industry representation and liquidity. It represents approximately 3% of the total market capitalization of the U.S. domestic equity market.

The S&P SmallCap 600/BARRA Growth Index is a subset of the S&P SmallCap 600 Index consisting of those companies with the highest price-to-book (P/B) ratios. Twice a year, the S&P SmallCap 600 is split in half by market capitalization (not by number) and sorted by P/B ratio. Those stocks with the highest relative P/B ratios are then assigned to the Growth Index.

The S&P SmallCap 600/BARRA Index is a subset of the S&P 600 SmallCap Index consisting of those companies with the lowest price-to-book (P/B) ratios. Twice a year, the S&P SmallCap 600 is split in half by market capitalization (not by number) and sorted by P/B ratio. Those stocks with the lowest relative P/B ratios are then assigned to the Value Index.

136

The S&P 100 Index is a subset of the S&P 500 Index. It is comprised of one hundred "blue chip" stocks chosen from the S&P 500 Index by Standard & Poor's. The Index is market capitalization weighted and represents approximately 40% of the market capitalization of all listed U.S. equities.

The S&P Global 100 Index is comprised of one hundred stocks selected for inclusion based on size, liquidity and sector representation. It is a subset of the S&P Global 1200 Index and tracks the performance of large trans-national companies that are of major importance in the global markets.

The S&P Europe 350 Index seeks to measure the performance of the leading companies in the following countries: Austria, Belgium, Denmark, Finland, France, Germany, Ireland, Italy, the Netherlands, Norway, Portugal, Spain, Sweden, Switzerland and the United Kingdom. The stocks in the Index are chosen based on market size, liquidity, industry group and geographic diversity.

The S&P/TSE 60 Index measures the performance of selected large capitalization Canadian equities from ten different economic sectors. The Index is market capitalization weighted with constituent weights adjusted, by Standard & Poor's, based on available share float.

The S&P Latin American 40 Index is comprised of selected equities trading on the exchanges of four different countries. The four countries represented in the index are Mexico, Brazil, Argentina, and Chile.

The S&P/TOPIX 150 Index is comprised of companies representing approximately 70% of the market value of the Japanese equity market. TOPIX is an acronym for the Tokyo Stock Price Index. The Index includes 150 highly liquid securities selected from each major sector of the Tokyo market.

The S&P Global Energy Sector Index measures the performance of companies Standard & Poor's believes to be part of the energy sector of the global economy. It is a subset of the S&P Global 1200 Index.

The S&P Global Financial Sector Index measures the performance of companies Standard & Poor's believes to be part of the financial sector of the global economy. It is a subset of the S&P Global 1200 Index.

The S&P Global Healthcare Sector Index measures the performance of companies Standard & Poor's believes to be part of the healthcare sector of the global economy. It is a subset of the S&P Global 1200 Index.

The S&P Global Technology Sector Index measures the performance of companies Standard & Poor's believes to be part of the information technology sector of the global economy. It is a subset of the S&P Global 1200 Index.

The S&P Global Telecommunications Sector Index measures the performance of companies Standard & Poor's believes to be part of the telecommunications sector of the global economy. It is a subset of the S&P Global 1200 Index.

The Russell Indexes

The Russell 3000 Index represents approximately 86% of the market capitalization of all U.S. equity securities. It is a market capitalization weighted index consisting of the largest publicly traded companies domiciled in the U.S. or its territories.

The Russell 3000 Growth Index is a subset of the Russell 3000 Index, consisting of those companies with the highest price-to-book ratios and higher forecasted growth rates. It is a capitalization weighted index representing approximately 50% of the total market capitalization of the Russell 3000 Index.

The Russell 3000 Value Index is a subset of the Russell 3000 Index, consisting of those companies with the lowest price-to-book ratios and lower forecasted growth rates. It is a market capitalization weighted index representing approximately 50% of the market capitalization of the Russell 3000 Index.

The Russell 2000 Index represents the market capitalization of approximately 6% of all U.S. equity securities. It is a capitalization weighted index consisting of the 2,000 smallest companies, based on market capitalization, from the Russell 3000 Index.

The Russell 2000 Growth Index is a subset of the Russell 2000 Index, consisting of those companies with the highest price-to-book ratios and higher forecasted growth rates. It is a market capitalization weighted index representing approximately 50% of the total market capitalization of the Russell 2000 Index.

The Russell 2000 Value Index is a subset of the Russell 2000 Index, consisting of those companies with the lowest price-to-book ratios and lower forecasted growth rates. It is a market capitalization weighted index representing approximately 50% of the total market capitalization of the Russell 2000 Index.

The Russell 1000 Index is a capitalization weighted index of U.S. equities consisting of the 1,000 largest companies from the Russell 3000 Index. It represents approximately 80% of the total market capitalization of all U.S. equity securities.

The Russell 1000 Growth Index is a subset of the Russell 1000 Index, consisting of those companies with the highest price-to-book ratios and higher forecasted growth rates. It represents approximately 50% of the total market capitalization of the Russell 1000 Index.

The Russell 1000 Value Index is a subset of the Russell 1000 Index, consisting of those companies with the lowest price-to-book ratios and lower forecasted growth rates. It represents approximately 50% of the market capitalization of the Russell 1000 Index.

The Russell MidCap Index represents approximately 19% of the market capitalization of all U.S. equity securities. It is a capitalization weighted index consisting of the 800 smallest companies in the Russell 1000 Index.

The Russell MidCap Growth Index is a subset of the Russell MidCap Index, consisting of those companies with the highest price-to-book ratios and higher forecasted growth rates. It represents approximately 50% of the total market capitalization of the Russell 1000 Index.

The Russell MidCap Value Index is a subset of the Russell MidCap Index, consisting of those companies with the lowest price-to-book ratios and lower forecasted growth rates. It represents approximately 50% of the market capitalization of the Russell 1000 Index.

The Dow Jones & Company Indexes

The Dow Jones Industrial Average is perhaps the best known stock market barometer in the world. It is comprised of thirty large capitalization companies from various economic segments. The Dow is a price-weighted stock average; meaning component stocks are weighted based on their trading price, not market capitalization. Therefore, the higher the actual trading price per share of a stock in the Dow, the greater its impact on the overall average.

The Dow Jones U.S. Large Cap Growth Index is designed to track the performance of the U.S. large cap growth segment of the equity market. Each year Dow Jones selects the largest U.S. stocks by market capitalization. After the list is compiled, Dow Jones will use a proprietary model to identify the growth stocks within the large cap universe for inclusion in the index.

The Dow Jones U.S. Large Cap Value Index is designed to track the performance of the U.S. large cap value segment of the equity market. Each year Dow Jones selects the largest U.S. stocks by market capitalization. After the list is compiled, Dow Jones will use a proprietary model to identify the value stocks within the large cap universe for inclusion in the index.

The Dow Jones U.S. Small Cap Growth Index is designed to track the performance of the U.S. small cap growth segment of the equity market. Each year Dow Jones selects the smallest U.S. stocks by market capitalization. After the list is compiled, Dow Jones will use a proprietary model to identify the growth stocks within the small cap universe for inclusion in the index.

The Dow Jones U.S. Small Cap Value Index is designed to track the performance of the U.S. small cap value segment of the equity market. Each year Dow Jones selects the smallest U.S. stocks by market capitalization. After the list is compiled, Dow Jones will use a proprietary model to identify the value stocks within the small cap universe for inclusion in the index.

The Dow Jones U.S. Global Titans Index is designed to track the performance of the world's largest companies with global reach. Component companies are selected based on their market capitalization, assets, book value, sales/revenues and net profits. In essence, the index represents "The Biggest of the Big" and the "Bluest of the Blue."

The Dow Jones U.S. Total Market Index is designed to measure the performance of the U.S. equity broad market. The Index is comprised of all of the companies in the Dow Jones Large Cap Index, Dow Jones Mid Cap Index and Dow Jones Small Cap Index. The Index should represent approximately 95% of the market capitalization of all listed U. S. equity securities.

The Dow Jones U.S. Basic Materials Sector Index includes companies involved in the production of aluminum, chemicals, commodities, chemical specialty products, forest products, non-ferrous mining products, paper products, precious metals and steel.

The Dow Jones U.S. Chemicals Sector Index is comprised of companies involved in chemicals, household products/wares, commercial services, miscellaneous manufacturing, environmental control, pharmaceuticals, and diversified metals.

The Dow Jones U.S. Consumer Cyclical Sector Index is comprised of companies that include airlines, auto manufacturers, tire and rubber manufacturers, auto parts suppliers, casinos, toy manufacturers, restaurant chains, home construction companies, lodging chains, broad-line retailers, specialty retailers, footwear and clothing manufacturers, and media companies.

The Dow Jones U.S. Consumer Non-Cyclical Sector Index includes distillers and brewers, producers of soft drinks, consumer service companies, durable and non-durable household product manufacturers, cosmetic companies, food retailers, tobacco and agricultural companies.

The Dow Jones U.S. Energy Sector Index is comprised of companies that include oil equipment and services companies, major oil and secondary oil companies and pipelines. It also includes companies involved with the production of coal, oil field equipment and services companies, and natural gas.

The Dow Jones U.S. Financial Sector Index is designed to measure the performance of the financial sector of the U.S. equity market. Component companies include major banks, regional banks, diversified financial companies, insurance companies, real estate companies, savings and loan associations, and securities firms.

The Dow Jones U.S. Financial Services Sector Index is designed to measure the performance of the financial services industry segment of the U.S. equity market. It is a subset of the Dow Jones U.S. Financial Sector Index. Component companies include banks, savings and loan associations, specialty financial firms, and other financial services firms.

The Dow Jones U.S. Healthcare Sector Index is designed to measure the performance of the healthcare sector of the U.S. equity market. Component companies include health care providers, biotechnology companies and manufacturers of medical supplies, advanced medical devices and pharmaceuticals.

The Dow Jones U.S. Industrial Sector Index is designed to measure the performance of the industrial sector of the U.S. equity market. Component companies include aerospace and defense companies, equipment manufacturers, air freight companies, building materials manufacturers, packaging companies, heavy construction companies, railroads, shipbuilders, and trucking companies.

The Dow Jones U.S. Internet Sector Index is designed to track companies in two sub-groups, Internet Commerce and Internet Services. The Index components therefore include companies that derive the majority of their revenues from providing goods and/or services through an open network, such as a web site. Also, included in the Index are companies that derive the majority of their revenues from providing access to the Internet or providing enabling services to people using the Internet.

The Dow Jones U.S. Real Estate Sector Index is designed to measure the performance of the real estate sector of the U.S. equity market. Component companies include hotel and resort companies and real estate investment trusts (REITs) that invest in apartments, office and retail properties.

The Dow Jones U.S. Technology Sector Index is designed to measure the performance of the technology sector of the U.S. equity market. Component companies include those companies involved in the development and production of technology products, including computer hardware and software, telecommunications equipment, microcomputer components, integrated computer circuits and office equipment utilizing technology.

The Dow Jones U.S. Telecommunications Sector Index is designed to measure the performance of the telecommunications sector of the U.S. equity market. Component companies include fixed-line communications and wireless communications companies.

The Dow Jones U.S. Utilities Sector Index is designed to measure the performance of the utilities sector of the U.S. equity market. Component companies include electric utilities, gas utilities and water utilities.

The Nasdaq Stock Market Indexes

The Nasdaq 100 Index represents the one hundred largest non-financial companies listed on the National Market tier of The Nasdaq Stock Market. The Index is comprised of both U.S. and non-U.S. companies and includes the largest companies across major industry groups. Component companies are from industries such as computer hardware and software, telecommunications, retail/wholesale trade and biotechnology.

The Nasdaq Biotechnology Index is one of eight sub-indices of the Nasdaq Composite Index, which measures all common stocks listed on the Nasdaq. Component companies are primarily engaged in using biomedical research for the discovery or development of new treatments or cures for human diseases.

The Wilshire Indexes

The Wilshire 5000 Total Market Index represents the broadest index for measuring the performance of the U.S. equity market. Every U.S. headquartered equity security with readily available price data is included in the index. That is, virtually all regularly traded U.S. stocks are included in the index. The Index therefore provides one of the best representations of the performance characteristics of the entire U.S. equity market.

The Wilshire 4500 Index was created in 1983 by removing the 500 securities in the S&P 500 Index from the Wilshire 5000 Index. Therefore, the Wilshire 4500 Index is simply the Wilshire 5000, less the 500 stocks, which comprise the S&P 500 Index. The Index is comprised mostly of mid and small cap companies.

The Wilshire REIT Index is designed to measure the performance of the U.S. REIT market. The Index is comprised of U.S. companies whose main characteristics are the equity ownership and operation of commercial real estate, or companies that derive a minimum of 75% of their revenues from real estate related operations.

The Select Sector Indexes

The Basic Industries Select Sector Index is comprised of companies from the S&P 500 Index involved in such basic industries as integrated steel products, chemicals, fibers, paper and gold. The Index therefore, should measure the overall performance of the U.S. Basic Industries sector of the equity market.

The Consumer Services Select Sector Index is comprised of companies from the S&P 500 Index that will be affected by the consumer and changing consumer habits. Companies in the Index are from industries such as entertainment, publishing, prepared foods, medical services, lodging and gaming.

The Consumer Staples Select Sector Index is comprised of companies from the S&P 500 Index involved in the development and production of consumer products that cover cosmetic and personal care, pharmaceuticals, soft drinks, tobacco and food products.

The Cyclical/Transportation Select Sector Index is comprised of companies from the S&P 500 Index involved in the building materials industry, retailing, apparel, housewares, air transportation, automotive manufacturing, shipping and trucking.

The Energy Select Sector Index is comprised of companies from the S&P 500 Index involved in the development and production of crude oil and natural gas, and companies that provide drilling and other energy related services.

The Financial Select Sector Index is comprised of companies from the S&P 500 Index involved in a wide array of diversified financial services. Included in the Index are companies from investment management to commercial and investment banking.

146

The Industrial Select Sector Index is comprised of companies from the S&P 500 Index in industries such as the electrical equipment industry, the construction equipment industry, waste management services and industrial machinery products.

The Technology Select Sector Index is comprised of companies from the S&P 500 Index covering products developed by defense manufacturers, telecommunications equipment providers, integrated computer circuit and process monitoring systems companies, and microcomputer component manufacturers.

The Utilities Select Sector Index is comprised of companies from the S&P 500 Index that provide communication services, electrical power and natural gas distribution companies.

Summary

In this chapter, we discussed those companies most responsible for the creation and growth of the exchange-traded index funds marketplace. The undisputed leader is Barclays Global Investors. The iShares family of funds, created and managed by Barclays, is the largest and most diverse family of exchange-traded index funds with over eighty funds available. Other important players include State Street Global Advisors (streetTRACKS) and the Vanguard Group (VIPERs). Finally, we must never forget the true exchange-traded index funds pioneer: the American Stock Exchange. The AMEX was responsible for creating the first domestic exchange-traded index fund and they continue to be home to the vast majority of the funds traded today.

Part Three

Strategic Index Investing

Unlocking the Power of Exchange-Traded Index Funds

Chapter 9

ASSET ALLOCATION — THE KEY TO BUILDING A SOLID FOUNDATION

Overview

In Part 1, the two key components of Strategic Index Investing were introduced: building a strong foundation using strategies based on proven financial principles and access to the most efficient tools to implement the strategies.

In Part 2, we saw that exchange-traded index funds are the best investment tools available today. They provide significant portfolio management advantages over both traditional mutual funds and common stocks.

In Part 3, we focus on the strategies used in Strategic Index Investing. As we will see, each strategy discussed is easily implemented using exchange-traded index funds. In Chapter 9, asset allocation is introduced and explained. In Chapter 10, the asset allocation model is improved using strategic asset allocation. The four remaining chapters of Part 3 focus on active portfolio management strategies. Each strategy presented is designed to help the investor limit losses, protect profits, or take advantage of unique opportunities created by the markets.

Asset Allocation

Asset allocation is a scientific approach to portfolio diversification that allows each investor to construct the "best" portfolio based on his or her return objective, risk tolerance, and investment time horizon. Unlike the vast majority of portfolio management strategies used today, the goal of asset allocation is not to find the "hot" stock, predict which mutual fund manager will beat the market, or try to accurately time the market. Instead, the goal is to find the correct mix of assets that maximize expected return for a given level of acceptable risk. In this respect, asset allocation represents a return-optimizing portfolio management approach because it seeks to maximize return within the context of acceptable risk.

For our purposes, asset allocation provides four notable benefits:

- It allows the investor to compare various portfolios based on risk and return.
- It allows the investor to know in advance the possible return distributions for a given portfolio.
- It provides the investor with a diversified platform from which to implement active portfolio strategies.
- It provides the investor with a measuring stick to judge the effectiveness of active portfolio management decisions.

Every investor is different. From the level of risk they can tolerate to their investment time horizon. These differences can, and do, influence the way they invest. Whether the need is for income, growth, preservation of capital, or any other varied objective, asset allocation provides a framework for constructing the best portfolio possible. As such, asset allocation is the key to building a solid foundation for your portfolio and the first step in Strategic Index Investing.

Astonishing Findings

Even though the basic theories behind asset allocation were first developed in the late 1950s and early 1960s, it wasn't until the 1980s and 1990s that it became widely accepted and used by market participants. The first real world validation of asset allocation came in a landmark study, "Determinants of Portfolio Performance," published in the Financial Analysts Journal (July-August 1986) by Gary P. Brinson, L. Randolph Hood, and Gary L. Beebower. For the study, the researchers examined the investment performance of ninety-one large pension plans from 1974 to 1983. They were trying to determine what factors accounted for the differences in returns between the various pension plans.

The researchers identified three factors that accounted for the majority of the variation in investment returns between the pension funds. They were how the portfolios were allocated among different types of assets (asset allocation), the ability of the pension fund manager to pick winning stocks (security selection), and market timing. To everyone's surprise, the researchers concluded that asset allocation alone accounted for 93.6% of the variation in total returns achieved by the various pension funds. In contrast, security selection accounted for only 4.2% of the variation in returns while market timing accounted for 1.7%. In addition, other factors, including luck, accounted for 0.5% of the variation in returns. Exhibit 9-1 summarizes the findings of this landmark study.

A follow-up study in 1991 (by Brinson, Beebower, and Brian D. Singer) confirmed these results. The study showed that asset allocation accounted for a remarkable 91.5% of the variation in returns of the different institutionally managed portfolios analyzed.

It is important to note that both studies examined the investment results of some of the largest pension funds in the country ranging in size from $100 million in assets to well over $3 billion. Based on the size of the portfolios studied, it's not a far stretch of the imagination to assume they had access to the best available market research from some of the most prestigious investment managers in the world. In other words, the pension plan managers had access to the best and brightest talent on Wall Street.

Despite having access to the top investment minds in the country, the single biggest factor explaining variations in performance between the different funds was not the ability of the portfolio manag-

Exhibit 9-1:
Determinates of Portfolio Return Variance*

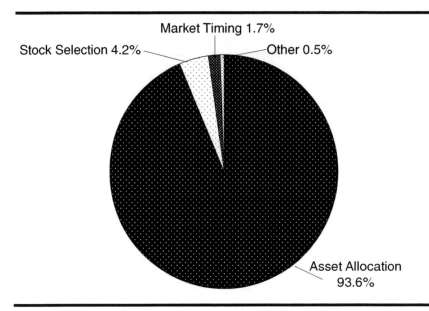

Market Timing 1.7%

Stock Selection 4.2%

Other 0.5%

Asset Allocation
93.6%

*Source: 1986 study by Gary P. Brinson, L. Randolph Hood, and Gary L. Beebower

ers to select the right securities or time the market correctly. The most important factor was how dollars were allocated between various types of assets. That is, the overall asset allocation of each portfolio represented the single most important factor in determining the variation of returns between the different portfolios.

These two studies, while focusing on large pension funds, have major implications for every investor. They show that it's not necessary to worry about such things, as which stock to buy or what actively managed mutual fund will do the best. It is also not necessary to try to time the market. Asset allocation theory shows us that the very activities most investors spend a great deal of time and energy on (security selection and market timing) are essentially a waste of time. In contrast, how an investor chooses to allocate dollars among different types of assets (asset allocation) is extremely important.

154

How Asset Allocation Works

In the early 1950s, Professor Harry Markowitz of the City University of New York introduced a revolutionary new approach to portfolio management, which subsequently became known as Modern Portfolio Theory (MPT). In his research, Professor Markowitz identified a mathematical relationship between the expected return, risk, and correlation among securities. The technique, which he called mean-variance analysis, showed how changing the allocation among different types of assets or groups of assets allows an investor to create a portfolio that maximizes return for a given level of risk. According to the theory, by simply changing the percentages invested in various types of assets every investor can create his or her optimal portfolio. The approach was so revolutionary that Professor Markowitz was later awarded a share of the Nobel Prize in economics for his landmark work.

Today, mean-variance analysis, more commonly known as asset allocation, forms the foundation of virtually every institutionally managed portfolio. In fact, it would be unthinkable for a large pension fund manager or portfolio consultant not to have a detailed asset allocation plan outlining exactly how a fund's dollars are to be invested. With the advent of computers, which can easily handle the vast amounts of data necessary to develop an asset allocation plan, it's possible for every investor, regardless of the size of their portfolio or level of expertise to develop a customized asset allocation plan.

Although the vast majority of investors will rely on asset allocation software or the help of a financial professional to determine their ideal asset mix, I've found that investors are far more likely to stick with a strategy if they have a basic understanding of how it works. Therefore, a brief overview of the main elements of asset allocation (expected return, investment risk, and correlation) is provided.

Expected Return

To create an asset allocation plan we must first calculate the expected return of the assets we wish to include in our universe. Expected return is simply the forecasted future return of an asset or group of assets. The more accurate the return forecasts are, the more accurate the asset allocation model will be. Unfortunately, there is no consensus on the best way to forecast the future or expected return of an asset or group of assets.

Theories and methodologies used to forecast future returns range from the very simple to extremely complex. The most common method is to use an asset's historic average return. The assumption is that over the long run the performance of an individual asset or group of assets will remain reasonably constant. Proponents of this method point out that while returns will fluctuate from year to year, sometimes dramatically, over time the average or mean return represents the best forecast of expected future returns. Also, using an asset's historic average return removes all human bias from the forecast because it's not necessary to make assumptions about future economic growth or market conditions.

Investment Risk (Standard Deviation)

Standard deviation measures the volatility of returns relative to the average return of a given security. In essence, standard deviation measures the likelihood that an asset's expected return will be different than its actual return, also known as risk. As the standard deviation of a given asset increases (greater risk), the probability that it will not return its average return also increases. Likewise, as the standard deviation of a given asset decreases (less risk) the probability associated with that security not returning its average return also decreases.

Studies have shown that the returns of financial assets follow a pattern of normal distribution. Therefore, based on the laws of normal distribution it's possible to make the following assumptions about the returns of any financial asset:

- Approximately 68% of an asset's returns will fall within one standard deviation of its mean return.

- Approximately 96% of an asset's returns will fall within two standard deviations of its mean return.

- Approximately 99.7% of an asset's returns will fall within three standard deviations of its mean return.

We can calculate the potential range of returns for any given asset or group of assets, using the rules listed above. For example, if the average or mean return of the S&P 500 Index was 12.9% and its standard deviation was 19.2%, between the period of 12/31/1925 and 12/31/2000, we can draw the following conclusions regarding expected future returns. There is roughly a 96% chance, or two standard deviations, that for any given year the return of the S&P 500 Index will fall between –27.5% and 53.5%. Therefore, an investor can rest assured, with a fairly high level of certainty (96%), that the worst one-year return they will experience using a fund tracking the S&P 500 Index is –27.5%. The best return they should anticipate, in any given year, is a gain of 53.5%.

In reality, the vast majority of actual returns for the S&P 500 Index will fall between these two extremes. And, we have no way of knowing, in advance, what the actual return will be. What the standard deviation tells us is the range of potential returns. By combining the range of potential returns of the S&P 500 Index with those of other assets it's possible to know the potential range of returns, and therefore the risk, for any given portfolio. Knowing the potential range of returns for a given portfolio makes it possible to easily evaluate and compare various portfolios and determine the one portfolio that best suits our objectives.

Exhibit 9-2:
Examples of Positive and Negative Correlation

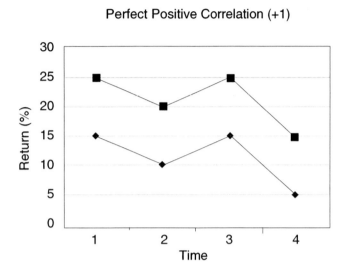

Perfect Positive Correlation (+1)

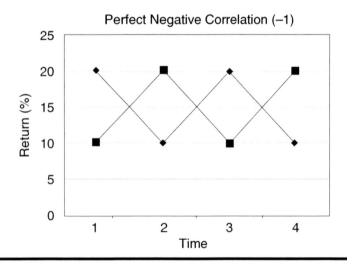

Perfect Negative Correlation (–1)

Correlation

The degree of correlation among assets is a key component of asset allocation. Correlation measures how closely related or linked the return of one asset is to that of another. For example, when comparing two different assets, asset A and asset B, they are said to reflect positive correlation if when asset A is moving up (or down) asset B is also moving up (or down). Negative correlation, in contrast, occurs if asset A is moving up (or down) while asset B is moving down (or up).

Correlation is measured on a scale that runs between the values of +1 and −1. If two assets move in "lock-step," they are said to have perfect positive correlation and are assigned a value of +1. On the other hand, if two assets move perfectly opposite each other they are said to be perfectly negatively correlated and have a correlation of −1. Exhibit 9-2 shows an example of two perfectly positively correlated assets and two perfectly negatively correlated assets.

Asset correlation is important because by combining assets with varying degrees of correlation it's possible to create a more diversified portfolio. In essence, when one asset is zigging the other is zagging. In fact, by combining two assets which are perfectly negatively correlated we can create a portfolio that will never fail. When one asset is losing value the other is gaining at the exact same rate. Exhibit 9-3 provides an example of combining two assets that are positively correlated and two assets that are negatively correlated. The top line in each graph signifies the price movement of the two assets when combined.

Unfortunately, finding two assets that exhibit perfect negative correlation is probably an impossible dream. They simply do not exist. Fortunately, it's not necessary. Even assets with a slight degree of negative correlation, when combined, offer substantial portfolio diversification benefits.

The Efficient Frontier

Once we have determined the expected return, standard deviation, and correlation of a group of assets it's possible to use the information to create the one portfolio that maximizes expected return for a given level of risk. In fact, for every level of risk it's possible to

Exhibit 9-3:
Why Correlation Matters

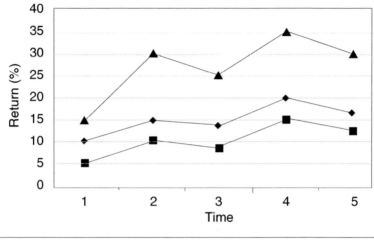

Combining Positively Correlated Assets

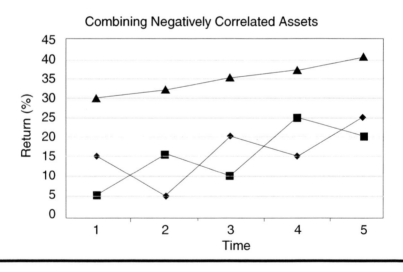

Combining Negatively Correlated Assets

create the one portfolio that maximizes expected return. We refer to these as "optimal" portfolios because they represent the most efficient mix of assets. By plotting the various optimal portfolios on a risk/return basis and then drawing a line connecting them, we get

Exhibit 9-4:
The Efficient Frontier

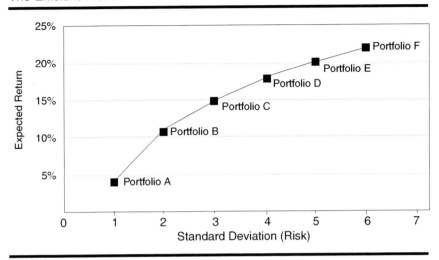

something that financial analysts refer to as the "efficient frontier."

An example of the efficient frontier is shown in Exhibit 9-4. As the exhibit shows, risk is plotted along the horizontal axis while expected return is plotted along the vertical axis. As risk increases so should expected return. For example, portfolio A has the least amount of risk and the lowest expected return. Portfolio F, in contrast, has the highest expected return and the highest amount of risk.

Regardless of where a portfolio falls along the efficient frontier, it represents the asset allocation that produces the highest expected return for the amount of risk taken. Therefore, it only stands to reason that any portfolio falling below the efficient frontier line does not represent the most optimal asset allocation mix and can be improved. For example, if a portfolio falls below the efficient frontier we can change its allocation and increase expected return without increasing risk or decrease risk without decreasing expected return.

Exhibit 9-5 shows an example of a portfolio that falls below the efficient frontier. In the exhibit, portfolio G falls below the efficient frontier line. Therefore, based on the principles of asset allocation we know it's possible to improve the portfolio. By simply changing the allocation of portfolio G it's possible to lower risk without decreasing expected return. This is represented by portfolio B. It's also possible to change the allocation of portfolio G and increase expected return without increasing risk. This is represented by portfolio D. Because portfolios B and D represent a more efficient asset allocation compared to portfolio G, an investor would never want to own portfolio G.

The implications of the efficient frontier for portfolio management are powerful. By focusing on the allocation among investment assets, instead of specific investments, an investor can create the one portfolio that produces the highest expected return based on the risk they are willing to assume. In this respect, asset allocation should be viewed as a portfolio optimizing discipline because it seeks to optimize return for a given level of risk or minimize risk for a desired rate of return. As such, asset allocation represents an extremely scientific approach to portfolio management and is the foundation of Strategic Index Investing.

Exhibit 9-5:
Using the Efficient Frontier to Find the Optimal Portfolio

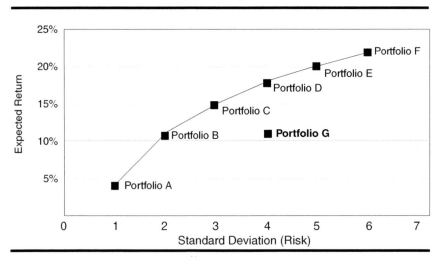

Asset Allocation at Work

Enough with the theories and formulas, it's time to show how asset allocation can be used to build diversified portfolios that really work. For asset allocation purposes, financial assets can be classified in broad terms like stocks, bonds, or cash or they can be subdivided further into smaller, unique asset classes based on factors such as company size, investment style, or industry sector. In this chapter, we focus on the three main asset classes (stocks, bonds, and cash). In Chapter 10, the benefits associated with changing the allocation among different types of stocks and bonds, a process commonly referred to as strategic asset allocation, are discussed.

For asset allocation to provide any meaningful benefits, the assets used must exhibit differing degrees of risk, expected return, and correlation, as discussed previously. By examining the historical performance data of stocks, bonds, and cash it's easy to see that each asset class does offer a unique level of risk and return. This is shown in Exhibit 9-6.

As might be expected, stocks have experienced a higher overall return compared to cash or bonds. The higher return, however, comes with a cost. Stocks have more risk than bonds or cash. Bonds offer less risk than stocks, but with a lower corresponding return. Cash, the least risky asset category, provides the lowest historic returns.

Exhibit 9-6:
Return and Standard Deviation of Equities, Bonds, and Cash (1928-2003)

Asset Class	Average Annual Return	Standard Deviation
U.S. Large Cap Equities	12.71%	24.95%
U.S. Long-Term Fixed Income	5.88%	12.09%
Money Market	4.29%	2.65%

Creating the Optimal Portfolio

Earlier in this chapter, it was stated that the goal of asset allocation is to create the optimal portfolio based on an investor's risk tolerance, performance objectives, and investment time horizon. By altering the percentage mix between stocks, bonds, and cash it's possible to create a series of portfolios with varying levels of risk and return. From the various portfolios it's possible for an investor to find the mix that best suits their needs. Fortunately for us, this is a relatively easy task given available asset allocation software and computer capabilities.

In Exhibit 9-7, five portfolios are shown. To keep the example simple, only two assets are included: stocks and bonds. The corresponding return associated with each portfolio, including "worst one-year loss" and "average loss" from 1970 through 2000 is shown.

Although extremely simplistic, the portfolios listed in Exhibit 9-7 show how altering the mix among stocks and bonds will alter the potential risk and return of the entire portfolio. As we can see, portfolio A, comprised entirely of equities, produced an average annual return of 14.84% over the time period shown. This portfolio

Exhibit 9-7:
Asset Allocation at Work

Portfolio Allocation	1970-2000			
	Number of Down Years	Average Loss	Worst 1-Year Loss	Average Annual Return
(A) 100% Stocks	4	-6.14%	-9.11%	14.84%
(B) 75% Stocks, 25% Bonds	4	-4.20%	-7.72%	13.96%
(C) 50% Stocks, 50% Bonds	4	-2.11%	-5.44%	12.86%
(D) 25% Stocks, 75% Bonds	2	-1.14%	-1.30%	11.42%
(E) 100% Bonds	2	-1.87%	-2.92%	9.31%

Source: Weisenberger, Inc.
Stocks: S&P 500 Index
Bonds: Lehman Aggregate Bond Index

experienced four down years with an average loss, in the down years, of -6.14%.

Portfolio D, consisting of 25% stocks and 75% bonds, experienced only two down years with an average loss of -1.14% in those years. This represents a dramatic reduction of risk compared to portfolio A. Portfolio D still produced a respectable 11.42% average annual rate of return, over the time period shown. As we might expect, the portfolio consisting entirely of bonds, portfolio E, produced the lowest average annual rate of return.

What does this mean to us? By simply changing the allocation between these two asset categories we were able to create portfolios with varying degrees of risk and return. In this very basic example it's easy to see that asset allocation is a powerful portfolio management approach. Every investor, regardless of risk tolerance, performance objectives, or investment time horizon can use asset allocation to construct a customized portfolio designed to meet his or her specific needs.

Quantifying Investment Objectives

To create a workable asset allocation plan you must be able to quantify your risk tolerance and objectives and set specific and attainable goals. To simply say you want to earn a lot of money in the stock market is not specific enough. Likewise, to say you want to earn 15% without taking any risk is unrealistic and unattainable.

The first part of asset allocation is to determine an overall investment objective. The investment objective answers the question, "Why are you investing?" Three common investment objectives are summarized below.

- **Preservation of Capital** — The main emphasis is on preserving the existing level of assets.
- **Income** — The main emphasis is on generating income to meet

current needs rather than on capital appreciation.
- **Growth** — The main emphasis is on generating capital appreciation rather than on preserving capital or income.

The investment objective sets the overall tone for the portfolio. In essence, it represents the big picture or how the investor wants the portfolio managed.

Risk Tolerance and Performance Goals

Next, an investor must determine the amount of risk they are willing to accept to achieve a given performance goal. Investment risk is defined as the possibility that the actual return on an investment may be different than the expected return. The greater the uncertainty of earning an expected rate of return, the greater the corresponding risk. In general, lower expected return equates to lower risk while higher expected return equates to higher risk.

For asset allocation purposes investors are often categorized based on the level of risk they are willing to assume. For example, it's possible to group investors into three very broad categories according to risk:

- **Conservative** — A conservative investor is anyone who cannot tolerate a loss in a given year in excess of 10% or may need access to their funds within the next three years.

- **Moderate** — A moderate investor is anyone who cannot tolerate a loss in a given year in excess of 20% or may need access to their funds within the next five to seven years.

- **Aggressive** — An aggressive investor is anyone who can tolerate a loss in a given year in excess of 20% and is not likely to need access to their funds within the next seven to ten years.

An investor's risk tolerance should be consistent with his or her primary investment objective. For example, it would be inconsistent for an investor to say that their investment objective is preservation of capital, but their risk tolerance is aggressive. Also, risk tolerance must be understood in light of the investment objective. For example, a conservative growth investor is very different from a conservative income investor.

The expected return for a given portfolio must also be in-line with the risk the investor is willing to accept. For example, if an investor wants to earn a potentially high return, they must be willing to accept greater risk. If an investor can't tolerate high risk, they must be willing to accept lower expected returns. This is commonly referred to as the trade off between risk and return and is one of the most basic of all financial principles.

Exhibit 9-8:
Investment Returns Resulting from Changing Asset Allocations

Investment Mix Equities/Bonds		Compounded Annual Return	Largest 1-Year Gain	Largest 1-Year Loss
100%	0%	11.6%	37.4%	-26.5%
90%	10%	11.3%	36.9%	-23.7%
80%	20%	11.0%	36.3%	-20.8%
70%	30%	10.6%	35.8%	-17.9%
60%	40%	10.2%	35.2%	-14.9%
50%	50%	9.8%	34.6%	-11.9%
40%	60%	9.3%	34.1%	-8.7%
30%	70%	8.9%	34.7%	-5.9%
20%	80%	8.4%	34.7%	-6.0%
10%	90%	7.9%	36.6%	-6.9%
0%	100%	7.3%	40.4%	-9.2%

Source: Ibbotson Associates, Inc.
Data based on returns from 1960-2000
Equity returns based on S&P 500 Index
Bond returns based on 20-year U.S. Treasury Bonds

In Exhibit 9-8, we see the risk and return characteristics associated with several different portfolios comprised of stocks and bonds. The exhibit also shows the largest one-year gain and loss associated with each portfolio. As the exhibit shows, the various portfolios range from ultra aggressive (100% equities) to ultra conservative (100% bonds). Using the portfolio statistics shown in Exhibit 9-8, it's possible to reach the following conclusions, for various growth investors. All conclusions are based on the risk tolerance parameters discussed previously (conservative, moderate, and aggressive):

- A conservative growth investor should have no more than 40% of their portfolio in equities at any time.
- A moderate growth investor should keep the equity portion of their portfolio to a minimum of 50% and a maximum of 70%.
- An aggressive growth investor should keep between 80% and 100% of their portfolio in equities.

The acceptable asset allocation ranges for each of the three investor types listed above are shown in Exhibit 9-9.

As we have seen, asset allocation is a very scientific approach to portfolio management that allows every investor to develop the optimal portfolio that is right for them. Asset allocation also allows the investor to know the potential return distribution and risk associated with a portfolio prior to investing. Allowing the investor to easily compare various portfolios and find the one "optimal" portfolio that best meets his or her needs. Therefore, it should be considered a key part of building a solid portfolio foundation and an important aspect of Strategic Index Investing.

Exhibit 9-9:
Acceptable Allocation Between Equities and Bonds

Investor Type	Equity Allocation Minimum	Maximum	Bond Allocation Minimum	Maximum
Low Risk Investor	0%	40%	60%	100%
Moderate Risk Investor	50%	70%	30%	50%
High Risk Investor	80%	100%	0%	20%

Asset Allocation Myths and Misconceptions

Before concluding our overview of asset allocation, it is important to address several commonly held myths and misconceptions. They are the following.

Myth 1: The older you are the less you should have in equities. This is perhaps one of the most prevalent myths today. As a general rule of thumb many financial professionals recommend that a person keep their age in bonds. For example, using this theory a fifty-year-old investor should allocate 50% of their portfolio to bonds and 50% to equities. Likewise, a seventy-five-year-old investor should allocate 75% of their portfolio to bonds with only 25% in equities. Therefore, as you grow older the dollars allocated to equities would naturally decrease while the dollars allocated to bonds would increase.

To assert that a person must give up the potential offered by equities simply because they are growing older is ridiculous. The percentage of total assets that an investor allocates to equities should not be a function of age, but instead based on their financial situation, risk tolerance, investment goals, and time horizon. Age can and should be a consideration, but it should not be the only factor considered. If your financial situation permits and if you have a high tolerance for risk, then allocating 100% of your portfolio to equities is acceptable.

One caveat is that you must also incorporate additional risk management strategies to minimize market risks. Risk management strategies are discussed later in this section. As we will see, the key to long-term market success is managing risk, not allocating a predetermined portion of your portfolio to bonds based on your age. Don't forget, fixed income investments, such as bonds, also carry risks including the loss of purchasing power during inflationary periods and loss of principal due to default.

Myth 2: All an investor needs to own is the S&P 500 Index. This myth became popular during the great bull market of the 1990s when growth stocks clearly and substantially outperformed value stocks. Large cap stocks, in general, outperformed small and mid cap stocks over this same time period, leading many to assert the need to own only large cap growth stocks. Since the S&P 500 Index is predominately a large company growth index, it, by default, became the index of choice for many investors during this time period.

About this same time, the merits of asset allocation in general were being questioned. Many claimed asset allocation wasn't relevant in this new market environment because large company growth stocks would always do well. Therefore, all an investor needs to own are large company growth stocks. Then, the unimaginable happened: a market correction that hit large company growth stocks particularly hard.

For several years the market seemed to be a one-way street with growth stocks in high gear. However, because today's winners are often tomorrow's losers, it is likely that regardless of how well a particular asset class performs in the short run, it's simply a matter of time before gravity sets in. When it does, and it always will, the investor who stays true to their asset allocation strategy, instead of chasing the "hot" asset category, will be rewarded.

Myth 3: Asset allocation is the only risk management an investor will ever need. Unfortunately, the strongest proponents of asset allocation most often put this myth forward. They typically point to the diversification benefits associated with asset allocation in conjunction with this argument. While I agree that asset allocation provides tremendous risk management benefits, it is wrong to consider it your only line of defense. Other risk management strategies, such as dynamic stop-loss orders, protective puts, and covered call writing, which we will discuss in later chapters, are also important.

Summary

Asset allocation is a long-term portfolio management approach that helps the investor determine a suitable mix of assets based on their investment objectives, risk tolerance, and investment time horizon. Regardless if an investor is managing hundreds of millions of dollars on behalf of a pension plan or hundreds of dollars in an IRA, asset allocation is important. The risk and return of every portfolio is influenced by how that portfolio is allocated, whether the allocation is done consciously or unconsciously. Therefore, the question isn't whether or not asset allocation matters, because it does. The question is whether or not you have given any consideration to how your current asset mix impacts the overall risk and return of your portfolio.

Chapter 10

STRATEGIC ASSET ALLOCATION

Asset Class Investing

In Chapter 9, we saw that asset allocation – how a portfolio is divided among different types of assets – is the primary determinant of risk and return over time. For years, proponents of asset allocation focused almost exclusively on the interaction of three broad-based asset categories: stocks, bonds, and cash. Little, if any, attention was given to the allocation *among* different types of stocks or bonds.

Today, the asset allocation decision is more complex than simply determining the optimal mix among stocks, bonds, or cash. As we will see, it's possible to create literally hundreds of sub asset groups or classes from the two broad asset categories of stocks and bonds. By changing the allocation among these different asset classes or groups it's possible to improve the overall asset allocation plan.

The process of "fine-tuning" a portfolio by changing the allocation among different asset classes is known as strategic asset allocation. In this chapter, we examine the merits of strategic asset allocation. First, an overview of common equity and bond asset classes is provided. Next, a series of portfolios are created to show how changing the allocation among groups of equities and bonds will change the risk and return of the overall portfolio. The importance of rebalancing a portfolio on a consistent basis is also discussed. Finally, the chapter concludes by showing why exchange-traded index funds are the best investment product to use when implementing a strategic asset allocation plan.

Why Strategic Asset Allocation Matters

Why is strategic asset allocation necessary? Just as changing the allocation among stocks, bonds, and cash will alter a portfolio's risk and return, research has shown that changing the allocation among different types of equities and bonds will also change a portfolio's

Exhibit 10-1:
Example of Strategic Asset Allocation

Portfolio A 75% Equities — 25% Bonds		Portfolio B 75% Equities — 25% Bonds	
Equities:		**Equities:**	
S&P 500 Index	75.0%	Large Cap Blend	15.0%
		Large Cap Value	15.0%
		Mid Cap Blend	20.0%
Total Equities	75.0%	Small Cap Value	15.0%
		International	10.0%
		Total Equities	75.0%
Bonds:		**Bonds:**	
Lehman 25+ Yr.Tsy. Index	25.0%	U.S. Tsy.Sht. Term	10.0%
		U.S. Tsy.Long Term	15.0%
Total Bonds	25.0%	Total Bonds	25.0%
Total Portfolio	**100.0%**	**Total Portfolio**	**100.0%**

Risk & Return Statistics*		
	Portfolio A	**Portfolio B**
Average Annualized Return	1.89%	6.10%
Standard Deviation	11.84%	10.84%

* From 12/31/1998 through 12/31/2003. All performance numbers are based on annual rebalancing.

risk and return. This is shown in Exhibit 10-1.

As the exhibit shows, portfolios A and B have the identical over-all asset allocation: 75% equities and 25% bonds. The similarities end there. The equity portion of portfolio A is represented by a single broad-based index, the S&P 500 Index. No distinction is made between different types or classes of equities. The bond portion of portfolio A is also represented by a single index, the Lehman Brothers 20+ Year Treasury Index. No distinction is made between different types or classes of bonds.

Portfolio B, in contrast, is allocated among distinct equity and bond asset classes. For example, the equity portion of portfolio B is allocated among five equity asset classes. This includes asset classes based on company size (large cap, mid cap, and small cap), investment style (value stocks), and geographic location (international stocks). The bond portion of portfolio B is allocated between short-term bonds and long-term bonds.

As a result, for the five-year period ended 12/31/2003, portfolio B produced an average annual return of 6.10% compared to 1.89% for portfolio A. The standard deviation (risk) of portfolio A was 11.84% compared with 10.84% for portfolio B. Keep in mind; the higher return and lower risk produced by portfolio B resulted from "fine-tuning" the overall allocation, or strategic asset allocation. Not by changing the overall mix between stocks and bonds.

Common Asset Classes

The first step in the strategic asset allocation process is to subdivide equities and bonds into unique asset classes or groups. To provide any meaningful benefits, each new asset class created must consist of securities with similar characteristics or attributes. For example, it makes sense to group stocks of small companies together because they tend to react in similar ways to changing economic or market factors. Likewise, it doesn't make sense to group utility stocks with technology stocks because they typically react differently to changing economic or market factors.

The objective is to create asset classes that exhibit unique risk and return characteristics. If the securities included in the various asset classes are too dissimilar, they will be of no value for strategic asset allocation purposes. While some stocks in the group are going up others will be going down. The newly created asset class will act more like a broad-based index instead of a unique asset class.

For strategic asset allocation purposes, equities are typically grouped or divided by market capitalization (size), investment style (growth or value), economic sector, industry group, or geographic location. Bonds are typically grouped by maturity, issuer, or credit quality. A brief description of the most common equity and bond asset classes is provided below.

Company Size/Market Capitalization

Company size or market capitalization tells us the value market participants are placing on an entire company at a precise moment in time. It's calculated by multiplying the price per share of a company's stock by the total number of shares issued and outstanding. For example, as of January 31, 2004 IBM had approximately 1.7 billion shares issued and outstanding. The closing price of IBM, on that day, was $100 per share. To calculate IBM's market capitalization we simply multiply 1.7 billion shares outstanding by $100 per share, which gives us $170 billion.

The most common size classifications are the following:

- **Large Capitalization (Large Cap)** – Large cap stocks are typically stocks of corporations with a total market value of $10 billion or more. Because large companies are often seen as mature and well established, their stocks tend to be less volatile than the share price of smaller, less established companies.

- **Mid Capitalization (Mid Cap)** – Mid cap stocks typically fall between the $1.5 billion to $10 billion range. They offer the growth potential associated with small cap stocks but with the greater stability associated with large cap stocks.

- **Small Capitalization (Small Cap)** – Small cap stocks are typically newer, less established companies. They usually have a market value of $1.5 billion or less, and tend to be more volatile than large or mid cap stocks. Small cap stocks typically offer a higher potential return.

Occasionally, financial analysts use a fourth size-based asset class called micro cap. As the name implies, micro cap stocks are the smallest companies traded based on total market capitalization. Due to their limited liquidity and sparse institutional coverage we will not include micro cap stocks in any of our strategic asset allocation models.

Investment Style — Growth vs. Value
Common stocks are often grouped using quantitative ratios that classify them as either "growth stocks" or "value stocks." Growth stocks tend to exhibit faster than average gains in earnings and are expected to grow more rapidly than the economy in general. They typically have high price/earnings ratios relative to the overall stock market and often make little or no dividend payments to shareholders.

Value stocks, in contrast, are typically well established businesses that are temporarily out of favor with investors, reflected in their unusually low price/earnings ratios. While growth stocks may tend to shine in a strong economy, value stocks may outperform during sluggish markets or periods of increased stock market volatility and uncertainty.

Industry Group or Economic Sector
Equities are often grouped according to the industry or economic sector in which they operate. Companies within a particular industry

or economic sector tend to be influenced by similar factors such as the overall economic climate, regulatory environment, or supply and demand for their product. This can, and does, cause the value of these companies to rise or fall in unison. For example, the price per share of most utility companies will tend to respond the same way when interest rates rise. Likewise, shares of technology stocks tend to do well during periods of strong economic growth and low interest rates.

Geographic Location

Corporations based outside the United States issue stocks, which trade on exchanges throughout the world. Typically, foreign company stocks are grouped based on the specific country or geographic region where they are domiciled and traded. Foreign company stocks are also commonly grouped based on the economic condition and stability of the underlying country where they operate, such as developing or emerging economy stocks.

Combining Size and Style

It is possible to create additional equity asset classes by combining companies of a certain size (large cap, mid cap, and small cap) and investment style (growth or value). The most commonly used size and style asset classes are shown in Exhibit 10-2.

Exhibit 10-2:
Combining Asset Size and Style

Company Size	Investment Style	
	Growth	Value
Large Cap	Large Cap Growth	Large Cap Value
Mid Cap	Mid Cap Growth	Mid Cap Value
Small Cap	Small Cap Growth	Small Cap Value

Bond Asset Classes

For strategic asset allocation purposes, bonds are often grouped or classified by maturity, issuer, or credit rating.

Maturity — The maturity date is the date on which a bond's principal or face value is repaid to the investor. Maturity date is important because shorter-term bonds are typically less volatile than longer-term bonds. The three main bond asset classes, based on maturity, are long-term (ten years or more), intermediate-term (one to ten years), and short-term (less than one year).

Issuer – An authority that borrows money through the sale of bonds is referred to as the issuer. Bonds are typically issued by governments, corporations, government agencies, or municipalities. Each type of bond issuer provides its own unique level of risk and return.

Credit Rating – A bond's credit rating measures the possibility of default by the issuer based on an analysis of the issuer's financial condition. Bonds are typically placed into one of two broad categories, based on credit rating: investment grade or high yield (junk bonds). Investment grade bonds are bonds backed by financially sound companies. Junk bonds are backed by companies of questionable financial strength and typically offer a higher expected return to offset their higher risk compared to investment grade bonds.

Evaluating Asset Classes

The process of grouping stocks and bonds by common characteristics, as we did in the previous section, is more than just an academic exercise. For strategic asset allocation to provide any meaningful benefits, the various asset classes must exhibit differing degrees of expected return and risk. If they don't, the investor would do better to allocate the equity and bond portion of their portfolio to a single broad-based index. It would certainly mean a lot less work. If the various asset classes discussed above, however, exhibit differing levels of risk and return, then it's possible to improve the portfolio's

Exhibit 10-3:
Year-by-Year Performance of Various Asset Classes

Index Name	1992	1993	1994	1995	1996	1997	1998	1999	2000	2001	2002
Russell 1000	8.93%	10.18%	0.39%	37.77%	22.45%	32.85%	27.02%	20.91%	-7.79%	-12.45%	-21.65%
Russell 1000 Value	13.58%	18.07%	-1.98%	38.36%	21.64%	35.18%	15.63%	7.35%	7.02%	-5.59%	-15.52%
Russell 1000 Growth	4.99%	2.87%	2.62%	37.18%	23.12%	30.49%	38.71%	33.16%	-22.42%	-20.42%	-27.88%
Russell 2000	18.41%	18.88%	-1.82%	28.45%	16.49%	22.36%	-2.55%	21.26%	-3.02%	2.49%	-20.48%
Russell 2000 Value	29.14%	23.77%	-1.54%	25.75%	21.37%	31.78%	-6.45%	-1.49%	22.83%	14.02%	-11.43%
Russell 2000 Growth	7.77%	13.37%	-2.43%	31.04%	11.26%	12.95%	1.23%	43.09%	-22.43%	-9.23%	-30.26%
Russell 3000	9.59%	10.88%	0.19%	36.80%	21.82%	31.78%	24.14%	20.90%	-7.46%	-11.46%	-21.54%
Russell 3000 Growth	5.22%	3.69%	2.20%	36.57%	21.88%	28.47%	35.02%	33.83%	-22.42%	-19.63%	-28.03%
Russell 3000 Value	14.90%	18.65%	-1.95%	37.03%	21.59%	34.83%	13.50%	6.65%	8.04%	-4.33%	-15.18%
Lehman Aggregate Bond	7.40%	9.75%	-2.92%	18.47%	3.63%	9.65%	8.69%	-0.82%	11.63%	8.44%	10.26%
MSCI EAFE	-12.17%	32.56%	7.78%	11.21%	6.05%	1.78%	20.00%	26.96%	-14.17%	-21.44%	-15.64%

Source: BGI

overall asset allocation through the use of strategic asset allocation.

In Exhibit 10-3, we see that the various asset classes do exhibit different levels of risk and return. It is possible to use these return differences to construct a more efficient portfolio.

Another important consideration is the extent to which the asset classes are correlated. As we saw in Chapter 9, correlation shows the degree to which assets move in unison. By combining assets that exhibit limited correlation it's possible to increase a portfolio's expected return without increasing risk. Exhibit 10-4 shows the amount of correlation between various asset classes.

As Exhibit 10-4 shows, there is a 96.37% correlation between the S&P 500 Index and the Russell 1000 Index. This should be expected because both indexes are comprised primarily of large cap stocks. An investor, therefore, would realize a very limited amount of benefit, from a diversification point of view, by owning exchange-traded index funds tracking both indexes. An investor should probably own one or the other, but not both.

On the other hand, the S&P 600 Value Index has a 50.67% correlation with the Russell 1000 Growth Index. Therefore, it's possible to combine these two indexes and create a portfolio that has a higher expected return with less risk than a portfolio comprised of either index individually. The reason for this is that these two indexes show negative correlation with one another, as we can see from the exhibit.

After reviewing Exhibits 10-3 and 10-4, it's easy to see that the unique asset classes we created have different levels of risk, return, and correlation. Therefore, it is possible to use the principles of strategic asset allocation, in conjunction with some of the asset classes listed above, to improve the overall allocation of any given portfolio.

Strategic Asset Allocation at Work

The goal of strategic asset allocation is to add value by changing the allocation among different classes of equities and bonds. Fortunately

Exhibit 10-4:
Percent Correlation Between Various Russell and S&P Style/Size Indexes (12/31/97 to 12/31/01)

	S&P 500	S&P 500 Growth	S&P 500 Value	S&P 400	S&P 400 Growth	S&P 400 Value	S&P 600 Growth	S&P 600 Value
Russell 3000 Growth	92.29	83.05	71.18	73.60	86.00	41.38	81.22	52.15
Russell 3000 Value	86.71	62.61	93.17	69.54	68.36	54.96	64.05	56.00
Russell 1000 Index	96.37	80.29	85.01	76.16	83.91	48.97	78.08	55.88
Russell 1000 Growth	92.61	83.45	71.30	72.32	84.60	40.59	79.11	50.67
Russell 1000 Value	86.09	61.79	93.13	67.68	66.23	53.89	61.31	53.93
Russell 2000 Growth	75.07	66.12	59.69	77.86	89.66	44.82	93.83	61.98
Russell 2000 Value	74.28	59.10	70.44	78.17	81.18	55.88	86.25	70.57
Russell Mid Cap Growth	81.53	72.61	63.76	79.49	93.15	43.92	88.38	55.61
Russell Mid Cap Value	81.21	58.20	87.67	75.21	73.27	60.05	69.00	60.16
Russell Mid Cap	87.22	71.18	78.97	84.62	92.66	54.52	87.59	62.14

Source: BGI

182

for us, it's easy to evaluate if this is possible. To do so, we begin our analysis with a very basic portfolio consisting of 60% equities and 40% bonds. For the equity portion of the portfolio the S&P 500 Index is used while the bond portion is based on the Lehman 20+ Year Treasury Bond Index. This portfolio will serve as the benchmark to judge the effectiveness of the strategic asset allocation changes we make.

Although it may seem rather basic, this is actually a very powerful portfolio. It doesn't require a lot of work to maintain, it's low cost, and it could very easily outperform the vast majority of all actively managed mutual funds in any given year. Exhibit 10-5 summarizes this portfolio's risk and average return from 1975 through 1995.

As Exhibit 10-5 shows, portfolio A produced an average annual rate of return of 13.21% with a standard deviation of 10.12% over the indicated time period. For most investors, this represents a very respectable risk and return profile. But, is it the best we can do? After all, it was stated earlier that strategic asset allocation allows the investor to improve a portfolio's overall asset

Exhibit 10-5:
Risk and Return of Portfolio A*, 1975-1995

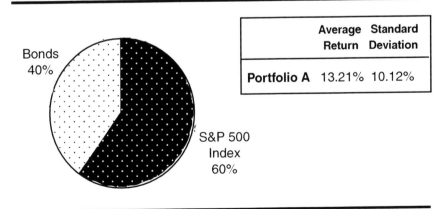

	Average Return	Standard Deviation
Portfolio A	13.21%	10.12%

Bonds 40%

S&P 500 Index 60%

* Based on Annual Rebalancing

allocation. Therefore, it should be possible to either increase the return or decrease the risk of the portfolio shown in Exhibit 10-5 through the use of strategic asset allocation.

The first change we will make is to add international equities to the portfolio. If we compare domestic stock indexes to foreign stock indexes it's easy to see that they exhibit a low degree of correlation. Therefore, it is possible to decrease risk and increase potential return by adding a foreign stock index to the portfolio. This is shown in Exhibit 10-6.

The amount allocated to the S&P 500 Index is decreased from 60% to 30%. The MSCI EAFE (Europe, Australia, and Far East) Index is added to the portfolio with a total allocation of 30%. By doing this, several positive things occur. First, the portfolio's average annualized return increased to 14.05% while standard deviation decreased to 9.49%. As we can see, allocating a portion of the portfolio to international equities has had an immediate and substantial impact on overall risk and return.

Since the S&P 500 Index and MSCI EAFE Index are both comprised primarily of large cap stocks, the next move is to cut both

Exhibit 10-6:
Risk and Return of Portfolio B*, 1975-1995

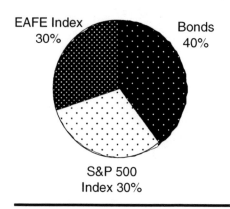

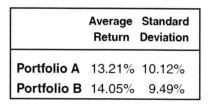

	Average Return	Standard Deviation
Portfolio A	13.21%	10.12%
Portfolio B	14.05%	9.49%

* Based on Annual Rebalancing

Exhibit 10-7:
Risk and Return of Portfolio C*, 1975-1995

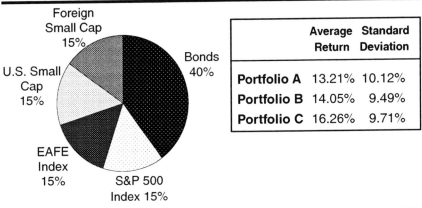

	Average Return	Standard Deviation
Portfolio A	13.21%	10.12%
Portfolio B	14.05%	9.49%
Portfolio C	16.26%	9.71%

* Based on Annual Rebalancing

positions in half and replace them with small cap stocks. There are two reasons for this. Small company stocks tend to offer a greater expected return compared to large cap stocks. And, small company stocks display a reasonably low correlation to large company stocks. To make these changes the S&P 600 SmallCap Index and the EAFE Small Company Index are added to the portfolio. The impact of the new allocation on the overall portfolio is shown in Exhibit 10-7.

The resulting change in risk and return, as shown in Exhibit 10-7, is truly remarkable. The portfolio's overall risk remained basically the same, while the average annual return jumped by over 200 basis points! By taking on a very small amount of additional risk, the portfolio's return increased dramatically.

Up to this point, the focus has been on "growth" stocks. It's now time to think "value." Value stocks are typically less volatile compared to growth stocks. They offer a great way to add return to a portfolio without adding additional risk. To demonstrate this, each of the existing indexes is cut in half again and a corresponding value index added. Exhibit 10-8 shows the risk and return characteristics associated with these changes.

Exhibit 10-8:
Risk and Return of Portfolio D*, 1975-1995

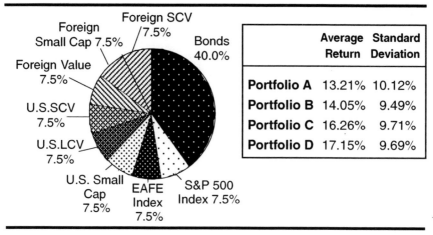

	Average Return	Standard Deviation
Portfolio A	13.21%	10.12%
Portfolio B	14.05%	9.49%
Portfolio C	16.26%	9.71%
Portfolio D	17.15%	9.69%

* Based on Annual Rebalancing

Once again, the changes to the portfolio yield amazing results. Overall risk decreases yet the portfolio's return increases. As we have seen, strategic asset allocation allowed us to dramatically improve the overall asset allocation mix of the initial portfolio. For example, average annual return increased by over 37% while risk decreased. Keep in mind, the dramatic improvements witnessed were not accomplished by using a market timing system, following the recommendations of the current "hot" stock analyst, or attempting to predict the "best" asset class to own. Instead, we followed a scientific approach based on sound financial principles and created a portfolio that optimized risk and return. The examples above demonstrate why strategic asset allocation is such a powerful management tool and an important part of Strategic Index Investing.

Strategic Asset Allocation and Short-Term Market Risk

In the previous section, strategic asset allocation was used to create a portfolio that produced superior long-term returns with less risk compared to the benchmark portfolio. Strategic asset allocation can also help moderate the impact of short-term market fluctuations, as well.

As most readers are probably aware, the market suffered dramatic losses from 1999 through 2002. For example, in 2002 the S&P 500 Index lost over 20% of its value while in 2001, it lost over 11% of its value. Other market indexes, such as the technology heavy Nasdaq 100 Index, saw even worse losses. From mid 1999 through 2002 it lost over 70% of its value.

How can an investor protect their portfolio from such dramatic short-term declines? The answer is with strategic asset allocation. To see how, we will examine two portfolios. The benchmark portfolio is comprised of 60% equities and 40% bonds. Equities are represented by the S&P 500 Index while bonds are represented by the

Exhibit 10-9:
Strategic Portfolio

Bonds:

iShares Lehman 1-3 Year Tsy. Index Fund	15.0%
iShares Lehman 7-10 Year Tsy. Index Fund	15.0%
iShares Lehman U.S. Aggregate Bond Index Fund	10.0%
Total Bonds	40.0%

Equities:

iShares Russell 1000 Index Fund	10.0%
iShares Russell 1000 Value Index Fund	5.0%
iShares S&P MidCap 400 Index Fund	10.0%
iShares Russell 2000 Index Fund	10.0%
iShares Russell 2000 Value Index Fund	5.0%
iShares MSCI EAFE Index Fund	10.0%
iShares DJ Select Sector Dividend Index Fund	5.0%
iShares Goldman Sachs Natural Resources Index Fund	5.0%
Total Equities	60.0%
Total Portfolio	**100.0%**

Lehman 7-10 Year Treasury Index. Our second portfolio, the strategic portfolio, is also 60% equities and 40% bonds, with one exception. It has been "fine-tuned" using strategic asset allocation. The strategic portfolio is shown in Exhibit 10-9.

As we can see, the strategic portfolio is allocated among eight different equity asset classes. They range from large cap value equities to sector specific equities represented by the Goldman Sachs Natural Resources Index. Ten percent of the portfolio is allocated to international equities. The bond portion of the portfolio is allocated among three indexes. They include short-term Treasury bonds, intermediate-term Treasury bonds, and corporate bonds.

The question for us is whether or not the strategic portfolio represents a better alternative than the benchmark portfolio. By examining Exhibit 10-10 it's easy to see the answer.

If you had any lingering doubts about the benefits associated with strategic asset allocation, Exhibit 10-10 should remove them. As we can see, the year by year performance of the benchmark portfolio, the strategic portfolio, and S&P 500 Index is shown in the exhibit. From 12/31/1999 to 12/31/2000 the S&P 500 Index lost 9.10% while the strategic portfolio gained 7.36% and the benchmark portfolio gained 0.43%. From 12/31/2000 to 12/31/2001 the S&P 500 Index lost 11.89% while the strategic portfolio gained 0.19% and the benchmark portfolio lost 4.40%. And, most remarkable, from 12/31/2001

Exhibit 10-10:
Performance Comparison of the Portfolios

1-Year Time Period	Strategic Portfolio	Benchmark Portfolio	S&P 500 Index
12/31/1999 to 12/31/2000	7.36%	0.43%	-9.10%
12/31/2000 to 12/31/2001	0.19%	-4.40%	-11.89%
12/31/2001 to 12/31/2002	-5.51%	-7.46%	-22.10%
12/31/2002 to 12/31/2003	23.15%	17.96%	28.68%

Source: RCM Data Management

to 12/31/2002 the S&P 500 Index lost 22.10% while the strategic portfolio lost 5.51% and the benchmark portfolio lost 7.46%.

A portfolio that protects you from large market losses is good. However, being too conservative often means missing out on the huge potential gains. As we can see from the exhibit, the strategic portfolio did extremely well when the market moved higher. From 12/31/2002 to 12/31/2003 the S&P 500 Index gained 28.68%. Over this same time period the strategic portfolio gained 23.15% and the benchmark portfolio gained 17.96%. Not only did the strategic portfolio provide protection during tough markets, it also participated nicely when the market snapped back. Critics might point out that in 2003 the strategic portfolio underperformed the market, as measured by the S&P 500 Index. While this is true, I'm sure no investor would be upset only earning 23.15% given that the portfolio dramatically reduced losses during the preceding three down years.

Systematic Rebalancing

As we have seen, strategic asset allocation represents a scientific and non-emotional approach to portfolio construction that allows the investor to customize their portfolio in an extremely efficient and systematic manner. To be effective, however, the portfolio must be rebalanced on a regular basis. Otherwise, the investor runs the risk of allowing the market to dramatically alter the intended risk and return characteristics of the portfolio.

For example, assume an investor allocated 15% of their portfolio to large cap growth stocks. Then, over the following year, growth stocks far outperform other stocks, increasing the investor's position in growth stocks to 25% of the total portfolio. As a result, the portfolio is riskier than initially planned. In Exhibit 10-11, we see how a diversified portfolio might shift over time if not properly rebalanced.

Exhibit 10-11:
The Importance of Rebalancing

Initial Portfolio:		Allocation One Year Later:	
Asset Class	**Percentage**	**Asset Class**	**Percentage**
Large Cap Growth	15.0%	Large Cap Growth	25.0%
Large Cap Value	15.0%	Large Cap Value	20.0%
Small Cap Blend	25.0%	Small Cap Blend	35.0%
International	10.0%	International	5.0%
Bonds	35.0%	Bonds	15.0%
Total	**100.0%**	**Total**	**100.0%**

As the exhibit shows, the initial allocation does not even resemble the allocation after one year. A major market rally changed the allocation of equities from an intended 65% to 85% of the total portfolio. As a result, the portfolio is riskier than intended and needs to be rebalanced.

Rebalancing Methods
The two most common rebalancing methods are "acceptable asset range" and "set percentage." Using an acceptable range method the investor decides on a maximum and minimum acceptable exposure for each asset class. For example, they might decide an appropriate range for large cap growth stocks is 15% to 25% of their overall portfolio. As long as the percentage invested in large cap growth stays within the range, no changes are made. If at any time large cap growth stocks move outside the accepted range, either above or below, the necessary changes are made.

A set percentage rebalancing method is a more rigid approach. The investor simply determines how often they are going to rebalance (quarterly, semi-annually, or annually) and then does so at the appropriate time. This method is far less time consuming and provides the purest way to keep a portfolio in-line with the investor's desired risk and return parameters.

When developing a rebalancing plan it's important to balance frequency with reality. While rebalancing monthly may be the truest way to keep the portfolio in-line with the original asset allocation plan, it's costly and time consuming. Similarly, rebalancing every five years would provide little benefit. We must try to strike a happy medium when deciding on a rebalancing strategy. For me, rebalancing a portfolio on a semi-annual basis works well, but I know many extremely qualified advisors who recommend quarterly or annual rebalancing. The key is to find what works for you and to stick with it.

Strategic Asset Allocation Tools

As we have seen, strategic asset allocation is a powerful approach to portfolio management. To take full advantage of the benefits it has to offer, the right investment tools must be used. When implementing a strategic asset allocation plan, investors have essentially four choices: traditional actively managed mutual funds, traditional index-based mutual funds, common stocks, and exchange-traded index funds. Although each investment product was discussed in Part 2, it's important to understand their unique advantages and disadvantages in the context of strategic asset allocation. Therefore, a brief overview of each follows.

Traditional Actively Managed Mutual Funds

Traditional actively managed mutual funds are one of the worst possible tools to use when implementing a strategic asset allocation plan. The entire theory on which strategic asset allocation is based is that individual stock selection is irrelevant. Yet, that is exactly what you are paying the mutual fund manager to do!

Every strategic asset allocation model ever created is based on the performance, correlation, and standard deviation of various market indexes. Therefore, it's imperative that the investments used exactly match the risk and return characteristics of the underlying in-

191

dex. As we have seen, most actively managed mutual funds do not accomplish this simple goal.

Actively managed mutual funds employ the services of portfolio managers. The portfolio manager's job is to outperform the market or a given asset category, although most do not. This creates several potential problems. Not only does the investor have to develop a strategic asset allocation plan that fits his or her objectives, they must continually monitor numerous active mutual fund managers to insure the fund stays true to its investment discipline. If or when they begin to deviate, the fund must be removed from the portfolio. In other words, using actively managed funds adds an additional layer of evaluation and monitoring to the asset allocation process, not to mention added expenses.

I'm always amazed when a financial advisor brilliantly explains to a client the logic behind strategic asset allocation, illustrating for them the many benefits associated with allocating dollars between different types of asset classes instead of trying to pick individual securities or timing the market. Then, in an amazing leap of fate, the advisor tells the client the plan will be implemented using actively managed mutual funds. One is contrary to the other. It's simply illogical to recommend actively managed mutual funds in conjunction with strategic asset allocation because the fund's performance depends solely on the ability of a fund manager to accurately predict which stocks will do well. In contrast, strategic asset allocation is based on the notion that individual security selection is all but useless.

Traditional Index-Based Mutual Funds
This brings us to the second vehicle commonly used to implement strategic asset allocation plans: traditional index-based mutual funds. While offering clear advantages over actively managed funds, they still fall short of exchange-traded index funds. As we have seen, traditional mutual funds can only be bought or sold at the end of the day. This limits the use of active risk management strategies, dis-

cussed in later chapters. Also, traditional index mutual funds offer investors a very limited number of indexes from which to choose. When building a strategic asset allocation plan, it's essential that the investor have access to a wide range of indexes based on asset size, style, economic sector, industry group, and geographic regions. Therefore, exchange-traded index funds, which offer investors access to a vast number of indexes, represent a superior choice compared to traditional index-based mutual funds.

Individual Common Stocks

Investors often use individual common stocks to implement a strategic asset allocation plan. Doing so, however, presents several key problems. The first is deciding which stock best represents a particular asset class. For instance, if your asset allocation calls for 25% in large cap growth, which large cap growth stock should you use? There are literally thousands available.

Furthermore, how can anyone be sure the individual stock purchased will move in unison with other large cap growth stocks? That is, the desired asset class might perform well and yet the stock selected may do poorly. When using individual stocks within a strategic asset allocation plan, it's difficult, if not impossible, to insure true asset class exposure. As such, individual stocks fall far short of exchange-traded index funds.

Exchange-Traded Index Funds

Exchange-traded index funds are the best tools to use when implementing a strategic asset allocation plan. They provide three key benefits not found together in any other investment product: pure asset class exposure (index-based), access to a wide selection of different types of indexes, and actively traded throughout the day.

If one believes in the logic and soundness of strategic asset allocation, then they must come to the conclusion that exchange-traded index funds are the best way to implement the plan.

Summary

Strategic asset allocation is the process of fine-tuning the overall asset allocation plan. It allows the investor to maximize the return of the equity and bond portion of the allocation while minimizing risk. For strategic asset allocation purposes, equities and bonds are divided into asset sub classes. The most common way to group equities is by size, investment style, industry or economic sector, or geographic location. The most common ways to group bonds is by maturity, issuer, or credit rating.

Once the initial strategic asset allocation plan has been implemented, it's necessary that the investor establish a system for rebalancing the portfolio. The two most used methods for rebalancing a portfolio are acceptable allocation range and set percentage. Rebalancing is important because it helps ensure that the portfolio remains true to its initial strategic asset allocation plan.

When implementing a strategic asset allocation plan, investors have four basic choices: traditional actively managed mutual funds, traditional index-based mutual funds, common stocks, and exchange-traded index funds. The best tools to use, by far, are exchange-traded index funds. They offer pure asset class exposure, access to a wide range of indexes, and intraday liquidity.

Chapter 11

ACTIVE PORTFOLIO MANAGEMENT STRATEGIES

Active vs. Passive

For millions of investors, creating a strategic asset allocation plan based on their goals and objectives, implementing the plan using exchange-traded index funds, and then systematically rebalancing the portfolio on a consistent basis will be enough. This approach, often referred to as passive investing, will most likely outperform the vast majority of all actively managed mutual funds since approximately 70% fail to beat the market in any given year. It will also be far more tax-efficient and considerably less expensive than a portfolio comprised of traditional actively managed mutual funds. Even though we refer to it as passive investing, it actually takes a great deal of planning, thought, and discipline, as we have seen.

For millions of other investors passive investing is not enough. They want to test their skills against other market participants in an attempt to "beat" the market. They want to use active risk management strategies to systematically limit losses, protect profits, or preserve capital. Whatever the motivation, active portfolio management offers a number of unique advantages for those willing to put in the effort.

Active portfolio management requires far more work than passive investing. Contrary to popular belief, it's not a part-time endeavor. Active portfolio management takes a great deal of time, attention to detail, discipline, and the will to succeed. If you are not prepared to commit the time and energy necessary, then you need to either find someone who is and pay them for their services, or limit the active strategies you implement.

Regardless of whether an investor wants to be passive or active, the first step is to create a strategic asset allocation plan, as we did in Chapter 10. The passive investor would rebalance accordingly and make few other changes. For the active investor, the strategic asset allocation plan provides two important functions:

- It serves as a launching pad for making active decisions. Prior to making any active portfolio management changes you must have a starting point. The strategic asset allocation plan serves as just that. It also provides a base to move back to when an active strategy is dismantled.

- It serves as a benchmark against which the success or failure of active decisions can be judged. The strategic portfolio serves as a measuring stick to determine if the active strategies implemented are benefiting the overall portfolio. If the passive portfolio continues to beat the active portfolio, you need to re-evaluate the strategies being used.

In this chapter, we introduce two active portfolio management strategies designed to work in conjunction with strategic asset allocation: tactical asset allocation and core-satellite portfolio construction. Both strategies provide a way for the investor to take advantage of perceived opportunities in the market. Both strategies allow the investor to enhance return and both are easily implemented using exchange-traded index funds.

Before discussing the merits of these strategies, we outline some of the reasons why an investor may want to consider implementing active portfolio management strategies, in the first place. The overview is by no means intended to list every potential reason. There are literally hundreds, if not thousands, of reasons why an investor may want to add active portfolio management strategies to his or her portfolio. The intention is not to discuss every possible reason, but simply to provide a broad overview of some alternatives.

Opportunities Created by Changing Market Cycles

Over the last few years investors, professional and individual alike, have found themselves in a quandary: firmly believing in the benefits of strategic asset allocation, yet wondering if it could be improved. Strategic asset allocation, after all, is somewhat rigid. The markets are not. They are driven by emotion and are prone to extremes to both the up and down side.

For example, during the mid-to-late 1990s staying true to a rigid strategic asset allocation model did not necessarily benefit investors. As interest rates continued their downward spiral and corporate earnings grew at record rates, the performance of growth companies far outpaced value companies. Likewise, the favorable economic conditions helped the market in general produce returns far above its historical norm. Investors who stayed true to a given strategic asset allocation model, emphasizing both growth stocks and value stocks, missed out on the potential to reap superior returns. Similarly, investors that stayed true to their overall asset allocation between stocks and bonds missed out, as well.

This sparked cries from many in the financial community that asset allocation was no longer relevant. While I believe declaring asset allocation irrelevant was a bit premature, those investors who stuck to their plan paid a heavy price for their intellectual purity. They forgot one very important rule: the market is not logical and often goes to extremes in both directions. The best way to take full advantage of these extremes is through the use of active portfolio management strategies.

How Opportunities To Profit Come About

Over time the economy will move from slow growth to rapid growth. It will move from recovery to expansion and back to recession. This is commonly referred to as the business or economic cycle and typically takes years to complete.

The stock market, just like the economy, is cyclical in nature. As the economy moves through various cycles, different types of equities produce different rates of return. For example, in a weak economy companies that tend to do well include consumer non-durable companies, energy companies, drug companies, and utility companies. Likewise, during periods of strong economic growth consumer cyclical and capital goods companies tend to perform well.

The size of a company will influence how the company's stock price reacts to changing economic conditions, as well. For instance, stocks of smaller companies, based on total market capitalization, tend to do well as the economy shows signs of early growth, while stocks of larger companies tend to do well when the economy is expanding rapidly. Other factors include whether a company is considered a growth company or a value company. Growth stocks tend to perform well during periods of strong economic growth while value stocks typically outperform growth stocks during periods of weak economic growth.

Over the course of an entire economic cycle, it's common to see the price per share of certain types of companies outperform the market in general as well as their own historical rate of return, sometimes by substantial margins. For example, from 1995 through 1999 large cap growth stocks far outpaced every other asset category. During this time period, large cap growth stocks, as measured by the S&P 500/BARRA Growth Index, gained an amazing 38.13%, 23.97%, 36.52%, 42.16%, and 28.25% compared to their historic average growth rate of 14.32%. In Exhibit 11-1 we see that it's common for some asset classes to significantly outperform their average return in any given year.

Exhibit 11-1:
Example of Asset Classes Producing Returns
Different than Their Historic Returns

Year	Asset Class/Index	Total Return for Year	20-Year Avg.Ann. Return*	Absolute Percentage Difference
2003	Small Cap/Russell 2000 Index	47.58%	12.29%	287.14%
2002	Large Cap Growth/Russell 1000 Growth Index	-27.88%	11.54%	341.59%
2001	International/MSCI EAFE Index	-21.21%	11.13%	290.57%
2000	Small Cap Value/Russell 2000 Value Index	22.83%	12.35%	84.86%
1999	Mid Cap Growth/Russell Mid Cap Growth Index	51.29%	12.16%	321.79%
1998	Large Cap Growth/Russell 1000 Growth Index	38.71%	11.54%	235.44%
1997	Large Cap Value/Russell 1000 Value Index	35.18%	13.56%	159.44%
1986	International/MSCI EAFE Index	69.94%	11.13%	528.39%
1985	International/MSCI EAFE Index	56.73%	11.13%	409.70%

*Average Annualized Return for 20-Year Period Ended 12/31/2003

As the exhibit shows, owning the right asset class at the right time can pay big rewards. The question is, "How do we take advantage of such opportunities?"

Prior to the creation of exchange-traded index funds, shifting a portfolio between various types of asset classes was difficult and cumbersome. It was virtually impossible to target specific asset categories with laser like efficiency using traditional mutual funds or individual stocks. Exchange-traded index funds, in contrast, make it possible for investors to quickly and efficiently overweight specific asset classes or the entire market, a process commonly referred to as tactical asset allocation.

Tactical Asset Allocation

Tactical asset allocation is the process of making small, temporary changes to a strategic asset allocation plan in an attempt to enhance overall return. The tactical changes should be short in duration, probably no longer than six to eight months. The objective of tactical asset allocation is not to change the overall strategic asset allocation plan, only to take advantage of perceived short-term market opportunities.

The two most common tactical changes are to over/under weight equities in general or over/under weight a specific asset class or style. The ease with which both strategies can be implemented, using exchange-traded index funds, is shown below.

Over/Under Weight the Market in General

There are times when an investor should be bullish. Likewise, there are times when an investor needs to minimize his or her exposure to equities. Exchange-traded index funds make it easy to quickly and efficiently overweight or underweight equities. For example, if an investor believed the market was entering a period of sustained over-performance they could make the changes shown in Exhibit 11-2.

As the exhibit shows, to take advantage of anticipated strength in equities the investor decreased the allocation in bonds from 25% to 10%. This was accomplished by selling shares of iShares Lehman 7-10 Yr. Treasury Index Fund and using the proceeds to purchase shares of iShares DJ Total Market Index Fund. Using exchange-traded index funds the investor can quickly and efficiently implement the desired tactical change. In a matter of minutes, if not seconds, the entire shift is completed.

The tactical change, shown in Exhibit 11-2, does not mean the investor is suddenly less risk adverse. At some point in the future, when they feel equities no longer present an attractive opportunity, the portfolio will be adjusted back to the original strategic asset allo-

Exhibit 11-2:
Example of "Tactical" Shift with a Bias to Equities

Initial Strategic Asset Allocation

Investment	Percent of Portfolio
iShares Russell 1000 Fund	20.00%
iShares Russell 2000 Fund	20.00%
iShares DJ Total Market Fund	20.00%
iShares Europe 350 Index Fund	15.00%
iShares Lehman 7-10 Yr. Tsy. Fund	25.00%
Total	**100.00%**

Portfolio After Tactical Changes

Investment	Percent of Portfolio
iShares Russell 1000 Fund	20.00%
iShares Russell 2000 Fund	20.00%
iShares DJ Total Market Fund	35.00%
iShares Europe 350 Index Fund	15.00%
iShares Lehman 7-10 Yr. Tsy. Fund	10.00%
Total	**100.00%**

---

cation. Of course, this assumes the investor's risk tolerance, investing time horizon, or return objectives have not changed.

As we mentioned earlier, there are literally thousands of ways to decide when to overweight or underweight equities in general. One such way is based on seasonal trading patterns. Two of the most commonly used seasonal trading patterns are the November Effect and the January Effect.

Anticipating a Seasonal Move
The November Effect takes advantage of the observation that over the last forty-five years (October 1954-October 1999), between 75% and 100% of the annual returns of the Dow Jones Industrial Aver-

Exhibit 11-3:
The November Effect — Performance of Dow Jones Industrial Average

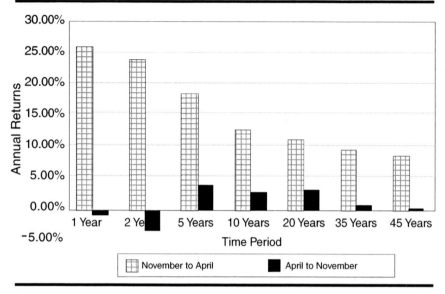

Source: Dow Jones

age have occurred during the November to April period. Further-more, less than 10% of the Dow's annual gain was made in the April to November time period. This phenomenon is shown in Exhibit 11-3.

An investor can easily take advantage of the November effect using the DIAMONDS, which track the Dow Jones Industrial Aver-age. Assume an investor is holding the portfolio shown in the top of Exhibit 11-4. To take advantage of the November Effect they would simply make the changes shown in the portfolio on the bottom of the exhibit, on the first day of November.

As the exhibit shows, the investor moved 20% of their total portfo-lio from bonds to the DIAMONDS in early November. Following the strategy, the investor will liquidate the position in April and move back to their initial allocation of 25% bonds and 75% equities. As we will see in later chapters, the investor could initiate a "bearish" position in April by selling shares of the DIAMONDS short. Selling short allows an investor to benefit from any seasonal weakness that might occur.

Another seasonal trading pattern that some investors follow is the January Effect. The January Effect refers to the tendency of small company stocks to perform well during late December through late January. To take advantage of the January Effect an investor would simply make a tactical change overweighting small company stocks around mid-December. Again, the entire change can take place easily and efficiently in a matter of minutes using exchange-traded index funds, such as the iShares Russell 2000 Index Fund or the iShares S&P SmallCap 600 Index Fund.

Exhibit 11-4:
Tactical Move Designed to Take Advantage of "November Effect"
Using Exchange-Traded Index Funds

Initial Strategic Asset Allocation

Investment	Percent of Portfolio
iShares Russell 1000 Fund	20.00%
iShares Russell 2000 Fund	20.00%
iShares DJ Total Market Fund	20.00%
iShares Europe 350 Index Fund	15.00%
iShares Lehman 7-10 Yr. Tsy. Fund	25.00%
Total	**100.00%**

Portfolio After Tactical Changes

Investment	Percent of Portfolio
iShares Russell 1000 Fund	20.00%
iShares Russell 2000 Fund	20.00%
iShares DJ Total Market Fund	20.00%
DIAMONDS	20.00%
iShares Europe 350 Index Fund	15.00%
iShares Lehman 7-10 Yr. Tsy. Fund	5.00%
Total	**100.00%**

Over/Under Weight by Style or Size

A second popular tactical change is to overweight or underweight a portfolio by company style or size. Professional money managers have long known that properly managing asset size and style offers the greatest chance to add value to the portfolio management process. Before the creation of exchange-traded index funds, managing a portfolio by asset size and style was nearly impossible for retail investors. Now, with exchange-traded index funds, it's easy.

The potential advantages associated with properly managing a portfolio based on asset style and size is shown in Exhibit 11-5. The first portfolio consists entirely of the iShares Russell 1000 Index Fund while the second portfolio shows the returns generated by perfectly allocating dollars between growth stocks and value stocks. The Russell 1000 Growth Index and the Russell 1000 Value Index are used to represent growth and value stocks.

As the exhibit shows, from 1990 through 2001, the average annual rate of return for the Russell 1000 Index was 14.54%. By shifting perfectly between growth stocks or value stocks each year, the annualized rate of return jumps to 21.44%. This is almost double the average return of the entire market, as measured by the Dow Jones Total Market Index.

It should be obvious that an investor would never be able to perfectly time asset classes as was done in Exhibit 11-5. What the exhibit does make clear, however, is the potential reward offered by correctly allocating funds between different asset classes. The difference between a 14.54% average annual return and a best case scenario of 21.44% average annual rate of return is clearly enough to justify the time and effort necessary to try to capture excess return through style management.

The best way to actively manage a portfolio by asset style is to first build a style neutral portfolio as shown in Exhibit 11-6. The style neutral portfolio acts as a springboard for making tactical changes. If interest rates are rising and corporate earnings are slowing, a tilt towards value makes sense. Likewise, if the economy is

Exhibit 11-5:
Buy-and-Hold Compared to Switching Between Growth and Value*

Buy-and-Hold Using Russell 1000 Index Fund			Perfectly Switching Between "Growth" and "Value"		
Year Ending	Value	Return	Year Ending	Value	Return
12/31/90	$100,000.00		12/31/90	$100,000.00	
12/31/91	$133,040.00	33.04%	12/31/91	$143,270.00	43.27%
12/31/92	$144,920.47	8.93%	12/31/92	$162,726.07	13.58%
12/31/93	$159,673.38	10.18%	12/31/93	$192,130.67	18.07%
12/31/94	$160,296.10	0.39%	12/31/94	$197,164.49	2.62%
12/31/95	$220,839.94	37.77%	12/31/95	$272,796.79	38.36%
12/31/96	$270,418.51	22.45%	12/31/96	$335,867.41	23.12%
12/31/97	$359.250.99	32.85%	12/31/97	$454,025.56	35.18%
12/31/98	$456,320.60	27.02%	12/31/98	$629,778.85	38.71%
12/31/99	$551,737.24	20.91%	12/31/99	$838,613.52	33.16%
12/31/00	$508,756.91	-7.79%	12/31/00	$897,484.19	7.02%
12/31/01	$445,416.67	-12.45%	12/31/01	$847,314.82	-5.59%
Annualized Return		**14.54%**	**Annualized Return**		**21.44%**

*Performance numbers based on Russell 1000 Index, Russell 1000 Growth Index, and Russell 1000 Value Index.

expanding and corporate earnings are growing, a tilt towards growth makes sense.

An example of a tactical change favoring value and a tactical

Exhibit 11-6:
Example of Style Neutral Portfolio

	Value Stocks	Neutral/ Blend	Growth Stocks	Total Allocation
Large Capitalization	0.00%	70.00%	0.00%	70.00%
Mid Capitalization	0.00%	20.00%	0.00%	20.00%
Small Capitalization	0.00%	10.00%	0.00%	10.00%
Total Portfolio	**0.00%**	**100.00%**	**0.00%**	**100.00%**

change favoring growth, from the initial style neutral portfolio, is shown in Exhibit 11-7. To complete the tactical changes shown in the exhibit the investor would simply purchase shares of the corresponding exchange-traded index funds that track the desired underlying asset classes.

Limitations on Tactical Changes

Tactical asset allocation allows the investor to take advantage of many different and unique market situations. It should always be remembered, however, that for every action there is a reaction. Any change to the overall strategic asset allocation will change the portfolio's risk and return characteristics, so changes should be minimized and only done when strong evidence exists to warrant such actions.

Exhibit 11-7:
Example of Tactical Style Shifts (Growth Portfolio and Value Portfolio)

Growth Portfolio	Value Stocks	Neutral/ Blend	Growth Stocks	Total Allocation
Large Capitalization	0.00%	45.00%	25.00%	70.00%
Mid Capitalization	0.00%	10.00%	10.00%	20.00%
Small Capitalization	0.00%	0.00%	10.00%	10.00%
Total Portfolio	**0.00%**	**55.00%**	**45.00%**	**100.00%**

Value Portfolio	Value Stocks	Neutral/ Blend	Growth Stocks	Total Allocation
Large Capitalization	20.00%	50.00%	0.00%	70.00%
Mid Capitalization	15.00%	5.00%	0.00%	20.00%
Small Capitalization	5.00%	5.00%	0.00%	10.00%
Total Portfolio	**40.00%**	**60.00%**	**0.00%**	**100.00%**

Before executing any tactical shift, the investor must consider the following:

- **How much of the portfolio should be committed to each position?** A good rule of thumb is to make the tactical move large enough to impact the overall portfolio but not so big as to dramatically decrease portfolio returns should it turn out to be wrong.

- **Is the projected differential return enough to warrant the risk?** Often times, investors make the mistake of looking at absolute returns instead of the differential between expected returns and average returns. For example, consider the following two assets. Asset 1 has an average return of 15% while asset 2 has an average return of 6%. If the forecasted expected return for asset 1 is 17% and asset 2 is 12%, which represents the better investment? Asset 2 has the lower expected return, but offers the greatest return differential compared to its average return, making it the more attractive alternative.

- **The number of tactical shifts at any one time should be limited.** It is imperative that the tactical plays be kept to a manageable level; otherwise they can quickly get out of hand and lead to potential losses. A good rule is to have no more than two to three tactical allocations going at one time. This is a subjective number and could certainly be increased should market conditions warrant.

- **If it is not working, don't be afraid to admit your mistake and get out.** Investors often let pride get in the way of investing. They feel that taking a loss is admitting they made a mistake. I believe the opposite is true. It shows courage to admit a tactical move was a mistake and close out the position. Prior to making any tactical change the investor should know and understand all possible ramifications, and have an exit strategy in place should the move turn out to be a mistake.

Core-Satellite Portfolio Construction

In the previous section, we saw how to make tactical changes to the strategic asset allocation plan. Typically, the changes were made by "tweaking" investments already in the portfolio. An example of a tactical change is increasing a portfolio's exposure to large cap growth stocks from 10% of the portfolio to 15%.

What if an investor wants to do more than simply tweak an existing position? What if they want to move money into an entirely different type of asset, which they do not already own? To do this, we use a "Core-Satellite" strategy.

As its name implies, a core-satellite portfolio is comprised of two parts: the core and the satellite. The "core" represents the larger portion of the portfolio while the "satellite" is the smaller portion. Depending on how aggressive or conservative the investor wishes to be, the core holdings can range anywhere from 70% to 90% of the total portfolio. The satellite portion of the portfolio, therefore, would fall between 10% and 30% of the entire portfolio.

Similar to tactical asset allocation, the investor first creates the appropriate strategic asset allocation plan based on their risk tolerance, investment goals, and time horizon, among other things. This forms the investor's core holdings. The satellite portion is then invested in any one of a number of different ways, which will be discussed later in this chapter.

An example of a core-satellite portfolio strategy, using exchange-traded index funds, is shown in Exhibit 11-8. As the exhibit shows, the hypothetical investor is anticipating two sectors will do well, technology and financial services. They are also anticipating the equities of two specific countries will do well, Brazil and Spain.

The result is a core portfolio that satisfies a given set of return

Exhibit 11-8:
Example of Core-Satellite Portfolio

Investment	Percent	Total
Core Holdings:		
iShares Russell 1000 Index Fund	20.00%	
iShares Russell 2000 Index Fund	20.00%	
iShares S&P 400 MidCap Index Fund	15.00%	
iShares EMU 350 Index Fund	10.00%	
iShares Lehman 7-10 Yr. Tsy. Index Fund	15.00%	
Total Core Holdings		80.00%
Satellite Holdings:		
iShares MSCI Brazil Index Fund	5.00%	
iShares MSCI Spain Index Fund	5.00%	
iShares Dow Jones U.S. Financial Sector Index Fund	5.00%	
iShares Dow Jones U.S. Technology Sector Index Fund	5.00%	
Total Satellite Holdings		20.00%
Total Portfolio		**100.00%**

and risk parameters with the satellite portion offering the investor a chance to add value by actively selecting different areas of the market on which to focus. Again, unlike a tactical allocation, we don't simply overweight or underweight already existing investments. Entirely new investments are made in the satellite portion of the portfolio.

The percentage allocated to the satellite portion of the portfolio determines how much added risk the investor is willing to assume. For instance, if an investor had 90% of their portfolio invested based on their overall strategic asset allocation and only 10% in various satellite holdings, they would be taking far less risk than an investor with a 75% to 25% split. Therefore, the amount designated for the satellite holdings is a function of the investor's own risk tolerance and desire to actively pursue other investments.

The objective of using a core-satellite strategy is to provide the ability to add value by investing in various industry sectors, countries, or specific stocks all within a strategic asset allocation framework. How the investor determines their strategic allocation is straightforward enough. However, the investments held in the satellite portion of the portfolio will typically vary greatly from one investor to the other.

Several common ways to invest the satellite portion of a portfolio are the following:

- **Sector Rotation Strategies** – A popular use of sector or industry based exchange-traded index funds is to develop a sector rotation strategy. To do so, the investor simply determines the different sectors they wish to invest in and allocates an equal portion of the satellite to each. A good rule of thumb is to never place more than 5% of the total portfolio in any single sector.

- **Actively Managed Mutual Funds** – Some actively managed mutual fund managers are able to produce superior results, albeit they are few and far between. Using a core-satellite strategy allows the investor to incorporate actively managed mutual funds with a portfolio of exchange-traded index funds.

- **Individual Stock Strategies** – Many investors like to own shares of individual common stocks. The reasons why vary. They may work for the company. They may have inherited the stock. Or, they may be looking to hit a home run. Regardless of the reasons why, the core-satellite strategy allows the investor to keep the majority of their portfolio in a systematic investment strategy while only risking a portion on individual stocks.

- **Country Specific Investments** – Another way to invest the satellite portion of a portfolio is to make specific country investments. If an investor believed the economy favored a particular country or area of the globe they could use exchange-traded index funds and a core-satellite portfolio approach to easily gain access to the desired area. Again, as with a sector rotation strategy, I recommend investing no more than 5% of the total portfolio in a given country index.

The core-satellite strategy offers the investor tremendous flexibility to manage their portfolio. It's the perfect strategy for the investor who wants a portion of their portfolio to track the market, yet also wants a chance to hit a home run with a portion of his or her portfolio. Best of all, exchange-traded index funds make it very easy to implement and maintain the strategy.

Summary

As the economy and markets change, opportunities are created. To take advantage of these opportunities investors can make tactical changes to their strategic asset allocation plan or implement a core-satellite approach. Tactical asset allocation involves making small, targeted changes to the portfolio. The core-satellite approach, on the other hand, gives the investor a way to balance the benefits associated with strategic asset allocation with the desire to hit a home run.

Chapter 12

EXIT STRATEGIES —
PROTECTING YOUR PORTFOLIO

The Exit Strategy

Will Rogers once said, "The return of my money is more important than the return on my money." He was right. The first rule of investing is to protect your capital. It's too hard to make money in the market to simply watch it evaporate when the averages turn lower. The best way to protect capital is with a *sell* or *exit* strategy.

In Chapter 10, strategic asset allocation was shown to provide comprehensive risk management through diversification. The difference between using an exit strategy and strategic asset allocation is that an exit strategy is designed to move the investor out of the market to protect them from a major loss. Strategic asset allocation, in contrast, keeps the investor in the market but minimizes market risks through scientific diversification. An exit strategy provides an extra layer of protection above and beyond that offered by strategic asset allocation.

There are three basic reasons why an investment should be sold. First, your goals or objectives change and the investment no longer fits your needs. Second, the investment achieves your performance objectives. The third reason to sell an investment, and the focus of this chapter, is based on a predetermined exit strategy.

In this chapter, exit strategies are discussed. First, the key components central to all exit strategies are evaluated. Next, we show specific examples of how exit strategies work. The advantages and disadvantages associated with using exit strategies are outlined. Finally, we conclude by explaining why exchange-traded index funds are the best investment product to use in conjunction with the exit strategies discussed in this chapter.

Creating an Effective Exit Strategy

I have often heard investors say that knowing when to sell is the hardest part of investing. They may be right. Selling an investment is difficult because of the emotions tied to the process. Too often investors view selling, particularly for a loss, as a sign of failure. They take it personally. Even selling an investment for a gain can be emotionally difficult. Our fear is that as soon as we sell the investment it will move higher without us on board.

To improve as investors we must remove the emotional baggage that makes selling so difficult. From my experience, only one thing can help eliminate the emotional difficulties associated with selling. Notice that I said *help* eliminate. To become completely impartial is probably an impossible goal. After all, whenever your financial future is at stake it's hard to be impartial. The best way I've found to ease the anxiety surrounding the sell decision is to establish a clear, concise, and detailed exit strategy based on logic, not emotions.

Unfortunately, when it comes to selling most investors tend to shoot from the hip. Over the years, I've heard hundreds of different ways sell decisions are made. A few of the more interesting ones are listed below:

- If it doesn't go up in a few months I'll sell it.
- My brother (insert any relative) will tell me when it's time to sell.
- I'll buy some now and if it goes down I'll buy more.
- I'm not worried about the 50% drop; it's a long-term investment.

- I'm sure my broker will tell me when it's time to sell.
- I got the idea from a magazine. I'm sure they will let me know when I should sell.
- A friend of mine, who knows someone at the company, will tell me when to sell.

Be honest, you have used at least one of the above at some point in your life, probably with less than stellar results. Hopefully, after reading this chapter, you will never need to rely on any of the above-mentioned "strategies" again.

Important Considerations When Creating an Exit Strategy

Exit strategies are an important part of risk management. For an exit strategy to provide any meaningful benefits, however, several important factors must be considered. They include the following:

1. **Markets are dynamic.** In the short-term markets change by minutes and seconds, while over the long-term they offer both bull and bear market cycles. For an exit strategy to work, it must be dynamic.

2. **Markets tend to move higher over time.** This is an undeniable truth; therefore, an exit strategy should be designed to keep the investor in the market as much as possible and on the sidelines as little as possible.

3. **Markets can move dramatically lower over the short-term.** While it's true that equity markets tend to move higher over time, it cannot be overlooked that markets also experience sharp corrections. In fact, it's common to see the market post dramatic losses over relatively short periods of time.

4. **Trading is costly.** Trading is costly in terms of potential capital gains taxes owed and actual out of pocket trading related expenses. An exit strategy, therefore, should not create excessive trading and must provide the investor with the flexibility to consider the tax consequences of their actions.

The final component necessary to create a successful exit strategy is the investor. It takes mental toughness to stay true to an exit strategy over the long-run. At some point, every investor will be tested. They will experience doubt and uncertainty. I can assure you that at some point you will sell an investment for a loss only to see it move dramatically higher. When this occurs, you must be strong and have enough confidence in your strategy not to second guess your actions.

Most investors second guess sell decisions because they feel the market always goes up after they sell. Contrary to popular belief, the market does not know, or for that matter care, when you sell. It's simply human nature to second guess our actions, regardless of what we are doing. It's also human nature to remember those times when an exit strategy didn't work and forget those times when it protected us. Therefore, for an exit strategy to provide any meaningful benefits it must give the investor the confidence not to second guess their every move. To do this, the strategy must be logical, systematic and based on sound financial principles.

Stop-Loss Orders – A Key Part of the Exit Strategy

Professional investors have long known that stop-loss orders are one of the most powerful risk management tools at their disposal because they provide a systematic and non-emotional way to limit losses and protect profits. Simply put, a sell stop-loss order is an order placed with a broker to sell if, and only if, a certain price (called the stop price) is reached by the underlying security.

To see how a sell stop-loss works, we will use the following example. Assume an investor owns 100 shares of iShares S&P 500 Index Fund (IVV) with a cost of $100. They want to limit their loss on the investment to 10% or $1,000. To do this, the investor can enter a stop-loss order with a stop price of $90 ($100 cost basis - ($100 x 10%)). As long as the price per share of IVV remains above $90, nothing happens. If the price per share of IVV falls to $90, the stop order is activated and becomes a market order. The 100 shares of IVV are immediately sold at the best available price.

The process is automatic and simple. The investor doesn't need to watch the price of IVV throughout the day. They don't need to continually call their broker and check the market. If the price per share of IVV drops to $90, the sale occurs automatically. The investor could be playing golf or fishing, it doesn't matter. The order is executed in a timely manner. As we can see, the beauty of a stop-loss order is in its simplicity and ease of use.

Stop-loss orders provide several important benefits:

- They provide a non-emotional, systematic, and disciplined platform by which to make decisions.

- They help the investor remain focused regardless of market conditions.

- They help reduce portfolio risk and investor anxiety.

- They help the investor avoid second guessing every transaction because sales only occur when the investment trades at a predetermined price.

- They operate automatically and efficiently.

- They can keep you from losing large amounts of money.

Even though stop-loss orders provide a number of significant benefits, as we saw above, we must remember that markets are dynamic, changing continually. To provide any meaningful protection, our stop-loss order must also be dynamic and move with the market. Not simply provide a static level of protection. The answer is to use a *trailing* or *dynamic* stop-loss order.

Making a Stop-Loss Order Dynamic

When used correctly, a stop-loss order is a powerful risk management tool. The problem is that most investors rarely use them correctly. They fail to adjust the stop price as the underlying security moves higher limiting the overall effectiveness of the order.

For example, assume an investor purchased 100 shares of IVV (iShares S&P 500 Index) at $75 per share and immediately entered a stop-loss order at $69.38 per share. This represents a 7.5% stop-loss ($75 – ($75 x 7.5%)). The investor is protected since the stop-loss order will be activated if the price of IVV drops to $69.38 per share.

We know that if the price per share of IVV falls to $69.38 the stop-loss order will be activated and the shares sold. But what happens if the price per share of IVV moves higher? When the price of the underlying security moves higher, the stop price needs to be adjusted. If the stop-loss price is not adjusted, to reflect the increase in the price of IVV, unrealized profits are left unprotected. This is shown below.

Initial Transactions:
Purchase 100 shares of IVV at $75.00 = $7,500
Initial stop-loss price (7.5%) : $69.38
Maximum anticipated loss: ($75 - $69.38) x 100 = ($562) or 7.5%

One Year Later:
Price of IVV is $100.00
Unrealized profits: ($100 - $75) x 100 = $2,500
Unadjusted stop-loss price : $69.38
Stop price (if adjusted) : $92.50 = 100 - (100 x 7.5%)

Two Years Later:

Price of IVV is $69.38

Stop-loss activated at $69.38

Gain or (Loss): ($75 - $69.38) x 100 = ($562)

Lost Profits: ($92.50 - $69.38) x 100 = ($2,312)

The investor, in the example above, lost $2,312 by not adjusting the stop-loss price to reflect the increase in the price of IVV. This is based on a 7.5% stop-loss price and IVV at $100 per share ($100 − (100 x 7.5%)). The stop-loss order provided some benefit, by limiting the loss to a maximum of 7.5% of the initial investment, but it clearly didn't do as much as possible.

The answer is to make the stop-loss order dynamic. A dynamic stop-loss order is a stop order that trails the price of the underlying security as it moves higher. For instance, a 7.5% dynamic stop-loss order always trails the closing price of the underlying stock by 7.5%. On any day that the shares of IVV close at a new post purchase high the dynamic stop-loss price is adjusted accordingly. The new stop-loss price is always 7.5% under the new high closing price.

For example, an investor buys 100 shares of IVV at $75 per share and immediately enters a stop-loss order at $69.38 or 7.5% below the purchase price. On any day that IVV closes at a new post purchase high the stop price is increased, always trailing the closing price by 7.5%. On any day that IVV does not close at a post purchase high, the stop-loss price is not adjusted. Remember, we never decrease the stop-loss price, only increase it. An example of a dynamic stop-loss order in action is shown in Exhibit 12-1.

As we can see from the exhibit, when the closing price per share of IVV makes a new high the stop price is increased to keep pace, always trailing the post purchase high closing price by 7.5%. On any day that IVV does not close at a new post purchase high no changes are made. As long as the price per share of IVV continues to increase the shares will not be sold. Eventually, one would expect the price of IVV to retreat and activate the stop price, at which time the order becomes a

Exhibit 12-1:
Hypothetical Dynamic Stop-Loss Order (7.5% Stop Price)

Date	Closing Price	Action (Buy or Sell)	Price	Stop-Loss Price = 7.5%
Day 1	$102.00	**Buy**	$102.00	$ 94.35
Day 2	$103.50			$ 95.74
Day 3	$104.00			$ 96.20
Day 4	$101.50			n/c
Day 5	$100.75			n/c
Day 6	$ 99.00			n/c
Day 7	$102.85			n/c
Day 8	$104.75			$ 96.89
Day 9	$105.50			$ 97.59
Day 10	$107.75			$ 99.67
Day 11	$103.00			n/c
Day 12	$106.00			n/c
Day 13	$109.25			$101.06
Day 14	$108.70			n/c
Day 15	$113.00			$104.53
Day 16	$109.25			n/c
Day 17	$107.00			n/c
Day 18	$105.75			n/c
Day 19	$104.68			n/c
Day 20	$103.28	**Sell**	$104.53	

market order and the shares are sold at the best available price.

The benefits associated with using dynamic stop-loss orders are the following:

- Losses are always limited to a fixed percentage. As the price moves higher the investor continually benefits since the stop-loss price is raised accordingly.
- Dynamic stop orders offer the investor discipline and continuity.
- Dynamic stop orders help keep investors focused during all types of market cycles.

- Dynamic stop orders avoid the need for market timing.
- Dynamic stop orders offer a non-emotional and systematic framework for making hard decisions.

Dynamic stop-loss orders, when used correctly, help keep the investor in the market as the market is trending higher and out of the market while it's trending lower. They are powerful tools that form the backbone of the exit strategy used in Strategic Index Investing.

Keeping Track of Dynamic Stop Orders
Dynamic stop-loss orders are powerful risk management tools, as we have seen. To be effective, they require ongoing monitoring and adjustments. To help keep track of a single, or multiple stop-loss orders you need a system. To do this, I recommend using a spreadsheet similar to the one shown in Exhibit 12-2.

A spreadsheet allows the investor to easily track and adjust multiple stop-loss orders on a daily or weekly basis. On the days that the underlying investment moves up, to a new post purchase high, the dynamic stop price is raised. On the days that the price moves lower or is unchanged the dynamic stop-loss order is not changed. In only a few minutes daily, using the spreadsheet shown in the exhibit, it's possible to keep track of your stop-loss orders and add a level of risk management to your portfolio not possible with most investment strategies.

When determining how often to adjust a dynamic stop-loss order, the investor must weigh the need for accuracy with the time commitment necessary. The preferable method is to monitor and adjust all stop-loss orders on a daily basis. This, however, may not be feasible for every investor. In that case, weekly will certainly work. I would not recommend monthly. The markets are far too volatile to only monitor and adjust your stop-loss orders twelve times per year.

Exhibit 12-2:
Example of Dynamic Stop-Loss Monitoring Worksheet

Exchange-Traded Index Fund Monitoring Worksheet				
Fund Name/Ticker:		**Stop-Loss %:**		
Date	**Closing Price**	**Stop-Loss Price**	**Buy/ Sell**	**Gain/ Loss**

Benefits of Stop-Loss Orders

To appreciate how important dynamic stop-loss orders are within the context of risk management, we will examine the benefits they offer. When used correctly, stop-loss orders provide three essential benefits. They help 1) limit losses, 2) protect unrealized gains, and 3) preserve capital. As a result, portfolio volatility should decrease while return consistency should improve.

Limit Losses

Stop-loss orders help to limit investment losses. This is important because portfolio losses have an exponential characteristic: any subsequent profit must be *greater* than the loss. For example, if a portfolio decreases by 25% over the course of a year, simply earning 25% the following year will not bring the portfolio back to where it was before the loss occurred. A return of 33%, and not 25%, is required to get back to pre-loss values. Exhibit 12-3 shows the exponential nature of losses.

As the exhibit shows, allowing losses to accumulate makes it all but impossible to effectively grow a portfolio. Stop-loss orders provide the means necessary to limit losses before they occur, or before they become too large.

Protect Unrealized Gains

Stop-loss orders help to protect profits. The importance of protecting profits was made clear over the last several years. When the

Exhibit 12-3:
The Exponential Nature of Losses

Percentage Loss	Gain Necessary to Get Back to Break-Even
10.0%	11.1%
15.0%	17.6%
20.0%	25.0%
25.0%	33.3%
30.0%	42.8%
40.0%	66.7%
50.0%	100.0%
75.0%	300.0%

market corrected in early 2000, many investors saw large profits, which had taken years to accumulate, literally vanish in a matter of days. Still worse, many saw nice profits become devastating losses. Exhibit 12-4 shows just how quickly unrealized profits can turn into losses without a plan to protect them.

Imagine the joy and then frustration of the individual who started with a $25,000 investment in EMC Corp. in August of 1996. In a matter of only a few years the investment ballooned to well over $400,000, a gain of some 1,500%. Then, in only a few months, profits were wiped away as the price of EMC dropped, reducing a spectacular gain of over $380,000 to a mere $1,600.

If you think it's unlikely that an investor would simply watch as his or her shares of EMC collapsed, think again. A study done by the New York Stock Exchange in the late 1990s found that on average, when a stock's price gets cut in half, it's typically sold less than 10% of the time. According to the study, if the price of a stock drops from $100 per share to $50 per share, only 1 out of 10 investors actually sell. The other nine simply watch and do nothing to protect their gains. The effective use of stop-loss orders can help you protect profits and avoid the same mistakes made by 90% of all investors.

Exhibit 12-4:
The Market Gives and the Market Takes Away

Company	Initial Investment 8/31/1997	Value of Investment at High Point	Value of Investment 7/31/2002	Dollars Given Back
Sun Microsystems	$25,000.00	$269,521.00	$15,376.00	$254,145.00
EMC Corp	$25,000.00	$410,486.00	$26,445.00	$384,041.00
Cisco Systems	$25,000.00	$244,770.00	$41,252.00	$203,518.00
Nortel Networks	$25,000.00	$179,513.00	$ 2,117.00	$177,396.00
SPDRs "Spiders"	$25,000.00	$ 43,085.00	$25,116.00	$ 17,969.00
Intel Corp.	$25,000.00	$ 82,298.00	$18,086.00	$ 64,212.00
Ciena Corp.	$25,000.00	$158,000.00	$ 4,250.00	$153,750.00

Preserve Capital

Stop-loss orders help preserve capital. There is an old saying: "He who learns to run away lives to fight another day." Every investor should write this down and read it daily. An obvious, yet rarely discussed benefit associated with cutting losses and protecting profits is that more dollars are available to invest when the market eventually turns around and moves higher.

History tells us that some of the biggest percentage gains in the market have occurred *after* the worst declines. If an investor holds tight as the market declines, failing to limit losses or protect profits, as many buy-and-hold investors do, they will have less capital to work with when the market eventually advances. However, if an investor takes precautionary action and limits losses during the decline they will have more capital to invest when the market begins its next move to the upside. Exhibit 12-5 shows some of the tremendous gains that have historically followed steep market downturns.

Without a strategy in place to limit a portfolio's decline the spectacular gains shown in the exhibit do little more than get the investor back to where they were before the decline occurred. It's virtually impossible to effectively grow a portfolio by simply treading water. Opportunities to make spectacular gains, like those shown in Exhibit 12-5, are too few and far between to miss. The only way to take advantage of such opportunities is to limit losses and protect profits. Stop-loss orders allow investors to do both.

An Exit Strategy Can Help Lower Volatility and Improve Consistency

A natural by-product of limiting losses, protecting profits, and preserving capital is a decrease in portfolio volatility and more consistent returns over time. From my experience, lower portfolio volatility helps keep investors focused and confident about achieving their desired goals. In contrast, high portfolio volatility tends to cause investors to pull out of the market, often abandoning investment goals and objectives completely. And, while lower volatility does not nec-

225

Exhibit 12-5:
S&P 500 Index Advances Following Bear Markets

Bear Market Time Period	Subsequent Advance
September 1929 - June 1932	177.27%
July 1933 - March 1935	131.64%
March 1937 - March 1938	62.24%
November 1938 - April 1942	157.70%
May 1946 - March 1948	259.39%
August 1956 - October 1957	86.35%
December 1961 - June 1962	79.78%
February 1966 - October 1966	48.05%
November 1968 - May 1970	73.53%
January 1973 - October 1974	125.63%
November 1980 - August 1982	228.81%
August 1987 - December 1987	353.00%

essarily insure better long-term performance it certainly decreases investor anxiety and fear.

Potential Problems and Other Considerations

It would be nice to end this chapter by boldly proclaiming that dynamic stop-loss orders are the magical tool that will allow you to make untold amounts of money in the stock market without ever losing a dime. Nothing would make me happier. Unfortunately, there is no such thing as a safe, automatic way to make money in the markets.

Every tool or strategy has a downside, including dynamic stop-loss orders. With that said, it's time to look at some potential problems that might arise when using dynamic stop-loss orders in conjunction with exchange-traded index funds. Keep in mind, even when we consider the following, the benefits associated with dynamic stop-loss orders far outweigh any potential problems.

Finding the Correct Percentages

In the examples shown in this chapter we used a 7.5% or 10% stop-loss price. There is nothing magical about these numbers. Unfortunately, there is no set rule that tells us the "best" percentages to use for a given exchange-traded index fund.

When determining the percentages to use, we must balance the amount we are willing to lose with the realities of the markets. For example, trying to protect an equity portfolio from normal market fluctuations, such as 4% to 6%, is not realistic. By setting the stop price too close to the price of the underlying security we increase the likelihood of being "whipsawed." Whipsaw is a term used to describe the continual buying and selling of an investment.

If the percentages being used continually cause the investor to be whipsawed, then one of two things must be done: the percentages should be increased or the investor should stay on the sideline and wait for the market to settle down. Keep in mind, broad-based indexes will tend to be less volatile than narrowly focused indexes, such as sector indexes. Therefore, a 10% stop-loss may make sense for a broad-based index while applying a 10% stop-loss to a technology based index does not. In the end, the investor must balance their need for protection with the historical volatility of the underlying exchange-traded index fund.

Keeping Gains From Becoming Losses

One problem inherent with the use of dynamic stop-loss orders is that gains can turn into losses. For example, if shares of IVV are purchased at $100 per share and subsequently move up to $107.50, a paper gain of 7.5% exists. This is calculated as follows, (($107.50-$100)/$100). If a 7.5% dynamic stop-loss is being used then the actual stop-loss price is $99.43. Therefore, if stopped out a loss of $0.50 per share would occur, despite the investment posting a nice gain of 7.5% at one time.

To counter this problem, a strategy I've seen used with very good results is to never let a 5% profit (or any number you are comfortable with) turn into a loss. For example, if any position increases in value by at least 5%, on a closing basis, the investor would set the stop-loss price at the purchase price (break-even). If the position subsequently moves lower the investor doesn't let a nice gain turn into a loss. Once the position moves up approximately 8.2%, the 7.5% dynamic stop-loss would be reinitiated because at that point the stop price would be above the purchase price of $100 per share.

$$\$108.20 \times 7.5\% = \$8.12$$
$$\$108.20 - \$8.12 = \$100.08 \text{ Stop-Loss Price}$$

This strategy helps to avoid the problem of feeling as if you let something slip away. Unfortunately, when using stop-loss orders it is inevitable that some profits will be given back. Keep in mind, at any time prior to the investment reaching the stop-loss price, you can cancel the order and sell outright. For example, if an investment moves up 15% over a relatively short period of time, you might decide to simply sell it and lock in the nice gain.

Taxes

In an account that offers tax advantages, such as an IRA or 401K, whether a trade generates a capital gain or loss is irrelevant. In a taxable account, however, an investor must consider the potential tax implications of trading decisions. Because any system designed to cut losses and protect profits will create gains and losses, we must always be cognizant of the tax implications of our actions.

At the same time, it's foolish to forgo active risk management strategies for the sake of avoiding taxes. I know many investors who would happily pay a portion of their capital gains to Uncle Sam if they could go back and sell their investments at prices from several years back. Too often investors use potential tax liability as an excuse not to sell. Instead, they must weigh any tax liability with the need to manage risk and try to reach a happy medium.

Transaction Costs

Similar to the negative impact of taxes, transaction costs can also have a negative impact on a portfolio. Risk management strategies tend to increase trading and therefore trading related costs. The actual fees and charges paid by investors to buy or sell shares will vary dramatically. If one uses a deep discount broker, the transaction costs will be less than if the trades are done through a full service broker. However, using a discount broker usually means no help when implementing various strategies.

A popular alternative to paying a commission on each individual transaction is to pay a yearly fee based on the size of your account. This is often referred to as a wrap account. With a wrap account the investor knows, in advance, the amount they will pay regardless of the number of transactions made over the course of the year. Since exchange-traded index funds already have total expenses that are dramatically lower than traditional mutual funds, even when the wrap fee is considered the investor will usually pay less, on a yearly basis, than they would with a portfolio of traditional mutual funds.

Selling at a Price Substantially Different Than the Stop Price

One common risk associated with all exchange-traded securities, whether individual stocks or exchange-traded index funds, is that they can open for trading at a price substantially higher or lower than the price at which they closed the previous day. In fact, during periods of extreme market volatility, the price per share of any traded security can and will open at a price very different than its previous day's closing price. When this occurs, it can have a negative impact on your stop-loss order.

For example, assume an investor had a stop-loss order to sell shares of IVV with a stop of $100. If the market in general opens dramatically lower and shares of IVV open at $95 per share the investor will not be filled at $100. Instead, they will receive a price around $95 or roughly 5% under the stop price. Remember, a stop-loss order becomes a market order when the price of the underlying security trades at or below the stop price. A market order is filled at the best available price, in this example, $95 per share.

To avoid this problem, some investors like to use stop-limit orders. A stop-limit order is an order that becomes a limit order when the stop price is hit. For example, assume our investor had an order to sell 100 shares of IVV at $100 stop with a limit of $100. When the share price of IVV trades at or below $100 per share the order becomes a limit order to sell 100 shares at $100 or better. In the example above, the order would not be filled because the best available price is $95 per share. If the price per share of IVV continues to drop the investor suffers. The stop-limit provided virtually no protection. For this reason, I rarely use stop-limit orders.

When the price per share of an exchange-traded security opens above or below its previous day's closing price, it's called a "gap" opening. An example of the potential problems associated with gap openings is shown in Exhibit 12-6.

To avoid these potential problems the investor can always cancel their order prior to the opening, although I would not recommend it. In reality, the number of times that an investor will be adversely impacted by a gap opening should be minimal, especially when using exchange-traded index funds tracking broad-based indexes.

Why Exchange-Traded Index Funds

As we have seen, dynamic stop-loss orders offer numerous benefits. But, why couldn't we use stop-loss orders in conjunction with a portfolio of individual stocks or traditional mutual funds? After all, other investments exist besides exchange-traded index funds.

An advantage exchange-traded index funds have over traditional mutual funds is intraday pricing. Without the ability to transact busi-

Exhibit 12-6:
Example of "Gap" Openings

Closing Price of Previous Day	Stop Price	Opening Price	Actual Sell Price	Difference
$ 98.00	$ 97.00	$94.00	$94.00	- 3.09%
$104.50	$102.00	$99.00	$99.00	- 2.94%
$102.25	$102.00	$91.50	$91.50	-10.29%
$ 65.50	$ 65.00	$60.25	$60.25	- 7.31%

ness throughout the day, traditional mutual funds are at a tremendous disadvantage. Additionally, because of the way they are structured, investors cannot buy or sell shares of traditional mutual funds using stop orders, completely eliminating the use of this powerful portfolio management tool for mutual fund shareholders.

Exchange-traded index funds also offer advantages over common stocks when using stop-loss orders. They include the following:

- **Less Volatility** – Individual common stocks are far more volatile than a basket of securities. Individual stocks are more prone to wild swings causing the investor to be whipsawed more often, which makes it more difficult to use stop orders effectively.

- **Less Emotional Attachment** – It is far easier to become attached to an individual company than an index. Exchange-traded index funds therefore offer investors emotional separation.

- **Less Reaction from Unexpected Announcements** – When a company makes an unexpected announcement, whether good or bad, often times the stock will react dramatically. Again, with an index-based investment an unexpected announcement by one of the companies comprising the index should have a minimal impact on any fund tracking the index.

Summary

An exit strategy provides investors with a systematic, non-emotional, and disciplined way to manage the risks associated with investing. In Strategic Index Investing the primary tool used to implement an exit strategy are stop-loss orders. Without a clearly defined exit strategy investors are at the mercy of the markets. This can cause them to make decisions by the seat of their pants at the worst possible times. With an exit strategy the investor is in control, making key decisions according to a plan instead of reacting emotionally to the market.

Chapter 13

OPTION STRATEGIES USING EXCHANGE-TRADED INDEX FUNDS

The Options Market

"To my mind, this Exchange is unquestionably the most exciting and potentially important experiment now occurring in the securities industry." These remarks by U.S. Senator Harrison A. Williams, Chairman of the Securities Subcommittee of the Senate Banking Committee, were made in April 1973 to mark the one-year anniversary of the Chicago Board Options Exchange (CBOE).

I'm sure most of those in attendance had no idea just how accurate the Senator's remarks would prove to be. In a little less than thirty years, trading volume on the four main option exchanges has exploded. In 2003, over 250 million option contracts were traded with daily volume routinely exceeding one million contracts. Since each option contract normally represents 100 shares of an underlying common stock, option trading volume is equivalent to more than 100 million shares of common stock daily. In only a few years, options have gone from being virtually non-existent to one of the most used and most dependable risk management tools available.

Today, millions of large organizations routinely use options to manage investment risks and enhance return. For example, corporations, banks, insurance companies, university endowment funds, pension funds, and mutual fund companies all consider options an integral part of their overall portfolio management strategy. With the introduction of options on some exchange-traded index funds, individual investors now have access to the same powerful option strategies once reserved for large institutional investors.

Although institutional investors have long embraced the use of options, tremendous confusion and reluctance still exists among individual investors. Some have misconceptions about the risks associated with options. Others have heard horror stories of unsuspecting investors losing their life savings in an ill-fated option trade. Or, perhaps they associate options with get-rich-quick schemes. We've all seen the claims, "How I turned $10,000 into $10 million trading options."

Given the outlandish and false claims often associated with options it's no wonder many investors are leery. It is normal to avoid the things we don't understand; that's basic human nature. Instead of avoiding options and missing out on the many benefits they have to offer, investors must educate themselves on the proper use of options. Option contracts, after all, are simply tools. No different than a hammer or a saw. In the hands of an expert carpenter a hammer can be used to build many wonderful and beautiful things. In the hands of a reckless vandal a hammer can be used to destroy many wonderful and beautiful things. The same is true of options. In the hands of an expert, they offer many benefits. If used recklessly, they can easily damage or destroy a portfolio.

Whenever I hear someone assert that options are risky, I cringe. If used properly, options are not risky. In fact, they represent one of the best ways to reduce investment risk and enhance portfolio return. In this chapter, we learn how to use options the right way. We begin with an overview of the components and unique terminology associated with options. Next, the exchange-traded index funds which offer underlying option contracts are listed. Finally, specific option strategies are introduced and explained which are easy to implement using exchange-traded index funds.

Option Fundamentals

To understand the option strategies put forth in this chapter, the reader must have a basic knowledge of how options work. Many readers will undoubtedly already be familiar with the characteristics of options and the specialized vocabulary associated with them. If so, please feel free to skip to the next section of this chapter. For those who wish to brush up on options or have a limited knowledge of how they work, the following review should prove beneficial.

An option contract is a financial instrument that gives the buyer, also referred to as the holder, the right but not the obligation to either purchase or sell a particular stock, at a fixed price, for a specified period of time. The key components of every option contract are: 1) the option type, 2) the underlying security, 3) the expiration month, 4) the strike price, sometimes referred to as the exercise price, and 5) the option premium which refers to the market price of the option. The main components of an option contract are explained below.

- **Option Type:** There are two types of option contracts: call options and put options. The option type will determine whether the holder of the option has the right to purchase or the right to sell the underlying security. A call option gives the holder the right to purchase the underlying security while a put option gives the holder the right to sell the underlying security. The option holder has the right, but not the obligation, to either purchase or sell shares of the underlying security depending on whether they hold a call or put. In contrast, an option writer (seller) has an obligation to either deliver shares (call) of the underlying security or purchase shares (put) of the underlying security if assigned.

- **Underlying Security:** The underlying security is the security subject to being purchased or sold upon exercise of the option contract by the holder. Option contracts usually cover 100 shares of the underlying security.

- **Expiration Month:** The expiration month is the date on which the holder's right to exercise the option contract ceases to exist, and therefore the option contract expires. Option contracts expire at 11:59 p.m. Eastern Standard Time on the Saturday following the third Friday of the expiration month. The last trading day is typically the third Friday of the expiration month.

- **Strike Price:** The strike price, also referred to as the exercise price, is the stated price per share for which the underlying security may be purchased by the holder, in the case of a call option, or sold by the holder, in the case of a put option.

- **Premium:** The market price of an option is called the premium and is the only component of the option contract that is not standardized. An option's premium is quoted in dollars and cents and will change throughout the day in response to changes in the value of the underlying security. To determine the dollar value of the option contract, at any given time, the premium is multiplied by the number of shares covered by the contract, usually 100 shares.

Additional Option Terminology

Additional option-related terms, which are important to know and understand prior to discussing specific strategies, are the following:

In-the-money: A *call* option is in-the-money if the price of the underlying security is above the strike price of the option contract. A *put* option is in-the-money if the price of the underlying security is below the strike price of the option contract. For example, a call option with a strike price of $50 is in-the-money as long as the underlying security is trading above $50 per share. Similarly, a put option with a strike price of $50 is in-the-money as long as the underlying security is trading below $50 per share.

Out-of-the-money: A *call* option is out-of-the-money if the price of the underlying security is below the strike price of the option contract. Similarly, a *put* option is out-of-the-money if the price of the underlying security is above the strike price of the option contract.

At-the-money: An option is said to be at-the-money if the strike price of the option is equal to the current market price of the underlying security.

Opening Transaction: An opening transaction on an option contract can be either a buy or sell. An investor who buys an option, which they are not short, is buying to open. An investor who sells an option, which they do not own is selling to open.

Closing Transaction: A closing transaction on an option contract can be either a buy or a sell. An investor who had previously written (sold) an option contract would buy the same option in order to close out their obligation. Similarly, an investor who is long an option would sell the same option to close the transaction.

Option Writer: The investor who sells an option in an opening transaction is called an option writer. The writer of an option contract creates a short position in the option they sell and is obligated to either buy stock if put to them (put option) or sell stock if called (call option).

Exercise: When an option contract is exercised, the holder exercises their right to either buy (in the case of a call option) or sell (in the case of a put option) shares of the underlying security. An option contract that can be exercised at any point prior to expiration is known as an "American-style" option contract. In contrast, "European-style" options can only be exercised on the expiration date.

Assignment: The receipt of an exercise notice is called an option assignment. The option writer receives the assignment and is obligated to either sell, in the case of a call option, or purchase in the case of a put option, shares of the underlying security at the specified strike price.

Option Contracts on Exchange-Traded Index Funds

Just as Senator Williams spoke of the exciting changes occurring within the options market in 1973, I believe that today we are seeing equally dramatic events. The creation of exchange-traded index funds, and more specifically, the ability to trade option contracts on some exchange-traded index funds, has literally revolutionized the way investors manage their portfolios.

For the first time in the history of the markets, individual investors can incorporate option strategies with a portfolio of index-based investment products (exchange-traded index funds). They can take advantage of the same option strategies used by professional portfolio managers to decrease risk and increase potential return. This is possible because of the large number of exchange-traded index funds that have underlying option contracts, shown in Exhibit 13-1.

As the exhibit shows, at present thirty-six exchange-traded index funds offer underlying option contracts. Traditional mutual funds, in contrast, are unable to offer underlying option contracts due to the outdated way they are structured. They effectively eliminate a wide range of portfolio management choices and strategies for investors. Traditional mutual fund shareholders are unable to take advantage of the exciting and important events that Senator Williams spoke so enthusiastically about some thirty years ago. Exchange-traded index funds, on the other hand, allow investors to easily implement a wide range of option-related strategies.

Exhibit 13-1:
Exchange-Traded Index Funds with Underlying Option Contracts

Fund Name	Trading Symbol
Broad-Based Funds:	
iShares Russell 1000 Index Fund	IWB
iShares Russell 1000 Growth Index Fund	IWF
iShares Russell 1000 Value Index Fund	IWD
iShares Russell 2000 Index Fund	IWM
iShares Russell 2000 Growth Index Fund	IWO
iShares Russell 2000 Value Index Fund	IWN
iShares Russell 3000 Index Fund	IWV
iShares S&P MidCap 400 Index Fund	IJH
iShares S&P MidCap 400 BARRA Growth Index Fund	IJK
iShares S&P MidCap 400 BARRA Value Index Fund	IJJ
iShares S&P 100 Index Fund	OEF
iShares MSCI EAFE Index Fund	EFA
S&P 400 MidCap SPDRs Fund	MDY
S&P 500 Index SPDRs Fund	SPY
FORTUNE 500 Index Tracking Stock	FFF
Nasdaq-100 Index Tracking Stock	QQQ
Vanguard Total Stock Market VIPERs	VTI
Vanguard Extended Market VIPERs	VXF
DIAMONDS	DIA
Sector Funds:	
iShares DJ US Financial Sector Index Fund	IYF
iShares DJ US Technology Sector Index Fund	IYW
iShares DJ US Telecommunications Sector Index Fund	IYZ
iShares Nasdaq Biotechnology Sector Index Fund	IBB
Select Sector SPDR-Materials Index Fund	XLB
Select Sector SPDR-Healthcare Index Fund	XLV
Select Sector SPDR-Consumer Staples Index Fund	XLP
Select Sector SPDR-Energy Index Fund	XLE
Select Sector SPDR-Financial Index Fund	XLF
Select Sector SPDR-Industrial Index Fund	XLI
Select Sector SPDR-Technology Index Fund	XLK
Select Sector SPDR-Utilities Index Fund	XLU
Fixed Income Funds:	
iShares Lehman 1-3 Yr. Tsy. Bd. Index Fund	SHY
iShares Lehman 7-10 Yr. Tsy. Bd. Index Fund	IEF
iShares Lehman 20+ Yr. Tsy. Bd. Index Fund	TLT
iShares Goldman Sachs Corp. Bd. Index Fund	LQD
iShares Aggregate Bond Index Fund	AGG

Source: AMEX

There are three powerful option strategies we will discuss which are suitable for most equity investors and easy to implement using exchange-traded index funds. They are covered call writing, buying protective puts, and protective collars. As we will see, when used in conjunction with exchange-traded index funds each strategy provides a unique way to limit investment risk and enhance return.

Covered Call Writing

The most commonly used option strategy today is covered call writing. It offers three substantial benefits. First, the strategy is no riskier than owning shares of a given stock or exchange-traded index fund. Second, the position can be profitable even if shares of the underlying investment remain unchanged or decrease slightly. Third, the covered call writer maintains ownership of the underlying security and is entitled to receive any dividends paid.

The following is an example of how covered call writing works. For this example, the S&P 500 Index Spiders (SPY) are used in conjunction with a six month call option. Additionally, to keep the example as simple as possible commissions are not considered. However, the applicable commissions or fees must always be taken into consideration when making an investment decision in the real world since they will have an impact on net performance. We also exclude dividends from all of the following examples.

On January 1, the following hypothetical covered call position is established.

Buy 100 shares SPY at $125
Sell 1 SPY June 135 Call at $3.50
Total Cost 100 shares of SPY = $12,500
Proceeds from Sale of Option = $350
Net Cost of Transaction ($12,500 - $350) = $12,150

This transaction is often referred to as a buy/write because shares of the underlying security are purchased at the same time the call option is sold or written. The action is to "buy" the underlying stock and simultaneously "write" a call option. The other way to initiate a covered call strategy is to write a call option against shares of a security that you already own.

In the example, the investor's cost basis or break-even point is reduced by the amount of the option premium received, which is $3.50 per share. As a result, the break-even price per share is lowered to $121.50 per share (purchase price of $125 less the premium received $3.50). Therefore, the price per share of SPY can drop by $3.50 or almost 3.0% between now and expiration and the overall position will still be profitable.

A major advantage of using options is that all possible outcomes are known in advance. For example, if the covered call strategy shown above is maintained until expiration, there are only three possible outcomes. All possible outcomes are shown in Exhibit 13-2 and explained below.

- **Possibility 1: Shares of SPY close below the strike price of $135 (out-of-the-money).** If this occurs the investor maintains their shares of SPY and the option contract expires worthless. They also keep the premium of $3.50 per share, or $350. The actual profit or loss incurred depends on the price of SPY at expiration. For example, if SPY is at $130 per share at expiration the investor realizes a profit of $850 or 6.9% even though it only represents an increase of 4% in the value of SPY. If the price per share of SPY is $120 at expiration, the investor realizes a loss of $150 or 1.23%. This is shown in Exhibit 13-2.

- **Possibility 2: Shares of SPY close above the strike price of $135 (in-the-money).** If SPY closes above $135 per share the call option will be assigned and the shares called away. If the shares are called away, the call writer is obligated to deliver

Exhibit 13-2:
Profit and Loss Analysis of a Covered Call Writing Strategy

	Market Price of SPY	% Change in Price	Dollar Gain/(Loss) of Position	Percentage Gain/Loss of Position
	$150.00	20.00%	$ 1,350.00	11.11%
	$145.00	16.00%	$ 1,350.00	11.11%
	$140.00	12.00%	$ 1,350.00	11.11%
Maximum Profit	$135.00	8.00%	$ 1,350.00	11.11%
	$130.00	4.00%	$ 850.00	6.99%
	$125.00	0.00%	$ 350.00	2.88%
Break-Even	$121.50	-2.80%	$ -	0.00%
	$120.00	-4.00%	$ (150.00)	-1.23%
	$115.00	-8.00%	$ (650.00)	-5.35%
	$110.00	-12.00%	$ (1,150.00)	-9.47%
	$105.00	-16.00%	$ (1,650.00)	-13.58%
	$100.00	-20.00%	$ (2,150.00)	-17.67%
	$ 95.00	-24.00%	$ (2,650.00)	-21.81%
Maximum Loss	$ -	-100.00%	$(12,150.00)	-100.00%

100 shares of SPY to the option holder at the agreed upon price of $135. At this point, the covered call writer realizes the maximum profit of $13.50 per share or approximately 11%, as shown in Exhibit 13-2.

- **Possibility 3: Shares of SPY close at the strike price of $135 (at-the-money).** The third possible outcome is that SPY closes exactly at $135 per share at expiration. If this occurs, the covered call writer most likely will not get assigned and therefore retain ownership of the stock. Again, this scenario is shown in Exhibit 13-2.

As we can see from the three outcomes listed above, covered call writing allows the investor to hedge his or her investment yet still have some growth potential. Also, since the covered call writer maintains ownership of the underlying security they are entitled to all dividends, making the strategy even more attractive. Finally, as is the case with most option strategies, the investor is able to evaluate all possible outcomes before initiating the position.

Potential Downside of Covered Call Writing

Like any investment strategy, covered call writing has some potential risks associated with it. The primary risk taken by a covered call writer, in addition to those risks taken by any other equity investor, is one of lost opportunity. Remember, writing the option creates an obligation for the writer that requires the potential sale of 100 shares of the underlying security, at the strike price, if assigned. In return for this, the option writer receives the option premium.

As we can see in Exhibit 13-2, the investor no longer participates as the price per share of SPY moves above the strike price of $135. This is because they are obligated to sell 100 shares at $135 per share. If the price per share of SPY is $145 at expiration, the lost opportunity cost would be calculated as follows.

Lost Opportunity = Current Share Price – (Strike Price + Premium)
Lost Opportunity = $145 – ($135 + $3.50)
Lost Opportunity = $6.50 per share

For those investors dreaming of owning a stock that doubles or triples in value, covered call writing is not a good strategy. For those investors who always look back and think of what might have been, it's not a good strategy. However, for those investors willing to accept modest returns with some downside protection covered call writing is a good strategy. There is a popular saying on Wall Street, "bulls and bears make money but pigs get slaughtered." This saying explains the logic behind covered call writing. The strategy forces the investor to take small, consistent gains instead of looking for one big hit.

Protective Puts

Investing in equities is risky. This truth must never be forgotten. Equities also represent one of the best ways to earn a high rate of return over time. Herein lies the dilemma faced by investors. How do you earn high returns and still limit risk?

In Chapter 12, dynamic stop-loss orders were shown to be a very effective risk management tool. However, they don't always work in every possible situation. For example, in the case of a security opening dramatically lower (gap opening). If an investor wishes to perfectly hedge an exchange-traded index fund position, a better alternative is to use protective puts.

A protective put is similar to an insurance policy for your investments. Most individuals would find it scary not to insure their home, car, or other valuable assets. Insurance helps to put one's mind at ease by protecting them from unforeseen disaster. Ironically, many of the same investors who would never consider going without car, home, or health insurance leave their most important assets — stocks, bonds, mutual funds — unprotected and think nothing of it. In fact, most investors never consider insuring their investments even though losing a substantial portion of their retirement account could cause untold financial hardships.

A protective put strategy is actually quite simple. It involves the purchase of one put option contract for every 100 shares of the underlying security the investor wishes to protect. This is shown in the following hypothetical example, assumed to have taken place on January 1.

Buy 100 shares of SPY at $95.00 per share
Buy 1 SPY June 90 put at $3.50
Total cost of the position = $98.50 per share

The total cost of the position is calculated by adding the option premium paid and the purchase price of SPY ($95 + $3.50 = $98.50).

The cost of insurance is 3.6% and is represented by the amount of premium paid for the put option. Similar to the covered call strategy, all potential outcomes associated with a protective put strategy are known in advance. The various profit and loss scenarios, if the protective put is held to expiration, are shown in Exhibit 13-3.

From the exhibit it's easy to see that as the price per share of SPY drops, the investor is protected. The investor's maximum loss is known in advance and is calculated as follows:

Max Loss = (Purchase Price + Option Premium) – Strike Price
Max Loss = ($95 + $3.50) – $90
Max Loss = $8.50 per share

Exhibit 13-3:
Profit and Loss Analysis of a Protective Put Position

	Market Price of SPY	% Change in Price	Dollar Gain/(Loss) of Position	Percentage Gain/Loss of Position
	$125.00	31.58%	$2,650.00	26.90%
	$120.00	26.32%	$2,150.00	21.83%
	$115.00	21.05%	$1,650.00	16.75%
	$110.00	15.79%	$1,150.00	11.68%
	$105.00	10.53%	$ 650.00	6.60%
	$100.00	5.26%	$ 150.00	1.52%
Break-Even	$ 98.50	3.68%	$ -	0.00%
	$ 95.00	0.00%	$ (350.00)	-3.55%
Maximum Loss	$ 90.00	-5.26%	$ (850.00)	-8.63%
	$ 85.00	-10.53%	$ (850.00)	-8.63%
	$ 80.00	-15.79%	$ (850.00)	-8.63%
	$ 75.00	-21.05%	$ (850.00)	-8.63%
	$ 70.00	-26.32%	$ (850.00)	-8.63%
	$ -	-100.00%	$ (850.00)	-8.63%

No matter how low the price per share of SPY is at expiration, the protective put buyer's loss will never exceed $8.50 per share. Unlike the covered call writer, the put buyer participates if shares of SPY increase in value. The break-even price is higher, as a result of the premium paid for the option, but there is no ceiling on potential profits. Similar to the covered call writer, the protective put buyer is entitled to any dividends paid.

The Put Holder's Decision

Unlike a covered call writer, the protective put buyer gets to decide if they want to exercise their put option. Because they are the owner of the put they have a decision to make if the price of the underlying security is below the strike price at expiration. For example, assume that at expiration the value of SPY has dropped by 25% to $71.25 per share. While not the outcome anticipated, the put buyer has an important decision to make.

The protective put gives the investor the right to sell 100 shares of SPY at $90 per share (the strike price). Therefore, we would anticipate that the put option would have a value of about $18.75 per share, or the amount by which the shares of SPY are in-the-money ($90-$71.25). Based on this assumption, Exhibit 13-4 shows how the position might look at expiration assuming an initial purchase of 1,000 shares of SPY and 10 put option contracts with a strike price of $90.

The numbers in the exhibit above are very straightforward. The investor has an unrealized loss of $23.75 per share or $23,750 on their investment in SPY (purchase price less current price multiplied by the number of shares owned). They also have an unrealized profit of $15.25 per share or $15,250 in the put option (current price less purchase price multiplied by the number of shares covered by the option contracts).

Even though the price per share of SPY has dropped by 25% since the date of purchase, the protective put buyer's loss is only $8.50 per share or about 8.6%. The protective put has done its job and helped hedge the majority of the loss. At this point the investor has a decision

Exhibit 13-4:
Example of Hypothetical Protective Put Held to Expiration

Cost of Shares	$95,000.00	
(1,000 shares x $95 per share)		
Current Value of SPY	$71,250.00	
Loss on 1,000 shares		**$(23,750.00)**
Total Cost of Protective Put	$ 3,500.00	
Current Value	$18,750.00	
Gain on Put Options		**$ 15,250.00**
Net Loss		**$ (8,500.00)**

to make. They can exercise the put option and sell 1,000 shares of SPY at $90 per share, realizing a net loss of $8,500. Or, they can sell the put, realizing a profit, and continue to hold the shares of SPY. An important note, the put must be sold "prior" to expiration.

If the investor sells the put option in the open market they will realize a profit of $15,250 ((18.75 – 3.50) x 10 contracts). The gain on the sale of the option will partially offset the unrealized loss in the shares of SPY. The investor now owns shares of SPY with a cost basis of essentially $79.75 (purchase price of SPY less the profit realized on the sale of the option). The profit in the put option helped offset the loss allowing the investor to own the shares at a much lower cost than the initial purchase price. However, the investor is no longer protected unless they purchase a new protective put option.

Protective Collars

Covered call writing and protective put buying are two very powerful option strategies that can be used in conjunction with exchange-traded index funds. It's possible to combine the benefits of both strategies into one with a strategy commonly referred to as a "collar."

To initiate a collar the investor simultaneously purchases put options and writes call options with differing strike prices and the same expiration month on the same underlying exchange-traded index fund. The protective collar strategy provides downside protection through the use of the put option and finances the purchase of the put, either in part or in whole, with the sale of the covered call option.

Using these two strategies together offers a truly unique way to access the equity markets. It allows the investor to know in advance their maximum potential profit and loss, assuming all positions are held to expiration. To see how a collar strategy works, we will assume an investor establishes the following hypothetical position on January 1.

Buy 100 shares of SPY at $100
Sell 1 SPY June 110 call at $4.00
Buy 1 SPY June 95 put at $5.00
Net Cost to Investor = $101 per share

In Exhibit 13-5, the potential profit and loss scenarios for this position are shown. Again, all calculations are based on the position being held intact to expiration.

As we can see from the exhibit, the break-even price of $101 is slightly above the actual purchase price. This is calculated by adding the purchase price per share of the exchange-traded index fund and the protective put, then subtracting the amount received for writing the call option (($100 + $5) –$4).

Similar to a covered call, the point of maximum profit is realized if SPY closes above $110 per share because we are obligated to sell the shares at $110 (the strike price). Also, similar to a protective put, the maximum loss will occur if the price per share of SPY is at, or below, $95.00 per share at expiration, the strike price of the put option. The maximum profit this position can produce is $9 per share.

Exhibit 13-5:
Profit and Loss Analysis of a Protective Collar Position

	Market Price of SPY	% Change in Price	Dollar Gain/(Loss) of Position	Percentage Gain/Loss of Position
	$125.00	25.00%	$ 900.00	8.91%
	$120.00	20.00%	$ 900.00	8.91%
	$115.00	15.00%	$ 900.00	8.91%
Maximum Profit	$110.00	10.00%	$ 900.00	8.91%
	$105.00	5.00%	$ 400.00	3.96%
Break-Even	$101.00	1.00%	$ -	0.00%
	$100.00	0.00%	$ (100.00)	-0.99%
Maximum Loss	$ 95.00	-5.00%	$ (600.00)	-5.94%
	$ 90.00	-10.00%	$ (600.00)	-5.94%
	$ 85.00	-15.00%	$ (600.00)	-5.94%
	$ 80.00	-20.00%	$ (600.00)	-5.94%
	$ 75.00	-25.00%	$ (600.00)	-5.94%

The maximum potential loss is $6 per share. This represents an attractive 1.5 to 1 profit to loss ratio (maximum potential profit divided by the maximum potential loss).

If the price per share of SPY drops dramatically the investor can sell the put and realize a profit while continuing to hold their shares of SPY. Likewise, if the price per share of SPY decreases the investor can purchase the short call option back, relieve their obligation to deliver shares of SPY in the future, and realize a profit on the call option transaction.

When To Use a Collar

This combination strategy is best for the investor who is not willing to take a large, unknown risk yet still wants the potential upside offered by equities. By using a protective collar strategy, the investor can easily determine their potential risk and reward in advance. It's a strategy that provides a great amount of certainty, something not available with most equity-related investments.

Protective collars are also an excellent strategy for the investor with a short-term time horizon who still wishes to participate in the growth potential of equities. Investors are often told that they must be long-term minded to invest in equities. What about the investor who wants to invest for six months or a year? Should they be banned from the markets? Absolutely not! A protective collar strategy is perfect because all potential outcomes are known in advance and the investor can literally choose the length of time they wish to be invested.

Advanced Option Strategies

There are two additional option strategies, which we will discuss, that are easy to implement and offer tremendous potential when used in conjunction with exchange-traded index funds. They are uncovered put writing (naked puts) and writing covered calls in conjunction with naked puts (combination). Both strategies are outlined below.

Uncovered Put Writing

When an investor sells a put option, as an opening transaction, they are obligated to purchase shares of the underlying security, at the strike price, if the option is assigned. For instance, if an investor sells a put option on shares of SPY with a strike price of $95 they are obligated to purchase 100 shares of SPY at $95 per share if the option is assigned. This is commonly referred to as a "naked" put writer or simply as a "naked" put.

In return for agreeing to purchase shares of SPY, at the strike price, the put writer receives the option premium. They keep the premium regardless of whether or not the option is assigned. Therefore, writing a put option is considered an income generating strategy.

For the following example we will assume shares of SPY are at $100 per share. On January 1, an investor sells 1 SPY June 90 put at

$2.50, which generates $250 immediately (100 shares x $2.50). In return for the premium received, the investor is obligated to buy 100 shares of SPY, at $90 per share, if the option is assigned. Exhibit 13-6 shows all possible profit and loss scenarios if the position is held to expiration.

As the exhibit shows, the maximum profit the naked put writer can earn is the premium received. In our example, the premium received is $250. The maximum profit occurs if the price per share of SPY closes above the option's strike price, which is $90, at expiration. The reason why is simple. If the option holder can sell his or her shares of SPY in the open market for an amount greater than $90, they will do so. The only reason the option holder would "put" shares

Exhibit 13-6:
Analysis of Naked Put Position

	Market Price of SPY	Amount (In)/Out of Money	Gain/(Loss) at Expiration
	$125.00	$ 35.00	$ 250.00
	$120.00	$ 30.00	$ 250.00
	$115.00	$ 25.00	$ 250.00
	$110.00	$ 20.00	$ 250.00
	$105.00	$ 15.00	$ 250.00
	$100.00	$ 10.00	$ 250.00
	$ 95.00	$ 5.00	$ 250.00
	$ 90.50	$ 0.50	$ 250.00
Maximum Profit	$ 90.00	$ -	$ 250.00
Break-Even	$ 87.50	$ (2.50)	$ -
	$ 85.00	$ (5.00)	$ (250.00)
	$ 80.00	$(10.00)	$ (750.00)
	$ 75.00	$(15.00)	$(1,250.00)
	$ 70.00	$(20.00)	$(1,750.00)
Maximum Loss	$ -	$(90.00)	$(8,750.00)

of SPY to the option writer is if the price per share of SPY is below the strike price of the option, or $90 per share.

Even if the price per share of SPY drops, from the time the option is written up to expiration, the naked put writer can still make a profit. As long as the price does not close below $87.50 per share or approximately 12.5% under its current value the naked put writer will realize a gain. The break-even point for a naked put writer is determined by subtracting the option premium from the strike price ($90 - $2.50).

At first glance, naked put writing may seem like a risky strategy. It's not. The risk involved with naked put writing is no greater than the risk associated with owning shares of an exchange-traded index fund. Because the naked put writer is obligated to buy 100 shares of the underlying security for each option contract sold, the worst possible outcome is the naked put writer ends up owning shares of the underlying security. Unlike equity ownership the naked put rider doesn't participate in the price appreciation of the underlying shares. For example, no matter how high shares of the underlying security may go, the maximum the naked put writer can make is the amount of the initial premium received.

Writing Covered Calls with Naked Puts
The last option strategy we will review is commonly referred to as a "combination." It entails writing covered calls and writing naked puts simultaneously. This strategy allows the investor to generate substantially greater amounts of option premium than possible by simply selling puts or calls independently. The following hypothetical example shows the benefits associated with a combination strategy. Again, we will assume the following transactions take place on January 1.

Buy 100 shares of SPY at $100 per share
Sell 1 SPY June 110 call at $4.50
Sell 1 SPY June 90 put at $3.50
Net Investment = $92.00 per share

This strategy offers the investor several important benefits. First, if shares of SPY remain unchanged, at around $100 per share, the investor realizes a profit of almost 8% over a six month period ($8 of option premium / $100 per share cost). Likewise, if the price per share of SPY drops by $8, or 8%, the investor still breaks even.

If the share price of SPY closes above $110, at expiration, the investor will realize a maximum profit of $18 per share, or about a 19% return, even though the price of SPY only increased by 10%, from $100 to $110. Exhibit 13-7 shows all potential outcomes related to this strategy, if held to expiration.

If the price per share of SPY falls below the strike price of the put, which is $90, the investor may have an additional 100 shares of SPY put to them at $90 per share. Because the investor is obligated to buy additional shares of SPY, this strategy is typically used when an investor wants to get into the market slowly and is willing to buy some shares now and average down in the future, should the price move lower.

For example, if an investor wants to own 200 shares of SPY, but doesn't want to purchase all the shares at once, this is an excellent strategy. By purchasing 100 shares now and selling a covered call combined with a naked put the investor benefits in two ways. If the shares of SPY move higher, they participate because they own 100 shares. If the shares of SPY move lower, they will have an additional 100 shares put to them, but at a price under the current market price. Therefore, the investor ends up with a total of 200 shares but presumably at a much lower average cost per share.

Summary

For the first time in the history of the markets investors have access to some of the most advanced portfolio management strategies ever offered. Using exchange-traded index funds in conjunction with options, investors can easily implement a number of portfolio manage-

Exhibit 13-7:
Profit and Loss Analysis of Option Combination Position

	Market Price of SPY	% Change in Price	Dollar Gain/(Loss) of Position	Percentage Gain/Loss of Position
	$125.00	25.00%	$ 1,800.00	19.57%
	$120.00	20.00%	$ 1,800.00	19.57%
	$115.00	15.00%	$ 1,800.00	19.57%
Maximum Profit	$110.00	10.00%	$ 1,800.00	19.57%
	$105.00	5.00%	$ 1,300.00	14.13%
	$100.00	0.00%	$ 800.00	8.70%
	$ 95.00	-5.00%	$ 300.00	3.26%
Break-Even	$ 92.00	-8.00%	$ -	0.00%
	$ 90.00	-10.00%	$ (200.00)	-2.17%
	$ 85.00	-15.00%	$ (1,200.00)	-13.04%
	$ 80.00	-20.00%	$ (2,200.00)	-23.91%
	$ 75.00	-25.00%	$ (3,200.00)	-34.78%
Maximum Loss	$ -	-100.00%	$(18,200.00)	-197.83%

ment strategies once available only to institutional investors. The most commonly used option strategies include covered call writing, protective put buying, naked put writing, collars, and combinations. Options, if used properly, allow investors to initiate equity positions with known outcomes. They allow investors to limit risk and enhance potential return. The versatility of options combined with exchange-traded index funds offer investors a wide range of powerful choices.

Chapter 14

ADVANCED PORTFOLIO MANAGEMENT STRATEGIES

Additional Strategies

In this, the final chapter of Part 3, the focus is on two advanced portfolio management strategies which are easily implemented using exchange-traded index funds. The first strategy allows the investor to profit if the market moves lower. The second strategy allows the investor to earn greater potential returns if the market moves higher, through the use of leverage.

While both strategies offer unique profit opportunities, they may not be suitable for every investor. Additionally, these strategies are only appropriate for certain taxable, non-retirement accounts. Government restrictions placed on retirement accounts (i.e., Individual Retirement Accounts, 401k, Pension, etc.) limit the types of strategies one may use. As always, before implementing any strategy discussed in this book, or any investment book for that matter, the investor should know and understand all risks and benefits.

The Market Does Not Always Go Up

The fact of the matter is that the market does not always go up. This shouldn't be a surprise to anyone. When the market does go up, investors earn the rate of return of the underlying investments they are holding. For example, if you own shares of the iShares S&P 500

Index Fund and the S&P 500 Index produces a total return of 15%, you should earn about 15%.

What options do investors have when the market moves lower, as we know it does from time to time? Historically, when the market moves lower most investors either stay in the market (buy-and-hold) or move to a money market account to protect their capital. By moving into a money market account they earn prevailing money market rates, regardless of how much the market may drop. For example, if an investor moves from the iShares S&P 500 Index fund into a money market fund, in anticipation of a market decline, they earn money market rates. They don't actually profit from the market moving lower, they only protect their capital. If the market subsequently decreases by 25%, the investor earns the prevailing money market rate, and that is it.

What if an investor wants to do more than simply preserve capital when the market moves lower? In fact, many professional investors believe it's far easier to make money in a bear market than in a bull market. The reason why is simple. While bull markets usually take years to complete, market corrections tend to be severe and relatively quick in duration. This is seen in Exhibit 14-1, which compares the ten worst one-day losses for the Dow Jones Industrial Average with the ten best one-day gains, over the last twenty years.

As the exhibit shows, the market typically drops much faster than it goes up. Professional traders, institutional money managers, and hedge fund managers have known this for years. They routinely implement strategies designed specifically to take advantage of opportunities, such as those shown in Exhibit 14-1. Unfortunately, individual investors have historically not been able to easily take advantage of such attractive profit making opportunities. That is until now.

Exhibit 14-1:
Ten Largest Single Day Percentage Gains and Losses
for Dow Jones Industrial Average since 1985

Days with Greatest Net Gain:

Date	Close	Net Point Change	Percentage Change
3/16/2000	10630.60	499.19	4.93%
7/24/2002	8191.29	488.95	6.35%
7/29/2002	8711.88	447.49	5.41%
4/5/2001	9918.05	402.63	4.23%
4/18/2001	10615.83	399.10	3.91%
9/8/1998	8020.78	380.53	4.98%
9/24/2001	8603.86	368.05	4.47%
5/16/2001	11215.92	342.95	3.15%
12/5/2000	10898.72	338.62	3.21%
10/28/1997	7498.32	337.17	4.71%
	Average Gain		**4.54%**

Days with Greatest Net Loss:

Date	Close	Net Point Change	Percentage Change
9/17/2001	8920.70	-684.81	-7.13%
4/14/2000	10305.77	-617.78	-5.66%
10/27/1997	7161.15	-554.26	-7.19%
8/31/1998	7539.07	-512.61	-6.37%
10/19/1987	1738.74	-508.00	-22.61%
3/12/2001	10208.25	-436.37	-4.10%
7/19/2002	8019.26	-390.23	-4.63%
9/20/2001	8376.21	-382.92	-4.37%
10/12/2000	10034.58	-379.21	-3.64%
3/7/2000	9796.03	-374.47	-3.68%
	Average Loss		**-6.94%**

Source: Dow Jones & Company

Selling Short

Exchange-traded index funds offer investors the ability to profit from a decline in the overall value of a given index by initiating a short position, also known as selling short or shorting. Selling short entails selling shares of a security, which you don't own. The short seller must first borrow the security they wish to sell short, typically from a brokerage firm, and then sell the borrowed shares in the open market. At some point in the future, the short seller must offset the short position. This can be accomplished by purchasing an equal number of shares in the open market or by delivering an equal number of the shares to the brokerage firm, which loaned them the shares initially.

Everyone knows that the way to make money in stocks is to buy low and sell high. This is also true when selling short. With one big exception: the process is reversed. Instead of buying an investment in anticipation of selling it at a higher price, the investment is sold in anticipation of buying it back at a lower price. The investor still makes money regardless of whether they buy low first and then sell high, or they sell high first and then buy low.

For example, if an investor feels strongly that the market will lose value over the next few months they could do the following: sell short 1,000 shares of IVV (iShares S&P 500 Index Shares). To sell 1,000 shares of IVV short, the investor must first borrow the shares from their broker. The 1,000 shares are then sold at the current market price. For this example we will assume the current market price per share of IVV is $75. Upon completion of the short sale, the investor's account will show a credit of $75,000 (1,000 shares sold at $75 per share). The investor's account will also show a negative position of 1,000 shares of IVV representing their obligation to repay the borrowed stock at some point in the future.

If the investor is right and the market drops, they make a profit. The maximum profit is realized if the price per share of IVV goes to zero, a very unlikely scenario when shorting shares of an exchange-traded index fund. However, if the price per share of IVV drops to

$50 and the investor decides to close out the short position, they will realize a profit, before expenses, of $25,000 (1,000 x ($75-$50)). Exhibit 14-2 shows various potential outcomes associated with this hypothetical short sale.

As the exhibit shows, if the price per share of IVV increases, a loss occurs. For example, at $100 per share the investor has an unrealized loss of $25 per share or $25,000 (1,000 x $25). In fact, when selling short the potential loss is theoretically unlimited since there is no limit to how high the price per share of IVV may go. At $175 per share the short seller realizes a paper loss of $100,000 (current price minus short sale price multiplied by the number of shares). At this point, the loss exceeds the $75,000 initially generated by the short sale, or a loss of 133%.

Because there is no limit to how high an equity-based investment may go, selling short is riskier than simply owning shares of an investment. The risk is far greater, however, when shorting shares of an individual common stock compared to shares of an exchange-traded index fund. The reason why is because exchange-traded index funds are index-based baskets of securities. Some funds are comprised of hundreds if not thousands of different securities. It's rare

Exhibit 14-2:
Analysis of Hypothetical Short Sale (1,000 shares @ $75 per share)

Market Price of IVV	Dollar Gain/(Loss)*	Percentage Gain/(Loss)
$150.00	$(75,000.00)	-100.00%
$125.00	$(50,000.00)	-66.70%
$100.00	$(25,000.00)	-33.40%
$ 75.00	$ -	0.00%
$ 50.00	$25,000.00	33.40%
$ 25.00	$50,000.00	66.70%
$ -	$75,000.00	100.00%

* Based on 1,000 shares

to see a broad-based index jump 15%, 20%, or more over the course of a few days. In contrast, shares of common stocks can easily move up rapidly due to a wide variety of reasons, such as a positive news story or a good earnings release. As we will see, there are strategies that can help reduce the risks associated with selling short.

The Mechanics of Shorting Exchange-Traded Index Funds

Shares of exchange-traded index funds represent ownership in a basket of securities. Therefore, many of the same rules that apply when shorting shares of individual common stocks don't apply to exchange-traded index funds. In fact, shorting shares of exchange-traded index funds is actually easier, less cumbersome, and safer than shorting shares of common stocks.

For example, shares of common stocks can only be shorted on an up-tick in price or a no change up-tick in price. An up-tick is any trade that is higher than the previous trade. For instance, if shares of ABC are trading at $25 per share and the following trade is $25.50, it would be considered an up-tick.

Shares of exchange-traded index funds, in contrast, can be sold short on either an up-tick or down-tick in price, making it much easier to execute a short sale, especially during periods of declining prices. Exhibit 14-3 summarizes the structural differences between shares of common stocks and shares of exchange-traded index funds when selling short.

Managing Risk When Selling Short

While many investors might feel a bit uneasy selling something they don't own, it should not keep them from exploring the possible benefits. When it comes to investing, we often miss out on opportunities due to fear or lack of understanding. If used properly, selling short can offer a number of substantial portfolio management benefits. This is not to say that it's a risk-free strategy, because it's not. From

Exhibit 14-3:
Differences Between Common Stocks and
Exchange-Traded Index Funds When Selling Short

	Exchange-Traded Index Funds	Common Stocks
Sell short on down-tick	Yes	No
Sell short on up-tick	Yes	Yes
Sell short on no change down-tick	Yes	No
Sell short on no change up-tick	Yes	Yes

my experience, however, once an investor fully understands the benefits and risks associated with selling short they are usually more than willing to try it.

Selling short does present several unique risk considerations that need to be addressed. When selling short, it's important that we limit our risk through the use of a comprehensive risk management strategy, similar to the way risk is managed when establishing long positions. Two very good risk management strategies to use are dynamic buy-stop orders and protective call options.

Dynamic Buy-Stop Orders
In Chapter 12, we saw how stop-loss orders can be used to limit the risks associated with owning an investment. What many investors may not realize is that stop orders can also be used when purchasing an investment. A buy-stop order is an order that becomes a market order to buy a given security if, and only if, the underlying security trades at the stop price. Because the short seller eventually must buy the shares back, a buy-stop order is a good way to manage risk.

For example, assume an investor sells short 1,000 shares of IVV at $75 per share. If the maximum they are willing to risk is 7.50% of the initial proceeds, a buy-stop order would be entered at $80.63 per share. This is calculated by adding 7.50%, the maximum acceptable loss, to the initial sell price of $75 per share ($75 + ($75 x .075).

To make the buy-stop dynamic, we would adjust the stop price on any day that shares of IVV close at a new post short sale low. The dynamic buy-stop price is never raised, only lowered. For instance, if shares of IVV subsequently closed at $72.50 per share the buy-stop would be lowered to $77.94 ($72.50 + ($72.50 x .075)) and so on. Eventually, we can expect the price per share of IVV to have a sustained rally of at least 7.50%. When the buy-stop order is activated 1,000 shares of IVV are purchased and returned to the lender. Exhibit 14-4 shows how a dynamic buy-stop order works, assuming an initial short sale at $75 per share and a 7.50% stop price.

Similar to the dynamic stop-loss order, the dynamic buy-stop order only works if it's continually monitored and adjusted accordingly. Handled properly, a buy-stop order will effectively lower the risks associated with selling short. If not handled properly, it provides only a limited amount of protection.

Exhibit 14-4:
Hypothetical Short Sale with a 7.5% Dynamic Buy-Stop

	Closing Price	Action	Price	Buy Stop Price
Day 1	$75.00	Sell Short	$75.00	$80.63
Day 2	$75.50			
Day 3	$76.00			
Day 4	$75.00			
Day 5	$74.25			$79.82
Day 6	$73.50			$79.01
Day 7	$74.00			
Day 8	$74.50			
Day 9	$73.00			$78.48
Day 10	$72.25			$77.67
Day 11	$70.00			$75.25
Day 12	$72.50			
Day 13	$73.25			
Day 14	$75.00	Cover Short	$75.25	

Protective Call Options

Another way to limit the risks associated with selling short is by purchasing a protective call option. A call option gives the holder the right, but not the obligation, to purchase shares of the underlying security at the strike price for a predetermined amount of time. If an investor is short shares of an exchange-traded index fund, owning a call option on the fund they are short offers them a way to repurchase the shares at a predetermined price in the future. As is the case with options, we know in advance the maximum gain and loss associated with the position.

For example, assume an investor sold 1,000 shares of IVV short at $75 and simultaneously purchased 10 IVV call options, with a strike price of $80, at $4. At any time prior to expiration the call option gives the investor the right to purchase 1,000 shares of IVV at the strike price of $80. In this situation, the maximum potential loss is $9 per share or $9,000. It is calculated as follows:

Maximum Loss = (Strike Price + Premium) –
Short Sale Price
Maximum Loss = ($80 + $4) – $75
Maximum Loss per Share = $9

Exhibit 14-5 shows the various profit and loss possibilities associated with the above transactions.

As the exhibit shows, the investor realizes a profit if the price of IVV drops below $71, the break-even price. Due to the cost of the call option, the break-even price is $4 under the initial short sale price. Therefore, if the price of IVV drops to $65 over the course of time, the investor realizes a profit of $6 per share ((short sale price + option premium) – strike price).

A clear disadvantage associated with using a protective call option to protect a short position is that the investor is only protected for a limited amount of time. Once the option expires the investor will have to make a decision if they wish to remain protected: close

Exhibit 14-5:
Example of Short Sale Combined with Protective Call

Market Price of IVV	Unrealized Gains	Unrealized Losses	Percentage Change
$95.00	$ -	$(9,000.00)	-12.68%
$85.00	$ -	$(9,000.00)	-12.68%
$80.00	$ -	$(9,000.00)	-12.68%
$78.00	$ -	$(7,000.00)	-9.86%
$76.00	$ -	$(5,000.00)	-7.04%
$75.00	$ -	$(4,000.00)	-5.63%
$71.00	$ -	$ -	0.00%
$70.00	$ 1,000.00	$ -	1.41%
$65.00	$ 6,000.00	$ -	8.45%
$60.00	$11,000.00	$ -	15.49%
$55.00	$16,000.00	$ -	22.54%
$50.00	$21,000.00	$ -	29.58%
$45.00	$26,000.00		36.62%

the short position or purchase another protective call option. Keep in mind, the cost to purchase another option contract decreases potential returns. With the purchase of each new option the investor's breakeven price decreases by the amount paid for the option.

Selling Short to Hedge

One of the most popular reasons to sell short is to hedge an existing position. For example, take an investor who owns 1,000 shares of IVV with a cost basis of $50 per share. If shares of IVV are currently trading at $100 per share the investor has unrealized gains of $50,000 ((current price - cost basis) x number of shares). What can the investor do if they are convinced the market is going to move lower over the next few months?

The most obvious answer is to sell the 1,000 shares of IVV realizing a taxable capital gain of $50,000. This will protect them against any further market weakness. It also creates a potentially huge tax liability. The taxes on a $50,000 gain could be as high as $25,000 depending on the investor's tax situation.

Another alternative is to hedge the position by selling short, a strategy often referred to as "short-against-the-box." To initiate the strategy, the investor sells 1,000 shares of IVV short at the current market price of $100 per share. They now have two separate investments in IVV, which are the following:

Long 1,000 Shares of IVV at $50 per share

Short 1,000 Shares of IVV at $100 per share

If shares of IVV drop, the short position gains dollar for dollar what is lost in the long position. If shares of IVV increase, the long position gains dollar for dollar what is lost in the short position. The investor has completely neutralized the market and eliminated the risk associated with the market going lower. Best of all, no taxable gains were created. As long as the short position is maintained the investor is perfectly hedged.

If the market moves lower, as the investor is anticipating, they can close out the short position at a profit. Any profits realized on the short position will offset the paper loss in the long position. Therefore, after closing out the short position the investor remains in the market, but at a much lower level. Best of all, their portfolio didn't drop in value with the market. This scenario is shown in Exhibit 14-6.

As the exhibit shows, a short-against-the-box strategy protects the investor from a market decline. Unfortunately, it also keeps them from profiting should the market increase in value. At some point, the investor must either buy back the shares they are short or deliver the shares they own to cover the short position. When this occurs, they will no longer be hedged.

Exhibit 14-6:
Example of Short Hedge Position

	Price of IVV	Current Value	Gain/(Loss)
Portfolio after Short Sale:			
Long 1,000 Shares IVV	$100.00	$ 100,000.00	
Short 1,000 Shares IVV	$100.00	$(100,000.00)	
Six Months Later:			
Long 1,000 Shares IVV	$ 80.00	$ 80,000.00	$(20,000.00)
Short 1,000 Shares IVV	$ 80.00	$ (80,000.00)	$ 20,000.00
Net Change to Portfolio			$0.00
One Year Later:			
Long 1,000 Shares IVV	$ 65.00	$ 65,000.00	$(35,000.00)
Short 1,000 Shares IVV	$ 65.00	$ 65,000.00	$ 35,000.00
Net Change to Portfolio			$0.00

Margin Trading

Another strategy investors can use to enhance return is buying on margin. Margin is the term used to describe a loan, made by a brokerage firm to an investor, for the purpose of purchasing securities. Almost all exchange-traded securities, including exchange-traded index funds, can be purchased on margin.

When shares of a given exchange-traded index fund are purchased on margin the investor is required to initially pay for 50% of the purchase amount in cash. The brokerage firm lends the investor the remaining 50% necessary for the purchase. The amount the investor can borrow depends on the initial margin requirements at the time of purchase. The Federal Reserve Board sets initial margin requirements for all brokerage firms, which have varied over the years from a low of 5% to a high of 100% required. Currently, the initial margin requirement is set at 50%.

The interest rate charged on the outstanding loan is called the margin rate and varies based on the brokerage firm, the size of the loan, and the current broker call rate. The broker call rate is to brokerage firms what the prime lending rate is to banks. To determine the margin rate to charge a given client, the brokerage firm starts with the broker call rate then adds basis points based on the amount borrowed. In general, the larger the loan the lower the rate you will be charged. Margin interest is usually calculated daily and charged monthly. If unpaid, it will simply increase the debit or loan balance due. In essence, it's the reverse of compounding. You pay interest on interest.

Margin allows the investor to leverage their portfolio increasing potential returns. For instance, if an investor has $50,000 available and wants to buy shares of the iShares Russell 2000 Growth Index Fund (IWO), at $50 per share, they can do one of the following. They can purchase 1,000 shares of IWO at $50 per share for a total investment of $50,000 and pay for the transaction fully. Or, they can purchase 2,000 shares of IWO at $50 per share for a total investment of $100,000. The investor deposits $50,000 with their brokerage firm and the brokerage firm loans them the additional $50,000 necessary to cover the purchase. Exhibit 14-7 shows the possible outcomes associated with the two hypothetical transactions.

As the exhibit shows, a 10% increase in the price of IWO produces two very different results. The cash purchase produced a 10% gain or $5,000, as would be expected. The margin purchase, in contrast, produced a gain of $10,000 (2,000 x $5) or 20%. The exact same percentage change in the price of IWO resulted in two very different outcomes. Margin allowed the investor to dramatically increase their return, earning double the amount possible with an all cash investment.

Assuming a margin loan rate of 7% and a six month holding period, the margin transaction has total costs of $1,750. This represents the interest due on $50,000, at 7%, for six months. We are assuming the investor paid the interest each month instead of letting it accrue. Even when the interest charges are considered, the margin

Exhibit 14-7:
Comparison of Profit and Loss With and Without Margin

Transaction	All Cash Transaction	Margin Transaction
Original Purchase:		
Number of Shares	1,000	2,000
Price Per Share	$ 50.00	$ 50.00
Dollar Outlay	$ 50,000.00	50,000.00
Loan from Broker	$ -	$ 50,000.00
Total Value	$ 50,000.00	$100,000.00
Profit at $55 per share:		
Number of Shares	1,000	2,000
Current Value	$ 55,000.00	$110,000.00
Investment Excluding Loan	$ 50,000.00	$ 50,000.00
Net Profit	$ 5,000.00	$ 10,000.00
Rate of Return	10.00%	20.00%
Loss at $45 per share:		
Number of Shares	1,000	2,000
Current Value	$ 45,000.00	$ 90,000.00
Investment Excluding Loan	$ 50,000.00	$ 50,000.00
Net Loss	$ (5,000.00)	$ (10,000.00)
Rate of Return	-10.0%	-20.00%

transaction produced a substantially higher rate of return. Keep in mind, the longer a margin balance is maintained the greater the costs associated with the investment and the less attractive it may be.

Risks Associated with Margin
Any time leverage is used risk is magnified. Margin is no exception. The downside of margin is that it magnifies all losses. For example, if we assume the shares of IWO, from the previous example, dropped by 10% instead of increasing by 10% we see a very different outcome.

The cash transaction will lose 10% or $5,000. However, the margin purchase results in a loss of $10,000 or 20%, as shown previously in Exhibit 14-7. As we can see, the margin investor lost twice the amount as the cash investor even though the price of the investment dropped the same for both. When margin interest is added to the equation, the net loss is even greater.

If the price of IWO continues to drop, the investor will reach a point where they will receive a margin call. A margin call is a request, from the brokerage firm, for an additional deposit of funds in order to increase the investor's equity in the account. If the price continues to drop, the firm will ask for additional monies from the client. While the NYSE sets minimum acceptable margin requirements, individual brokerage firms often set higher requirements, especially during periods of increased market volatility.

To avoid the potential risks associated with margin an investor can use one of the previously discussed risk management strategies, such as dynamic stop-loss orders or protective puts. Before using margin, an investor should also make absolutely certain he or she fully understands all margin rules and regulations. The worst possible way to learn the inner workings of a margin account is by receiving an unexpected margin call.

Summary

For those investors interested in more advanced portfolio management strategies selling short and margin present an interesting alternative. Selling short allows the investor to profit if the market moves lower. It also allows investors with large amounts of unrealized gains to perfectly hedge market risk without selling their investment and creating taxable gains. For more aggressive investors, buying on margin provides a way to increase returns through the use of leverage. However, with leverage comes greater risk.

Part Four

Building a
Better Portfolio

Chapter 15

BUILDING YOUR PORTFOLIO

How To Get Started

Everything presented up to now has been designed to help you do one thing: become a better investor. Some of the ideas presented, in the previous three sections, are undoubtedly new to you. They may contradict your most firmly held beliefs about investing. For example, if you've always followed a buy-and-hold strategy using traditional actively managed mutual funds, the ideas put forth in this book are nothing short of revolutionary.

Way back in Part 1, the two key components of Strategic Index Investing were put forth. They are 1) building a solid foundation using strategies based on proven financial principles and 2) implementing the strategies with the best possible investment tools. In Part 2, exchange-traded index funds were shown to be the best portfolio management tools available today, offering substantial advantages over traditional mutual funds and common stocks. In Part 3, portfolio management strategies based on proven financial principles were presented.

In Part 4, we bring together everything presented in the previous three sections with one goal in mind: to construct the most efficient portfolio possible. In doing so, the intention is not to detail every possible obstacle you might face in the real world. Portfolio management, after all, while based on scientific research is not an exact science. Many factors will impact your portfolio and influence your actions, which can never be completely accounted for in a book. Instead, the intention is to outline the steps necessary to build a fundamentally sound portfolio using the principles of Strategic Index Investing.

In this chapter, the steps which comprise Strategic Index Investing are introduced and explained. In Chapter 16, one of the most important, yet least understood aspects of portfolio management is discussed: the cost of investment advice. In Chapter 17, the final chapter of Part 4, a list of investing rules is presented designed to make you think about the portfolio management process.

Creating an Investment Policy Statement (IPS)

An Investment Policy Statement is a written document that serves as a road map of sorts for investors. Widely used by institutional money managers and pension fund administrators, the IPS is an important planning tool. Similar to a business plan, it lays out the key steps of portfolio management, such as the type of investments to be used, the overall asset allocation, and how performance will be measured. In fact, the Investment Policy Statement is such an important part of building a fundamentally sound portfolio that most professional money managers would never think of investing a dime of a client's money without one.

Portfolio management takes planning. Without a plan we often find ourselves blowing in the wind, changing directions with every new fad that happens along. Planning is not only important when investing. It's an important part of most major tasks we undertake. Would you think of going on an extended family vacation without planning? Of course you wouldn't. A big part of going on a vacation is planning the events you want to do and deciding how best to get there. There is also the need to estimate costs involved and travel time. It's sad, but many investors spend more time planning their summer vacation than they do charting their financial future.

The Investment Policy Statement is an important planning tool because it provides an overview of how the portfolio is to be managed. As such, it should be kept in a handy location and referred to frequently to insure that your portfolio remains on track. The Investment Policy Statement needs to contain the following:

1. The investor's goals, objectives, and acceptable risk tolerance.
2. The optimal strategic asset allocation mix.
3. A list of acceptable investment products and an implementation plan.
4. An overview of any active strategies that are to be used.
5. A clear review process to measure success, ongoing monitoring, and rebalancing.

As we can see, the Investment Policy Statement sets forth all relevant issues regarding how the portfolio is to be managed, specific guidelines that must be followed, and what standards will be used to measure performance and determine if the portfolio is achieving its stated objectives. The IPS provides a level of comfort, particularly during periods of market uncertainty because it represents a plan of action based on sound financial principles. In this respect, it can be thought of as a security blanket for the nervous investor.

Step 1: Identify Goals and Risk Tolerance

Before a single dollar is invested you must determine how much risk you are willing to accept in exchange for expected future returns. To identify your optimal portfolio, several important factors must be analyzed. These include, but are not limited to, investment time horizon, ability and willingness to assume risk, expected rate of return, liquidity requirements, overall investment objectives, and the amount of time you can commit to management of the portfolio. While rarely discussed, the last consideration is important because portfolio management does place demands on the investor's time. If you are not willing, or unable to commit the time necessary to effectively manage your portfolio, then it's imperative that you find help. Not to do so may have devastating results.

In Chapters 9 and 10, investors were classified by the amount of risk they were willing to assume. As we discussed, the three general types of investors based on risk tolerance are conservative, moderate, and aggressive. Rather than accept broad generalizations, it's possible to create risk and return profiles suited to meet the needs of virtually any investor. Looking to history for guidance and following the principles of asset allocation, we can create a range of investor profiles based on acceptable levels of risk and expected return for any given time period. Exhibit 15-1 shows the wide range of investor profiles, which can be created.

A problem all investors face is quantifying risk. For many, risk is a somewhat vague concept that is hard to visualize. A good way to help measure risk is to put it in terms of real dollars rather than sim-

Exhibit 15-1:
Example of Wide Range of Types of Investors

Investor Type	Expected Return	Standard Deviation
Ultra Conservative	5.96%	5.05%
Very Conservative	6.73%	5.81%
Strongly Conservative	7.78%	6.15%
Conservative	8.68%	7.36%
Somewhat Conservative	9.58%	8.89%
Slightly Conservative	10.04%	9.74%
Balanced/Conservative Bias	10.63%	10.90%
Balanced	11.45%	12.38%
Balanced/Aggressive Bias	11.90%	13.22%
Slightly Aggressive	12.42%	14.30%
Somewhat Aggressive	12.94%	15.42%
Aggressive	13.39%	16.30%
Strongly Aggressive	14.30%	18.22%
Very Aggressive	15.13%	19.93%
Ultra Aggressive	15.40%	20.64%

ply as a percentage. For example, it is one thing to say you are willing to accept a 10% loss over any given one-year time period in return for a certain expected return. It is quite another to say you are willing to lose $10,000, assuming your portfolio has a value of $100,000. Both represent a loss of 10%. By stating the potential losses in dollar terms it seems more tangible. Especially when you think about how hard it is to earn $10,000 and some of the things you could do with the money.

Finally, when setting portfolio goals and objectives it is important that you remain realistic and, most importantly, remain honest with yourself. There is an old warning that most of my former high school teachers had committed to memory. When passing out a test they would remind the class, "When you cheat on a test you are only cheating yourself." The same is true when setting investment goals. If you are not completely honest with yourself about the amount of risk you can handle, you are only hurting yourself.

Many times investors have told me that they would be willing to take on more risk if it meant they could earn a higher return. They think the potential to earn more money will allow them to endure the added risk. Let me be clear: it won't. If you cannot handle high risk and volatility, even the highest *potential* return will not help you cope. You will be unable to ride out the inevitable hard times and your overall portfolio will suffer. In the end, the only one that will get hurt, if you are not true to yourself and take on more risk than you can handle, will be you. Therefore, the first step in creating the best possible portfolio is to accurately and truthfully determine the amount of risk you are willing to assume.

Step 2: Develop a Strategic Asset Allocation Plan

Once you have a clear understanding of your tolerance for risk, expected return, and investment goals the next step is to determine the appropriate combination of investments that will allow you to achieve your goals. As discussed in Chapters 9 and 10, this is commonly referred to as asset allocation or strategic asset allocation. The asset mix you choose should reflect your liquidity requirements, tolerance for risk, targeted rate of return, income needs, and investment time horizon.

Asset allocation makes it possible to find the optimal portfolio to match the risk and return objectives of any investor. For example, in Exhibit 15-1 we listed a number of different investor profiles based on the level of risk and expected return suitable for various investors. Following the principles of asset allocation, it's possible to find the optimal portfolio that will satisfy each risk profile shown in the exhibit. The customized portfolio that satisfies each investor's risk and return objectives is shown in Exhibit 15-2.

As we can see from the exhibit, asset allocation provides a platform, which allows every investor regardless of risk tolerance, performance objective or timeframe to develop a well-diversified portfolio best suited for them. Also, asset allocation allows the investor to ride out the inevitable tough markets since they know the expected maximum loss and gain associated with their portfolio.

Step 3: Implementation

As we saw in Part 2, exchange-traded index funds are the best tool to use when implementing an asset allocation plan. There are several reasons why. They are index-based meaning they provide pure asset class exposure at all times. Exchange-traded index funds are also very cost-effective, tax-efficient, and offer a high level of portfolio management flexibility.

With over 125 exchange-traded index funds available, however, determining the appropriate funds to use is not necessarily a simple task. When comparing funds, the decision should first and foremost be based on the asset class we are attempting to track. For example, if the strategic asset allocation plan you are using calls for 25% in large cap growth stocks, then an exchange-traded index fund that tracks a

Exhibit 15-2:
Asset Allocation Needed to Achieve Desired Risk and Expected Return

Investor Type	Expected Return	Standard Deviation	Allocation Needed to Achieve Desired Risk and Expected Return						
			LCE	MSE	FE	FFI	LTB	ITB	MM
Ultra Conservative	5.96%	5.05%	0%	0%	0%	10%	10%	50%	30%
Very Conservative	6.73%	5.81%	5%	0%	5%	10%	0%	50%	30%
Strongly Conservative	7.78%	6.15%	10%	5%	5%	10%	0%	50%	20%
Conservative	8.68%	7.36%	15%	5%	10%	5%	0%	50%	15%
Somewhat Conservative	9.58%	8.89%	20%	5%	15%	5%	0%	45%	10%
Slightly Conservative	10.04%	9.74%	25%	5%	15%	5%	0%	45%	5%
Balanced/Conservative Bias	10.63%	10.90%	25%	10%	15%	5%	0%	45%	0%
Balanced	11.45%	12.38%	30%	10%	20%	0%	0%	40%	0%
Balanced/Aggressive Bias	11.90%	13.22%	30%	10%	25%	0%	0%	35%	0%
Slightly Aggressive	12.42%	14.30%	30%	15%	25%	0%	0%	30%	0%
Somewhat Aggressive	12.94%	15.42%	30%	20%	25%	0%	0%	25%	0%
Aggressive	13.39%	16.30%	30%	20%	30%	0%	0%	20%	0%
Strongly Aggressive	14.30%	18.22%	35%	25%	30%	0%	0%	10%	0%
Very Aggressive	15.13%	19.93%	40%	25%	35%	0%	0%	0%	0%
Ultra Aggressive	15.40%	20.64%	30%	35%	35%	0%	0%	0%	0%

LCE = Large Cap Domestic Equity
MSE = Mid/Small Cap Domestic Equity

FE = Foreign Equity
FFI = Foreign Fixed Income

LTB = Long Term Bonds
ITB = Intermediate Term Bonds

MM = Money Market

large cap growth index must be used. To do otherwise would jeopardize the integrity of the strategic asset allocation plan.

The best case scenario is to find an exchange-traded index fund that tracks the same index used in the asset allocation analysis. For example, if the asset allocation software you are using is based on historical performance data from the Russell 1000 Index, it only makes sense that you would want to find a fund that tracks the Russell 1000 Index. Likewise, if the asset allocation analysis is based on the historical performance data from the S&P 500/BARRA Growth Index, then you should try to find an exchange-traded index fund tracking that specific index.

Unfortunately, it's not always such a clear cut decision. If the asset allocation program or analysis does not specify a particular underlying index, then the investor must sometimes choose between competing exchange-traded index funds. For example, if the asset allocation plan calls for 25% in large cap growth, but does not specify which large cap growth index, the investor has a decision to make. When multiple exchange-traded index funds exist covering the same asset class but based on different underlying indexes, the investor must decide which fund works best for them. Exhibit 15-3 provides an overview of some of the asset class overlap that exists among different exchange-traded index funds.

When this occurs, the investor must decide which fund is best for them based on the strategies they intend to implement. For instance, if they intend to sell covered calls or buy protective puts in conjunction with a specific fund, then the fund chosen must obviously have underlying option contracts available. Another factor is the structure of the underlying index being tracked. As we have seen, there are several major Index Providers. Two of the biggest and best known Index Providers are Standard & Poor's and Frank Russell Company. Each has its own unique index methodology and rebalancing protocols. While not discussed in this book, it's important to understand that how an index is compiled and maintained will have an impact on the funds tracking it.

Exhibit 15-3:
Asset Classes Tracked by Multiple Exchange-Traded Index Funds

Asset Class	Exchange-Traded Index Fund	Symbol
Large Capitalization	iShares Russell 1000 Index Fund	IWB
	iShares S&P 500 Index Fund	IVV
	iShares OEX 100 Index Fund	OEF
	S&P 500 Index "Spiders"	SPY
	DIAMONDS	DIA
	streetTracks FORTUNE 500 Index Fund	FFF
Mid Capitalization	iShares Russell MidCap Index Fund	IWR
	iShares S&P 400 MidCap Index Fund	IJH
	MidCap "Spiders"	MDY
Small Capitalization	iShares Russell 2000 Index Fund	IWM
	iShares S&P 600 SmallCap Index Fund	IJR
	Vanguard Extended Market VIPERs	VXF
Broad Market	iShares Dow Jones Total Market Index Fund	IYY
	iShares Russell 3000 Index Fund	IWV
	Vanguard Total Stock Market VIPERs	VTI

When To Buy

After we have determined *which* exchange-traded index funds to use, the next step is to decide *when* to implement the plan. For example, if an investor intends to invest $100,000 they could do so all at once or invest a partial amount now and spread the rest over several months. This is sometimes referred to as averaging into the market. For the nervous investor placing a large sum of money in the market all at once is often difficult. By averaging into the market, they avoid some of the fears associated with making large investments.

Taking too long to implement a portfolio plan, however, may cause you to lose focus and be swayed to change from the initial asset allocation. This can happen if one asset class is not performing well and another asset class is doing extremely well. The temptation is to add dollars to the better performing asset class and avoid adding dollars to the asset class that is not doing as well. This can, and does, lead to problems since it creates a portfolio different from the initial strategic asset allocation plan. Therefore, when averaging into the market I would recommend not extending the period to over three months.

Furthermore, if you are employing risk management strategies, such as dynamic stop-loss orders, working into the market slowly provides no real benefits. From my experience, it is far better to implement the portfolio on a timely basis and then get on with the business of managing it.

Step 4: Active Portfolio Management Strategies

We now come to the most difficult step in Strategic Index Investing: adding active portfolio management strategies. Up to now, the overall approach has been very systematic and scientific. We developed a strategic asset allocation plan based on our goals, objectives, and risk tolerance then implemented the plan using exchange-traded index funds.

Active portfolio management, in contrast, allows the investor to depart from the overall passive plan. The active strategies used in Strategic Index Investing can be divided into two categories: strategies designed to minimize a specific risk and strategies designed to take advantage of a perceived opportunity.

Active Risk Management Strategies

Risk management strategies provide a number of significant advantages, as we have seen in previous chapters. Properly managing the risks associated with investing is a key determinate of success over time. The best way to manage risk is with diversification (asset allocation) and active risk management strategies. Two of the main risk management strategies we use in Strategic Index Investing are dynamic stop-loss orders and protective puts.

The decision to use active risk management strategies depends on several factors. These include: your tolerance for risk, your willingness to pay for "insurance" when buying protective puts, and the amount of time you wish to spend watching over the strategies. If you find that you are not willing or able to spend the time necessary, it may make sense to hire a professional money manager to help you manage risk. Finally, the decision should be based on the health of the overall market. If the market, in general, is strong there is obviously less of a need for active risk management strategies.

Active Return Enhancing Strategies

Active portfolio management strategies can also be used to take advantage of perceived opportunities, as we have seen. When the appropriate opportunity occurs, strategies exist that allow the investor to benefit. The primary return enhancing strategies used in Strategic Index Investing are tactical asset allocation, core-satellite allocation, covered call writing, and selling naked puts. All four strategies allow the investor to take advantage of opportunities and increase potential return. In addition, other advanced active strategies that are easily used in conjunction with exchange-traded index funds include selling short and buying on margin.

By definition, return enhancing strategies are far more subjective compared to risk management strategies. Ten different investors could look at the exact same information regarding the market and come up with ten different ideas about its meaning. Therefore, when implementing active strategies it's important to continually check performance and compare the active strategies against the passive asset allocation. If the strategies are not adding value, you should consider going in a different direction.

Exhibit 15-4 provides an overview of the active investment strategies covered in this book and when to use them. As the exhibit shows, active portfolio management strategies allow the investor to earn a positive return if the market is moving higher, lower, or remains unchanged. As such, they represent a key part of Strategic Index Investing. Several factors to consider when deciding whether or not to implement active portfolio management strategies include: the amount of time one is willing to commit, and the potential benefits associated with the strategies.

Step 5: Ongoing Monitoring, Evaluation, and Rebalancing

For the portfolio management process to be effective, we must continually answer the question, "How am I doing?" After all, we are not investing for the fun of it. The best way to ensure that your portfolio remains on track to accomplish the desired goals is with ongoing monitoring, evaluation and systematically rebalancing the portfolio on a regular basis.

Performance is by far the most important measurement of success or failure. In fact, most investors gauge success or failure on performance alone. With this in mind, it's important to remember that performance objectives should be investor specific based on the

Exhibit 15-4:
Overview of Active Portfolio Management Strategies
Used in Strategic Index Investing

Strategy	When to Use	Risk
Covered Call Writing	Flat or down market	Limited
Dynamic Stop-Loss Orders	To reduce risk	Limited
Protective Put	To reduce risk	Limited
Selling Short	Down market	Unlimited
Buy on Margin	Up market	Limited
Selling Naked Put Options	Up or flat market	Limited
Tactical Changes to Asset Allocation	Various	Limited
Sector Rotation Strategies	Various	Limited

level of risk one is willing to assume. Unfortunately, investors often judge success not on the level of risk they are taking, but by how others are doing or how the market in general is performing. This often leads to problems.

For example, if an investor determined, based on the risk they were willing to assume, that an 8% per year return was sufficient, we might assume they would be happy actually receiving an 8% return in any given year. If the market, however, as measured by the Dow Jones Total Market Index, produced a return of 16%, should they be happy earning 8%? Would it change your answer to find out that their portfolio was exactly half as risky as the Dow Jones Total Market Index?

Far too often, investors base the return they believe they should receive on what other investments are returning without consideration to the risk associated with them. It is important to remember; when evaluating a portfolio based on return, performance must always be evaluated in the context of risk. In other words, how much risk did an investor take to achieve a given return?

Simply comparing two portfolios, with varying degrees of risk, can be quite misleading. Exhibit 15-5 shows the one-year return of several hypothetical portfolios along with the standard deviation of each. As we can see from the exhibit, portfolio 1 produced the highest one-year return, which was 12.0%. Portfolio 2, in contrast, produced the lowest one-year return with a dismal 6.0%. Therefore, one might assume portfolio 1 is the better portfolio of the group.

When risk is considered a very different story develops. Portfolio 1 took on three times the risk of portfolio 2 but did not deliver three times the return. Two of the portfolios (portfolios 5 and 6) produced the exact same return. Despite producing the same return, portfolio 6 took on far greater risk than did portfolio 5. Therefore, on a risk adjusted basis portfolio 5 represents a better alternative.

Remember that it's not necessarily how much you earn that's important; what is important is how much risk you must take to earn a given return. Most importantly, the investor needs to determine a rate

Exhibit 15-5:
Comparing Portfolios by Both Risk and Return

	1-Year Return	Standard Deviation
Portfolio 1	12.00%	15.50%
Portfolio 2	6.00%	5.40%
Portfolio 3	8.00%	8.10%
Portfolio 4	9.00%	8.41%
Portfolio 5	10.00%	10.46%
Portfolio 6	10.00%	13.25%

of return that will get them to where they want to be. Once the desired rate of return is determined, it is crucial to structure a portfolio that has only the amount of risk necessary to achieve the expected rate of return. If an investor decides later that a higher return is necessary, given a change in their financial circumstances, the new higher expected return should be considered within the context of increased risk.

Finally, to ensure that a portfolio remains in-line with desired risk and return parameters, it's essential that it be rebalanced on a consistent basis. Rebalancing insures that the portfolio stays true to the investor's goals and is not altered by changes in the market. When an investor does not rebalance, they allow the market to set their allocation for them, something that is rarely a good idea.

A Continuing Process

Portfolio management is like an eternal circle. That is, the process never ends. This is shown in Exhibit 15-6, which summarizes the five steps that are part of Strategic Index Investing. In the exhibit, active portfolio management strategies have been divided into separate steps.

As the exhibit shows, the final step, "ongoing monitoring, evaluation, and rebalancing" takes us back to the planning stage. Each year, after doing a final year-end portfolio review, the investor must re-evaluate goals, objectives, risk tolerance, and investing time horizon. Any changes that may have occurred over the course of the year must be accounted for and the appropriate changes made to the portfolio. For example, if a change in employment means more disposable income, the investor may want to be more aggressive with their investment portfolio. Likewise, active strategies being used must be evaluated and adjusted, if necessary.

The point of the flowchart is to make clear that portfolio management is not a one shot solution. It is a never ending endeavor that takes time and effort if you want to succeed.

Summary

The Investment Policy Statement is a written document that lists each of the steps necessary for the portfolio management process to work. In Strategic Index Investing these steps include: 1) setting goals and determining your tolerance for risk, 2) determining the appropriate strategic asset allocation plan, 3) implementing the plan using exchange-traded index funds, 4) adding active portfolio management strategies, and 5) ongoing monitoring, evaluation, and rebalancing.

Exhibit 15-6:
Strategic Index Investing Process

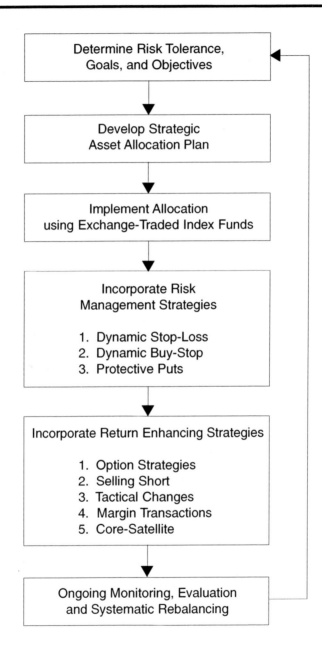

Chapter 16

FEES, COMMISSIONS, AND INVESTMENT ADVICE

The Cost of Investment Advice

We now turn our attention to one of the most important yet least talked about aspects of portfolio management: how to pay. Up to this point, every example given has excluded the effect of transaction fees or commissions. While many investors might wish these fees did not exist, they do. In the real world, investment advice is not free and it's the investor, either directly or indirectly, who pays.

Trying to determine the true costs associated with investing is difficult. After all, it's not like investment services come with price tags. You can't walk up and down the aisle of a brokerage firm comparing "investment advice" price tags to determine what services will be performed in return for the commissions paid. To the contrary, the vast majority of investors have absolutely no idea how much they are actually paying for investment advice, or what services they should expect in return for fees paid. In the absence of full and fair disclosure, investors are often cynical and untrusting of all investment professionals. They become averse to paying any investment related fees whatsoever.

Paying for investment advice is not necessarily a bad thing. There is nothing wrong with paying someone to help you manage your money should you need the help. Using a qualified, ethical, professional investment advisor is often the difference between success and failure. As long as the services performed warrant the fees paid, why wouldn't you? However, paying any amount of money for bad or inadequate investment advice is unacceptable.

To help the reader make a more informed decision, this chapter uncovers the mystery surrounding investment related fees. We examine several popular ways to pay for portfolio management services and discuss the total costs involved. Also, we look at several of the most important services an investment advisor can provide.

Discount vs. Full Service

Over the years, Wall Street has done an extremely poor job of explaining to investors the costs associated with investing. Much of the confusion results from the way traditional brokerage firms determine the commission to charge clients in the first place. The commission charged by a brokerage firm to execute a stock trade includes many costs, such as the cost of research, the broker's compensation, ongoing operating expenses for the firm, and the actual costs to execute the trade, just to name a few. When a trade is made, the investor only sees a single charge, the commission. They probably don't realize that this fee is designed to cover all related costs incurred by the brokerage firm during the normal course of business and not just the costs associated with actually executing the transaction.

Another problem with investment-related commissions is that the broker is rewarded for making transactions and not necessarily for doing what's best for the client. The brokerage firm also has a vested interest in high portfolio turnover. For example, if a broker regularly meets with a client. Helps the client develop a sound investment plan and then spends a great deal of time monitoring and reviewing their portfolio. Yet, doesn't make a transaction for the client the broker will not be compensated for their efforts. This can, and often does, lead to activities such as "churning." The practice of buying or selling securities designed to generate commissions for the broker, often to the detriment of the client.

When discount or low commission brokerage firms were first created, after the Securities and Exchange Commission (SEC) deregulated brokerage commission rates in the early 1970s, they were intent on portraying traditional brokerage firms as "bad guys." Some of the criticism was warranted but much of it simply confused investors even more.

To get business, discount brokerage firms told investors that the key to better performance was lower commission rates. They failed to point out that other factors, in addition to low commission rates, are important to investment success. Discount brokerage firms focused exclusively on one small part of investing, the costs associated with trading, because they were prohibited by law from rendering investment advice. They could execute a trade for an investor but not assist them in developing an overall investment plan or strategy. They were simply order takers. Therefore, discount brokerage firms had to minimize the importance of investment advice and convince investors that low costs were more important than good advice.

This created a quandary for investors. On the one hand, discount brokerage firms were telling them that all they needed to succeed was a cheap way to trade stocks while traditional brokerage firms were telling them that investment advice and better service was the answer. The investor was caught in the middle with nowhere to turn. That is, until the creation and widespread acceptance of fee-based investment accounts.

A Better Way To Pay for Investment Advice

In the late 1980s, a new way to deliver investment services was catching on. Once reserved for only the wealthiest of clients, fee-based or wrap accounts represent a revolutionary new way for investors to pay for investment advice and services. Wrap based accounts separate the cost of investment advice from the costs associated with transactions. Instead of paying hefty commissions on every transaction, investors are charged a flat percentage based on the size of their account.

The percentage charged for a wrap account generally varies based on the size of the account and level of service necessary. The fee is usually quoted based on an annual rate and charged quarterly. For example, an account with a 2% annual fee would be charged 0.50% quarterly (2% / 4). Exhibit 16-1 shows an example of how wrap accounts are typically priced using a sliding scale model.

Wrap fee accounts give the investment advisor the freedom to make recommendations and suggest changes, which they feel are in the client's best interest without the constant cloud of commissions hanging over their head. In this respect, they are one of the purest value for money propositions on Wall Street. There are two basic types of wrap accounts: wrap fee plus a small transaction charge on each trade or all inclusive.

Wrap Fee Plus Transaction Charges

Wrap accounts originated with independent portfolio management firms. They wanted to offer investors objective investment advice without being tied or obligated to a major Wall Street firm. The solution was to hold client assets with a discount broker, thereby offering the client the lowest possible commission charge on trans-

Exhibit 16-1:
Typical "Wrap" Account Fee Structure

Assets ($)	Annual Fee
100,000 - 249,999	2.75%
250,000 - 499,999	2.25%
500,000 - 749,999	1.85%
750,000 - 999,999	1.65%
1,000,000 - 1,999,999	1.25%
2,000,000 - 4,999,999	1.00%
5,000,000+	0.95%

actions. In return for managing the portfolio, the investment advisor charged the client a flat percentage fee. It represented the best of both worlds: low transactions costs and professional investment advice.

This type of account separates the costs of investment advice from the costs of investment transactions. The investment advisor receives the same percentage fee regardless of how much trading takes place. In fact, the only way to earn more is for the investment advisor to grow the account. Something most investors should appreciate.

Typical fees for this type of account range from 0.50% to 1.5% based on the level of advice and service required. The client also pays a transaction fee, which is usually a flat rate in the area of $5 to $25 per trade, based on the pricing schedule of the discount brokerage firm acting as the custodian. For example, using a deep-discount firm compared to a more traditional discount firm would result in lower transaction related fees.

Using a wrap fee plus transaction charges account the investor pays the investment advisor to manage their account, plain and simple. The transaction fee covers the cost of the transactions. There are no hidden fees or charges. If at any time the investor feels the investment advisor is not doing a good job, they can fire them. The investor is not tied to the investment advisor with long-term contracts or back-end surrender penalties, as is often the case when using products from a traditional brokerage firm.

All Inclusive

In an attempt to stem the outflow of funds moving to independent investment advisors, in the mid 1990s Wall Street brokerage firms introduced their own version of the wrap fee account. While it represented a welcomed alternative to commissions, the wrap fee accounts associated with Wall Street brokerage firms tend to charge a higher fee than those associated with pure money management firms. For example, it's common to be charged a 3% wrap fee if you have an account at a major brokerage firm.

Also, brokerage firms often encourage brokers to use proprietary products in wrap accounts. Meaning they are double dipping from the client's pocket. For example, the firm receives a management fee on the mutual funds inside the wrap account in addition to the wrap fee being charged the client. Additionally, large Wall Street brokerage firms prefer that their brokers use wrap accounts to simply raise money. They want them selling. The broker usually turns the portfolio over to a professional money manager and simply acts as an intermediary between the client and the money manager.

Understanding the Total Cost of a Wrap Account

In addition to any wrap or investment advisory fees, an investor must also understand the internal fees associated with the investments held in their portfolio. A wrap fee account comprised entirely of exchange-traded index funds will have lower total expenses compared to a wrap fee account comprised entirely of traditional actively managed mutual funds. As we saw in Part 2, exchange-traded index funds generally have lower internal operating expenses compared to mutual funds. Therefore, the investor pays less.

For example, consider a $250,000 portfolio with a 1% wrap fee. The investor is paying 1% per year or $2,500 for the investment advisor to manage their account. But, is this all? If the portfolio is comprised of exchange-traded index funds, the investor will pay approximately 0.35% in internal management fees. This is based on the average expenses associated with exchange-traded index funds, as discussed in Part 2. You will not see this expense, but as informed investors we know it's still important to consider. A portfolio comprised of traditional actively managed mutual funds, in contrast, could easily have internal expenses of 1.75% or more, as we saw in previous chapters.

When the internal expenses associated with the investments held in a wrap account are considered, we see the costs of the portfolios are very different. This is shown in Exhibit 16-2.

As the exhibit shows, the higher expenses associated with tradi-

Exhibit 16-2:
Hypothetical Comparison of Total Cost of "Wrap" Account
Using iShares and Traditional Mutual Funds

	Exchange-Traded Index Fund Portfolio	Actively Managed Mutual Fund Portfolio	Difference
Dollars Invested	$250,000.00	$250,000.00	
Average Fund Expense Ratio	0.35%	1.75%	
Total Yearly Operating Expenses (Avg. Fund Exp. x 250,000)	$ 875.00	$ 4,375.00	
Annual Wrap Fee (1%)	$ 2,500.00	$ 2,500.00	
Total Portfolio Expenses	**$ 3,375.00**	**$ 6,875.00**	**$3,500.00**

tional actively managed mutual funds mean the investor will pay an additional $3,500 per year compared to a portfolio consisting entirely of exchange-traded index funds. While the investor will not be charged separately for these internal fees, they decrease the overall return of the portfolio. A wrap fee account holding traditional actively managed mutual funds will generally be more expensive, all else being equal, than a wrap fee account holding exchange-traded index funds.

Therefore, using a wrap account to manage a portfolio of traditional mutual funds, or worse yet, a variable annuity does not make sense. Unless, and this is a big unless, the total expenses (wrap account fee plus mutual fund fees) are less than 1.0%. Otherwise, you are paying two people to do the same thing, and you are probably paying way too much. You are paying the investment advisor who created the portfolio and the various mutual fund managers to actually manage the portfolio.

Keep in mind, if using a wrap fee account that also charges commissions on each individual trade you must take this into consideration, as well. For example, if you make ten trades per year and each trade has a commission associated with it of $8.95 then the annual fees associated with the account must include the $89.50 for transaction fees ($8.95 x 10).

It's Portfolio Management, Not McDonald's

So you have decided to hire an investment advisor, pay a wrap fee, and let them manage your portfolio. What's the next step? After all, hiring a broker, investment advisor, or financial planner is not like ordering a hamburger at McDonald's. If you walked into a McDonald's restaurant anywhere in the country or, for that matter, anywhere in the world, and ordered a cheeseburger, french-fries, and a Coke you would know exactly what to expect, regardless of who owned or operated the McDonald's. The price may vary from city to city, but the basic product will be the same in taste, color, and smell.

Investment advice is different. You can sit down with five different financial advisors from the same firm, give each of them the exact same financial numbers, goals, and objectives, and receive five completely different portfolio recommendations. That's because every investment advisor is different, each with their own life experiences that will influence how they feel about the markets and investing in general. Some are overly optimistic while others always see disaster for the markets. Investment advice is not homogenous. It cannot be replicated like hamburgers.

A cookie cutter approach will not work when building a portfolio for a variety of reasons. However, I do believe there are several basic functions every investment advisor should provide and investors should be willing to pay them for doing so. I also believe there are some things investors should never pay an investment advisor to do.

One of the smartest things any investor can do is pay for risk management. Under risk management I include developing, implementing, and helping the investor stay true to a strategic asset allocation plan. Risk management includes ongoing portfolio monitoring and rebalancing. The process of developing and implementing a systematic buy/sell strategy is another example of risk management. Additionally, risk management could include buying protective puts or selling short to hedge a portfolio.

An investment advisor should be considered a professional risk manager first and foremost and not a soothsayer who can predict the future direction of the market or specific stocks. Most investment advisors would do their clients a tremendous benefit by putting away all their charts and computer programs designed to see into the future and instead focus on those things proven to add value, like risk management. Ironically, most investors rarely pay for professional risk management, and it shows.

Avoid Paying for Those Actions That Do Not Add Value
Recently, it has become popular to pay an investment advisor a yearly wrap fee to manage a portfolio of traditional actively managed mutual funds. This seems odd for several reasons. First, the investor is paying two different entities to manage his money: the investment advisor who picks and monitors the mutual funds and the actual mutual fund company, which picks and manages a portfolio of individual stocks. Often the combination of fees will exceed 3% or more of the total portfolio, as we saw earlier.

For the investor to be successful, both the investment advisor and fund manager must be able to accurately predict the future on a consistent basis, something that has been proven very hard to do. The investment advisor must be able to predict which actively managed funds will do at least as well as the market, and the fund's portfolio manager must be able to pick the stocks that will help them outperform the market.

I know what many of you are thinking. The investment advisor is on the same side of the table as the investor, watching out for them, searching out the best mutual funds and then monitoring those funds to ensure they do well. The story typically goes something like the following, "If the fund managers fail to perform we will fire them and find replacements." Hey, I've got a better idea. Why not fire the person who sold you the bad mutual funds in the first place? After all, it was their idea, wasn't it?

Strategic Index Investing, in contrast, eliminates a layer of fees because the investor is not paying both an investment advisor and a mutual fund manager. By using index funds, the need for high-priced mutual fund managers and the high fee structure often associated with actively managed mutual funds is eliminated. The investor pays the investment advisor to do those things shown to add value, such as developing a strategic asset allocation plan, implementing a risk management strategy, and rebalancing the portfolio on a regular basis.

Be Realistic About "Your" Money

Believe it or not, investment advisors are not humanitarians out to change the world. I've been in this industry for over twenty years and can assure you it is definitely an industry geared around making a profit. This is by no means bad because it allows qualified individuals to earn a living by providing a valuable service.

Like any profession, in return for the service, the investor pays a fee. Always remember, however, it's your money and in your best interest to know and understand how the money is being managed and what fees are being charged, both the fees you see and the fees you don't see. In the end, the responsibility is yours. After all, the ultimate success or failure of your investment plan will impact you and your family, not the investment advisor.

Final Thoughts on Fees and Free Lunches

I recently had the privilege of playing golf at one of the top private golf courses in Kansas. Along one of the fairways was a house that could have doubled as Buckingham Palace of the Midwest. I asked the person who had invited me if they knew who lived in this incredible mansion. His reply, while not surprising, reinforced a long held belief of mine: nothing about investment management is free.

He told me the homeowner was one of the top executives with a local no-load mutual fund company. "Imagine that," I quipped facetiously. "How do you think he can afford such a nice house working for a no-load mutual fund company?" "After all," I continued, "no-load mutual funds don't charge investors for the services they perform."

I'm always amazed at the number of investors who believe that by using a no-load mutual fund they avoid paying for investment advice. Even no-load mutual funds charge investors internal management fees. Some, in fact, are quite high. This brings us to one undeniable truth: you pay to have someone manage your money, whether you realize it or not. The questions you must ask yourself are: "who will you pay, how much will it cost, and what will you get in return?"

Summary

Investors have many choices regarding how to pay for investment advice. They must be knowledgeable about their alternatives in order to make informed decisions. One of the most innovative ways to pay for investment advice is with a wrap fee account. Instead of paying a large commission on each transaction, the investor pays a small fee based on a percentage of their account. Finally, never believe you are getting something for nothing when investing because you are not.

Chapter 17

THE ROAD YOU CHOOSE
TO FOLLOW

Final Thoughts

In closing, I want to leave you with several final thoughts on investing and life in general. How you choose to manage your money, whether intelligently or haphazardly, will determine the quality of life you ultimately enjoy. This is not meant to imply that one needs money to be happy. Happiness is not something you can buy.

Money does offer security and with security comes the freedom to live as you wish. Being financially secure allows you to do the things you enjoy as opposed to the things that must be done to meet basic survival needs. With this in mind, I leave you with the following thoughts.

- **Markets change, be flexible.** While this may seem overly obvious, investors continually get burned using last year's investment strategies. Buying last year's hot mutual fund or stock is a certain recipe for disaster. Don't rely on an investment strategy that only works in one type of market environment. Be able to change and be ready to do so. Always think flexibility first when investing.

- **Education is the key to success.** Never stop learning. We are fortunate to live in a country with the most open and accessible financial markets in the history of the planet. In many parts of the world people don't have access to the capital markets for one reason or another. We have access, yet education is needed. Education is so important to financial success that basic financial skills should be mandatory at every level in our public education system. If you want to succeed at investing, never stop learning. You will not regret it.

- **Time waits for no one.** Every day the clock is ticking. Taking us closer to when we will need our investment dollars. Time waits for no one. In other words, stop making excuses and start an investment plan today. Consider the following: $10,000 invested at 8% for thirty years grows to $100,662. However, $10,000 invested at 16% for fifteen years will only grow to $92,655. Amazingly, even earning twice the return does not make up for the loss of time. When investing, time can be our greatest ally or worst enemy. Use it to your benefit.

- **Diversification makes any investor look smart.** I have three words to say about this: diversify, diversify, diversify. This one basic principle alone will provide more risk protection than almost all others combined. Diversification, however, does not simply speak to the number of investments one owns. If an investor owns ten large cap growth funds are they really diversified? Proper diversification means diversifying across different types of assets (stocks, bonds, money market, and hard assets) as well as across different equity styles and classes (large cap, small cap, mid cap, growth, and value). Diversification is a crucial component of risk management, the benefits of which should never be underestimated.

- **Investing requires taking risks.** Be prepared to lose money. I don't want to burst anyone's bubble, but investing is risky. While it is possible to minimize risk, it can never be completely eliminated. As we know, there is a direct trade-off between risk and

302

return. The more an investor wants to earn the more risk they must be willing to bear. However, I believe the risks associated with not investing are far greater than any risks associated with investing. The markets offer unprecedented potential. Invest wisely and manage risk instead of letting risk keep you from enjoying the rewards the markets have to offer.

- **All things eventually regress to the mean.** Never forget this one basic statistical fact. Eventually, all things regress back to their long-term averages. I don't care what we are talking about. It could be the average number of speeding tickets issued over a specific time period, or the return of an index or a mutual fund. If a given investment, which has a long-term average return of 10%, has had five straight years of 20% plus growth you better be careful. Unless some new paradigm has completely changed the rules of the game, the returns will eventually regress to the mean. You can bank on it.

- **When a mutual fund disclosure reads: "past performance is no guarantee of future results," believe it.** For some reason investors love to own the top-performing mutual fund, whether they buy it before, or most often after, it has become a top-performing fund. More often than not a top-performing fund one year becomes a loser the next. Despite the fact that we are continually inundated with mutual fund ratings, tied primarily to performance, we must learn to accept that historic performance represents the past. It is by no means an indication of what the future holds, as the mandatory disclaimer indicates.

- **Think long-term but act in the moment.** Thinking long-term simply means staying focused on the big picture, staying focused on the long-term goals, and trying not to let the daily ups and downs of the market change the way we invest. Yet, we must also act in the moment. This means taking advantage

303

of situations the market gives. So often an investor will hide behind the veil of being a long-term investor, using it as an excuse not to make the hard decisions necessary. Instead, you must think long-term but make changes based on how the market is acting today.

- **No one can predict the future so be leery of those who claim such abilities.** Never forget that any investment strategy, which depends on someone consistently predicting the future to be successful, will eventually fail and probably fail in a big way.

- **Never be afraid to take a loss.** There is an old saying on Wall Street, "your first loss is usually your best loss," or said another way, "don't throw good money after bad." What this means is never be afraid to take a loss and move on. The proper use of stop-loss orders should help do just that. The worst decision is to average down when an investment is not working out. I always cringe when I hear an investor say they are going to average down. In a sense, they are saying the investment is doing so poorly they decided to invest more. Never, never, never average down and never be afraid to sell an investment at a loss.

- **Be willing to go against the prevailing market thought or trend.** Selling technology stocks would have been one of the hardest things to do in the spring of 1999. After all, everyone knew the market was going to keep going up. Only a fool would sell. All of America was going to retire early from profits made on technology stocks. Then, after the correction began everyone knew it would only be a short time before they went back up. Obviously, this did not happen. We all know how hard it is to go against the popular ideas. Selling when our friends and co-workers are buying. We learned this from our earliest days in school when most of us would do anything

304

to be accepted. Unfortunately, as grown-up investors it can be devastating to follow the crowd. When investing we must never be afraid to be different and go against popular investment themes.

- **Keep all emotions out of your investments.** Another aspect of this is never make an investment decision when in a bad mood or preoccupied. If you are following a systematic approach that is one thing, but if you are making a move outside of your plan be careful. Your mindset will definitely influence the decisions you make. When clients call me and want to make a trade outside their overall strategy, I often ask them to take a deep breath, count to ten and re-think the idea.

- **Know and understand why you are investing.** Don't ever make an investment to impress someone, either yourself or others. Trust me, they won't be impressed. All of us invest for very different reasons. You might be saving for retirement, to put a child through college, buy a new home, or a vacation home. Perhaps you are investing to help supplement your income. Regardless of the reasons, most of us usually place a great deal of importance on its successful outcome. With this in mind, know why you invest and always invest appropriately.

- **Don't believe everything you read.** This may seem a little odd coming from someone who has written a book about investing. Just because something is shown on television, printed in a magazine, in a newspaper, or in a book doesn't make it true. You have the responsibility to check the facts. After all, it's your money, if you don't check it out, who will?

- **Finally, always be positive.** While this alone may not improve your investment results, you will certainly be happier and any investment failures will be more bearable. I believe a positive attitude does carry over to how we invest and over the long-run will help to improve performance.

The Long and Winding Road

Always remember that successful portfolio management is not a destination, it's a journey. It is a long and never ending journey over a sometimes bumpy and unsure road. It will test your will to succeed and cause you to continually question all you believe to be true. It is also a journey, if done correctly, which holds untold rewards.

It's my sincere hope that this book will be a map of sorts to help you along that road. A guide that will help you maximize the correct portfolio management decisions you make and help minimize the incorrect decisions. And, in turn help you live a happier, more financially secure and rewarding life. In the end the decision is yours. You can move forward and prosper or do nothing. My sincere hope is that you move forward and enjoy much success using the strategies and ideas put forth in this book. Be well and invest wisely.

AUTHOR'S NOTE

This book is an attempt to help investors understand the reality and truth in relation to portfolio management and the financial markets. I have dedicated my life to this pursuit. That is why I founded Romey Capital Management, Inc. (RCM), a Registered Investment Advisory firm dedicated to delivering high quality portfolio management using the most advanced tools and strategies available.

Most people pay far too little attention to their investments. You have taken the first step to becoming a more informed investor. But, you must follow through. Exchange-traded index funds are the best portfolio management tools available today. They offer significant advantages above and beyond all other alternatives, as we have seen. However, you must have a plan to maximize the advantages they offer. Strategic Index Investing provides the plan. It allows every investor to construct the most efficient portfolio possible based on their specific needs and goals. I believe strongly in the benefits of this approach.

It is important to understand that there are literally only a handful of investment firms in the world that specialize in the exciting new approach to portfolio management discussed in this book. Romey Capital Management is one such firm. We are dedicated to helping investors improve investment performance through the use of Strategic Index Investing.

I invite you to keep in touch. To contact me, or to get information regarding the portfolio management services provided by RCM, please access my web page at:

www.RomeyCapital.com

I will be happy to answer any questions you may have about the ideas put forth in this book or portfolio management in general.

Additional Resources

In addition **to www.romeycapital.com,** there are several other resources I would recommend for those investors seeking more information on exchange-traded index funds. They are listed below.

www.ishares.com – This is the iShares home page. It is one of the best web pages available regarding exchange-traded index funds.

www.amex.com – This web site provides extensive information on every exchange-traded index fund traded on the American Stock Exchange.

www.streettracks.com – This web site provides detailed information on the streetTRACKS family of exchange-traded index funds.

www.spdrindex.com – This web page provides a number of research tools and information regarding exchange-traded index funds.

INDEX